COMPARATIVE JUSTICE

Off the Beaten Path

Victoria M. Time
Old Dominion University

W. Timothy Austin
Indiana University of Pennsylvania

Kendall Hunt
publishing company

Cover image © Shutterstock.com

Kendall Hunt
publishing company

www.kendallhunt.com
Send all inquiries to:
4050 Westmark Drive
Dubuque, IA 52004-1840

ISBN 978-1-5249-6907-3

Published in the United States of America

In memory of our fathers, John Edie Time and Willard Franklin Austin,
who were avid readers, and who would have enjoyed this book.

CONTENTS

FOREWORD

Comparative Criminal Justice Systems encourage critical thinking by introducing students and policy makers to different ways of organizing the administration of justice in the different parts of the world without ethnocentric assumptions that "our" ways must be superior to all others. [Max Weber], in *Economy and Society*, had offered an ethnocentric theory of ideal types of the administration of justice under the assumption that the Germanic tradition was superior to all other systems of administration because it was based on rational ideal bureaucratic rules and relied on trained professionals. [Zygmunt Bauman], in *Modernity and the Holocaust*, critiqued this Weberian obsession with rationality given that it lacked any emphasis on compassion and probably contributed to the rationalization of genocide during the holocaust and during German colonization in Africa. The lesson is that scholars should not believe that their country or any country has the best criminal justice system and so all should keep an open mind for chances to borrow, adapt, or innovate from the successes and failures of theirs and other countries. The criminal justice system is made for the people, the people are not made for the criminal justice system.

Having taught a section of Comparative Justice Systems for 4 years alongside Dr. Timothy Austin at Indiana University of Pennsylvania where he taught a section of the same class, I am pleased to say that we became close colleagues and have kept in touch since then. I am also delighted to note that Dr. Austin is known for his support for colleagues and students. I am not surprised to see that he has co-authored this book with one of his former doctoral students, Dr. Victoria Time, who is now a distinguished University Professor at Old Dominion. It was the dissertation topic of Dr. Time under the chairmanship of Dr. Austin on Fictional Crimes in the works of Shakespeare that attracted me to Indiana University of Pennsylvania, hoping that the department was open enough to creative scholarship.

This book testifies that the creativity of these two scholars has continued beyond the dissertation phase given the ease with which they introduce readers to interesting case studies of the families of law that tend not to be adequately covered in existing textbooks. Having done fieldwork in the Philippines and published about Singapore in the past, Dr. Austin is uniquely positioned to offer readers engaging contributions that lie off the beaten tracks in comparative justice systems. Also, having grown up in Africa where she obtained her first degree and Master's in Law, Dr. Time is able to contribute fresh perspectives on the developing countries sampled in this book. Their styles blend so well that it is difficult to say who drafted which chapters between the two of them.

On a recent visit to Singapore to present a workshop keynote, I was struck by some of the facts about the country that the authors summarized in this book. I was aware that the country was known to be strict with deviance and social control and this was reinforced by the flight attendant who announced that chewing gum was banned in the country as this book indicates. At my hotel, I told the front desk that the door from my room to the balcony was not locked and they smiled and told me that it was on a higher floor and that the country was relatively safe. The fascinating thing is that stricter punitiveness does not always lead to lower crime rates in other countries. I asked a Singaporean colleague whether the country also practices forgiveness as part of the criminal justice system the way that the first Prime Minister, Lee Kwan Yew, wrote that he forgave dozens of Malaysian army officers who were arrested for mutiny in the 1960s, alluded to in this book. They said that there was not much forgiveness and that penalties were almost certain, including the death penalty for some drug offenses. The book confirms much of this perception but also added the nuance that the country ensured support from the relatively well-to-do citizenry by building modern homes for almost all the citizens to create jobs for construction workers, prevent homelessness or shanty towns, and also to encourage the residents to participate in neighborhood watch schemes to prevent crimes on their apartment blocks. However, the country retains the use of caning as a legacy of British colonial rule long after Britain has abolished corporal punishment in the UK.

Ghana is another common law country profiled as being off the beaten track and, like Singapore, it retains the death penalty that was introduced by the British despite the fact that the British have since abolished this at home. I am hopeful that the discovery of huge oil deposits in Ghana would lead to prosperity and less repression in a country where one young military officer seized power and executed the former military rulers of the country as a corruption deterrent but without proof that the death penalty is a deterrent to corruption.

During my workshop presentation in Singapore, I wondered why the country punishes the possession of certain amounts of marijuana with the death penalty when the trend in other parts of the world was toward decriminalization and legalization of marijuana for medicinal and recreational purposes. At the same time, Singapore advertised huge amounts of tobacco at the airport for duty-free purchases despite the fact that tobacco kills millions of people worldwide annually but marijuana has never killed anyone. This book informs the readers that the country makes efforts to restrict public smoking of tobacco but I hope that the book will encourage Singaporeans to relax the authoritarianism with regard to marijuana and grant law-abiding adults the freedom to choose what to consume in the comfort of their own homes without posing a risk to anyone, especially given that marijuana has been an ingredient in traditional Chinese and Indian medicines for thousands of years.

The irony in this book is that the former colonial locations off the beaten track have continued to embrace the repressiveness of the colonial authorities long after regaining their political independence, whereas the former colonizers have granted more freedom to their own home citizens by abolishing some of the colonial legislations still embraced by the post-colonial locations. For instance, the Philippines hunted and killed thousands of citizens who were suspected of drugs offenses whereas the former colonizers who imposed the death penalty on their colonies have since abolished the death penalty for all crimes with the exception of the US where a majority of the states and the federal government retain capital punishment for murder. Hopefully a book like this will implicitly have a wider impact beyond the classroom by encouraging the increased decolonization of the criminal justice system even though the authors did not explicitly call for penal abolitionism.

Similar puzzles emerged for me while reading the chapters on the socialist family of laws with a focus on Cuba and North Korea. Given the socialist theory of the withering away of the law in a classless society, it is hopeful that the socialist regimes will strive to be more compassionate toward deviants and use their policy preference for education as a core mission of the justice system to get people to say no to things like drugs or treat them in hospitals when they get sick as is the case with alcohol and tobacco which remain legal even in socialist countries. Personally, I wish that Cuba had forgiven General Ochoa who led the heroic Cuban forces that forced South Africa to withdraw from Angola and pave the way for the independence of Namibia and for a negotiated ending of apartheid. Ochoa was executed for drug trafficking whereas even the capitalist countries have abolished the death penalty for drug offenses.

I hope that the book will encourage South Africans to use their hybrid criminal justice system to address the injustice of apartheid by redistributing land to the landless majority, building homes for the homeless, and by making education free at all levels as part of the original policy of truth and reconciliation as an alternative to punitiveness. Similarly, I hope that a book like this will indirectly persuade the people of North Korea to invest more in the welfare of their people and less in militarism given that social security is more likely to guarantee national security than missiles that were aimed at working people in other countries. Adherence to their socialist family of law principles should prioritize the reunification of Korea and the ending of hostilities between brothers and sisters in the Korean peninsula.

Brazil is one of the illustrations of the Germanic family of laws and it is claimed in the book that 91% of the citizens are literate. I hope that the marginalization of indigenous Brazilians and of the descendants of enslaved Africans will finally be ended in Brazil through equitable access to publicly funded higher education for all and through the elimination of the slums where the poor are forced to live in crime-infested hovels despite huge income from petro-dollars. Brazil continues the war on drugs against the poor while Portugal, the colonial power, has since decriminalized the possession of all drugs and, thereby, reduced the harm associated with drug use. The Czech Republic is another country in the Germanic family of laws and it may be benefitting from membership of the European Union with the requirement that all members must abolish the death penalty. Hopefully, such a standard of penal abolitionism will be globalized to end the brutalization of the conscience of the people by criminal justice systems that retain the barbaric practice of death penalty indirectly encouraging citizens to kill one another as punishment in the settling of scores. Jurisdictions with the death penalty also tend to record higher rates of homicide than abolitionist jurisdictions.

The countries used to illustrate the Islamic family of laws expose readers to less researched countries like Iran and Yemen. I hope that the chapters will indirectly encourage even non-Islamic countries to consider the principle of victim-forgiveness of offenders on the belief that their own transgressions will one day be forgiven. I hope that such forgiveness will be more widely applied in Islamic countries themselves by investing more in nonviolence and less in militarism given that much of those weapons that are manufactured in Western countries tend to fall into the hands of militant Islamic terrorists and result in genocidal wars.

Romania and Italy illustrate the Napoleonic family of laws based on Roman law and it is encouraging to know that both countries have evolved beyond the brutal eras of fascism and state capitalism to offer more compassionate criminal justice systems. I read somewhere that prisoners could be given discounts on their sentences if they write and publish a book in Romania. Similarly, the Italian army is said to be given the authority to grow medicinal marijuana for distribution to patients in Italy.

Finally, the Vatican is used to represent the canon family of laws. Hopefully, such church laws would be updated to end the arbitrary prohibition of priests and nuns from getting married and thereby hopefully reduce the huge scandal of the sexual abuse of children by Catholic clergy. It is true that sexual abuse of children is widespread worldwide but the Catholic Church appears to be struggling with this problem more than most and the marriage prohibition is not helping matters. Hopefully, church law will also recognize a woman's right to choose preventive health care under supervision from her physician. I am almost certain that the Vatican prison does not hold any woman for committing abortion and so the prohibition only succeeds in risking the lives of women, especially in postcolonial locations, who are forced to patronize quack doctors for procedures that could be done in safer clinics. In this direction, Pope Francis may be offering innovation by writing about the Joys of Love to the consternation of conservative Bishops who seem to think that allowing divorced couples to continue receiving communion or allowing same-sex couples to be a part of the church would be against the gospel of love even for the enemy as advocated by Christian ideology.

I highly recommend this thought-provoking book to all levels of readers within and beyond classrooms with the expectation that it will be the catalyst for increased law reforms in pursuit of enhanced social justice globally.

Biko Agozino
Virginia Tech

ABOUT THE AUTHORS

Victoria M. Time is University Professor and Professor of Criminology and Criminal Justice in the Department of Sociology and Criminal Justice at Old Dominion University, Norfolk, Virginia. Her education comprises two law degrees from the University of Cameroon; a master's degree in comparative law from George Washington University Law School; a master's degree in justice, law and society from American University in Washington, D.C.; and a PhD in Criminology from Indiana University of Pennsylvania.

Her research endeavors capture her various interests in comparative justice systems, contemporary legal issues, human rights, nation building, and crimes of culture. She has published extensively. Her first book titled *Shakespeare's Criminals: Criminology, Fiction, and Drama* portrays her interest in the English classics and criminological theories; while her second book titled *Women's Social and Legal Issues in African Current Affairs* demonstrates her interest in human rights and crimes of culture. Some of her numerous articles can be found in journals such as *Journal of Criminal Justice*; *International Journal of Comparative and Applied Criminal Justice*; *Women and Criminal Justice*; *Social Justice*, *Journal of Ethnicity in Criminal Justice*; among others. In addition, some of her other works can be found in numerous book chapters.

Victoria M. Time has travelled extensively in the United States and worldwide to present her research at conferences and symposiums on a variety of social and justice issues, and to teach as a visiting professor in foreign universities such as University of Kitakyushu, Japan, and Zhejiang University Guanghua Law School, China.

W. Timothy Austin received the PhD degree with distinction from the University of Georgia's Department of Sociology and Anthropology in 1972 after earlier preparation in anthropology and criminology from Florida State University. Research includes multiple ethnographic field ventures to Singapore, the Philippines, and the Crow Reservation funded by several Fulbright, NSF, and U.S. Institute of Peace grants. Teaching specialties at Indiana University of Pennsylvania over the past three decades focused on comparative justice systems and criminological theory. Several books include *Banana Justice: Fieldnotes on Philippine Crime and*

Culture (Praeger); and *Criminological Thought: Pioneers Past and Present* (co-authored with R. J. Mutchnick and Randy Martin, Prentice-Hall). Articles appear in such journals as *Criminology, Social Forces, Human Organization, Deviant Behavior, Criminal Justice and Behavior*, and *Practicing Anthropology*, among others.

CHAPTER 1
Thinking Comparatively

There are many ways to introduce the subject of comparative justice and not everyone would agree with the same approach. With this in mind, we offer a simple definition of comparative justice that is suitable for us, at least for the moment. That is, the study of the similarities and dissimilarities of diverse systems of social order. This brief and purposefully abstract definition only somewhat narrows our field of study. It is true that this book will identify selections of varied and sometimes overlooked justice systems from around the world. But, that is only part of the story. Let us back off for a moment and consider some of the varied ways that systems of social order might be viewed. Three rather slippery and overlapping perspectives of looking at human cultural diversity arise as especially significant when comparing justice systems: the spatial, the temporal, and the legal. Each merits separate consideration.

SPATIAL PERSPECTIVES

We begin with the spatial perspective because most readers likely perceive of comparative justice, first and foremost, in a geographical sense. Even though we live on a spherical earth, we tend to see and think of things as existing on a horizontal level. It is not surprising that when early explorers and social scientists, and later criminologists, began thinking comparatively they began by relating different cultural areas and nations of the world from geographical viewpoints. The age-old question of "What is on the other side of the mountain?" comes to mind. Yet, we do not have to think on a global scale when discussing the spatial aspects of comparative justice. In fact, we do not have to think beyond a single nation. Consider the United States of America. We could compare and contrast systems of social order in different regions of the nation (i.e., north versus south), different states (i.e., Texas versus Vermont), or different cities (i.e., New York versus Honolulu, etc.). Without question we could uncover a wide variation in how social order and particularly justice systems are defined, and how they emerged and are managed within the confines of a single nation.

Also, from a spatial perspective one could compare similarities and dissimilarities in rural and urban areas and surely never have to depart the nation of study. This was eloquently demonstrated by Émile Durkheim in the late 19th century when he examined differences in overall lifeways and, specifically, social organization patterns between the city of Paris and the surrounding French villages (1893). Durkheim found that one could compare health patterns such as suicides, physical illnesses, and other styles of social and emotional problems, to include lawbreaking, by contrasting big-city life with small-town life and without departing the nation's boundaries. Folk-oriented social features in the rural areas such as cultural homogeneity, family integrity, and altruism were associated with lower suicide rates and to less interpersonal conflict; consequently, Durkheim must be considered a comparative scholar (see, for instance, 1895; c.f., 1897).

Following in the footsteps of Durkheim, early rural sociologists continued to maintain comparative traditions in their studies of folk-urban distinctions that indirectly pertained to social deviance and norm-breaking between small-town agricultural communities that could be contrasted to urban areas (Smith, 1940; Sorokin, Zimmerman, & Galpin, 1930) and without necessarily departing a nation's boundaries. However, it was likely the early anthropologists were the first to think cross-culturally in an attentive and organized manner and from international points of view long before university courses on comparative justice began to thrive in the last quarter of the 20th century. Yet, the cultural anthropologists, in their studies of relatively unexplored parts of the world, did not limit their attention to crime and justice patterns. Instead, they more commonly concerned themselves with the overall lifeways of a society or segment of the world's people (i.e., frequently tribal areas) and only incidentally touched upon law and justice issues (Benedict, 1934; Linton, 1936; Lowie, 1920). Exceptions did emerge such as Maine's work on *Ancient Law* (1861), Malinowski's *Crime and Custom in a Savage Society* (1926), and Hoebel's *Law of Primitive Man* (1954).

Other reflections of comparative justice become important from spatial or geographic perspectives. Consider how humankind has shown high degrees of mobility from the earliest time of hunters and gatherers. Not unlike many lower animals, mobility was essential for people in the search for better resources and living conditions. It is not surprising that people would conflict with one another as they competed for scarce commodities, sometimes out of necessity and sometimes out of greed. Regardless, some human populations found the need to better themselves by plundering the resources of others—humans became aggressors and territorial. Ian Armit's writing on violence in the deep human past is instructive (2011).

Most nations of the world have suffered, and many continue to suffer, as one nation or people overtake the land and resources of others. Again, it is possible to focus on a single nation and compare how its inhabitants are, in fact, comprised of different peoples—the conquerors and the conquered. Very few of the approximately 220 nations of the world have managed to escape outside invaders and this frequently results in the longstanding stressful subjugation of the original inhabitants. In recent years this area of study falls under the theme of postcolonialism. The vast majority of nations of the world can be explored with this characteristic in mind, and this becomes another way that people and justice systems within the boundaries of a single nation can be observed and compared (see, for instance, the work of Agozino, 2003).

Any attempt to examine how a nation defines and manages social order and systems of justice must keep in mind the cultural mosaic of the world's countries resulting from invasion and annexation from without. As will be shown in subsequent chapters of this book, some nations are not as fortunate as others as foreign aggressors and trespassers continue to exert influence over original occupants, express themselves in different languages and customs, and struggle with the dominated over how social order and/or government systems should be maintained.

If we look for a moment at the USA, we see numerous examples of cultures and segments of society that sometimes conflict. Perhaps more than any other nation, the United States continues to be comprised of peoples from all world areas that have migrated into the country and that now reside either as nationalized citizens, lawful non-citizen residents, or even as undocumented and illegal outsiders. Again, our point being made is that by focusing within the borders of the USA, or within the boundaries of other countries, we can see a multitude of ethnic diversity. It is not so much that we need to compare and contrast one nation with another, but that we must not overlook the cultural mixture within specific nations.

Thus, for instance, one can spend a lifetime trying to understand the complexities of the approximately three million Native Americans who have endured considerable migration within the confines of the nation, many now living on federal reservations geographically secluded from the rest of the country's citizens. The conception of social order and justice on American Indian reservations is certainly distinct from that of off-reservation life. Thus, we are still thinking spatially, or geographically and comparatively, but within the borders of a specific nation.

Also, too often a people are dispersed from a homeland (i.e., diaspora) by war, natural disaster, or even economic ventures to include slavery, and are compelled to flee their homeland and sometimes cross over and occupy land of neighboring nations. Makeshift shelters and tent cities arise for many thousands of displaced persons who sometimes remain for years removed from their native land. As with reservation life for American Indians, and from a spatial perspective, such diaspora compounds the comparative issue. How is social order maintained in dispersed populations in what sometimes becomes near anarchic settings and how does this affect justice processing? The tent cities in the countries of Jordan, Turkey, and Haiti represent only a few examples of the complexities of considering comparative justice from spatial or geographic perspectives (For discussion of tent cities, see, for example, Kimmelman, 2014).

As a subdiscipline of criminology, it is not easy to precisely define the subject matter of comparative justice. The number of nations of the world is imprecise and, in fact, it is rather confusing to define what is meant by the concept of nation or nation-state. There are disputed territories around the globe making it unclear how to describe a nation's boundaries. Also, some nations hold onto lands or territories dispersed around the world that have some qualities of distinct cultural areas yet remain officially linked to or possessed by a homeland. The United Kingdom of Great Britain identifies 14 such territories (e.g., The British Virgin Islands, the Cayman Islands, Bermuda, etc.). The United States possesses five territories (e.g., American Samoa, Guam, Northern Mariana Islands, Puerto Rico, and the U.S. Virgin Islands), and any of these could arguably reflect unique justice systems worthy of discussion. Furthermore, and making matters more complex, how do we fit Russia, the Ukraine, and/or Crimea into a discussion of comparative justice? However, we must think beyond the spatial or geographic perspective.

TEMPORAL PERSPECTIVES

Comparison of various styles of social order is not limited to relating one place to another across geographic boundaries; one can also compare differences that take place over time. It may be that this viewpoint is so obvious that it is sometimes overlooked. That is, we are actually referring to a historical perspective that considers how systems of social order and justice have altered over the years. As noted earlier, the various perspectives of thinking comparatively overlap and it is difficult to discuss one without the other. Different spatial areas at diverse locations of the globe could be compared at one point of time, or a single nation could be segmented into many different time periods and examined for how social order may have changed over the course of history.

Rather than picturing yourself crossing the ocean in search of distant lands to explore for varied systems of social order, imagine yourself on a time machine in the middle of Washington, D.C., or for that matter, any city in any nation. You start the time machine so that you can view the flow of history as you go back in time while remaining in the same location. If you were to stop the machine at every previous decade or century, you would undoubtedly observe variation, sometimes profound, in human behavior and social custom. At each temporal stage, were it possible, you could depart the time machine and explore how persons resolve their interpersonal conflicts and how society generally tries to maintain peace and order. Although it is beyond the scope of this book, it is important to keep in mind that we could consider how systems of social order and justice have emerged at many time periods. Every nation of the world has a history, some extending thousands of years. To understand the present, it will often be necessary to give consideration to the past. In the temporal sense, comparative criminology or justice necessarily becomes comparative history.

To push this idea a bit further, we can make the point that with rare exceptions, every city was at some distant time in its past a village. For example, the modern-day metropolis of Istanbul in the Republic of Turkey was in an earlier era Constantinople. If we dig deeper into Constantinople's past, we find the ancient settlement of Byzantium. Each had its own distinct system of social order and justice. Similarly, the present-day city of Bagdad in the Republic of Iraq was in its distant past adjacent to the settlement known as Babylon. Thus, rather than exploring Durkheim's folk-urban distinctions from spatial perspectives, one can look at the progression of changes from folk to urban settlements from temporal or historic viewpoints.

We are concerned in this book with cross-cultural differences in how peace and order are maintained and we can explore different geographic locations (i.e., for instance, nations of the world) and also at various points in time. Some clarity can be added to this discussion if we consider how attempts to maintain peace and order, whether spatially or temporally, have been seen to fluctuate from informal to formal styles of social organization. As noted, both early anthropologists and sociologists labored over how the evolution of human society shifted from the simple to complex modes of social organization in the quest for ways to solve problems of survival. In order to endure, people found it functional to solve their problems in groups and communities rather than to go it alone. Only in communities were the various social institutions of family, economy, education, religion, and ultimately government, adequately fashioned (Homans, 1950; Linton, 1936; Park & Burgess, 1921).

What a perplexing and likely impossible task it would be to try to analyze all the systems of social order from both spatial and temporal standpoints throughout the more than several hundred often shifting nations and culturally distinct territories of the world.

LEGAL PERSPECTIVES

Fossil evidence suggests that humans have roamed the earth for about 200,000 years. However, only in the past four or five thousand years (i.e., 2 to 3% of human history) have people established laws aimed at officially instituting mandatory codes of conduct. It somewhat begs the question of how humans maintained systems of social order in the roughly 97% of their history prior to the evolution of law. Surely a legal system would require the existence of some form of government. Moreover, if we consider the early development of legal codes in ancient Egypt around 5,000 years ago (Theodorides, 1971), or King Hammurabi's legal codes in Babylon around 4,000 years ago (Chisholm, 1911), we must also presume that some system of implementation and enforcement of law must have existed or at least had been contemplated, no matter how primitive.

Importantly, for us to think comparatively we must realize that the development of the social institution of government, and subsequently of legal systems did not emerge in the same way, or at the same time periods around the globe. Legal systems are highly varied and dependent, in part, on the nature of other social institutions that help provide a backdrop for legal codes (i.e., family, economy, religion, etc.). The development of diverse traditions of law around the world provides another way for us to categorize and, thus, to compare justice systems. The variation of law into distinct traditions in different cultural areas of the world and at different time periods is sufficiently important to necessitate separate discussion in Chapter 2 of this book.

REFERENCES

Agozino, B. (2003). *Counter-colonial criminology: A critique of imperialist reason.* London: Pluto Press.

Armit, I. (2011). Violence and society in the deep human past. *British Journal of Criminology, 51*(3), 499–517.

Benedict, R. (1934). *Patterns of culture.* New York: Houghton Mifflin.

Chisholm, H. (1911). Babylonian law. *Encyclopedia Britannica* 3 (11th ed.). Cambridge University Press.

Durkheim, É. (1893). *The division of labor in society.* (Translated from the original by G. Simpson, 1933). New York: Macmillan.

______. 1895. *The rules of sociological method.* (Translated from the original by S. A. Solovay and J. H. Mueller). Chicago: University of Chicago Press.

Hoebel, A. E. (1954). *Law of primitive man.* Boston: Atheneum.

Homans, G. (1950). *The human group.* New York: Harcourt, Brace, and World, Inc.

Kimmelman, M. (2014). Refugee camp for Syrians in Jordan evolves into a do-it-yourself city. (July 4), *New York Times.*

Linton, R. (1936). *The study of man.* New York: Appleton-Century-Crofts, Inc.

Lowie, R. (1920). *Primitive society.* New York: Boni and Liveright.

Park, R. and Burgess, E. (1921). *Introduction to the science of sociology.* Chicago: University of Chicago Press.

Smith, T. L. (1940). *The sociology of rural life.* New York: Harper & Brothers.

Sorokin, P. A., Zimmerman, C. C., & Galpin, C. J. 1930. *A systematic source book on rural sociology.* Minneapolis: University of Minnesota Press.

Theodorides, A. (1971). The concept of law in ancient Egypt. In J. R. Harris (Ed.), *The Legacy of Egypt* (2nd ed.). London: Oxford University Press.

CHAPTER 2

Families of Law

As we categorize and compare systems of justice we realize the many benefits of such an endeavor. It is always necessary to study the system of a particular country in a larger context rather than in isolation because it is only then we see the strengths and weaknesses of a particular system. At first glance, a beginning student of criminal justice may be left with the impression that the criminal justice system is limited in its influence by the functions and decisions of agents in law enforcement, the judiciary, and corrections. While this is correct, it is a simplistic view of the criminal justice system because agencies not directly associated with the criminal justice system impinge on its workings, even if indirectly, and on the behavior of people.

Churches, and schools for instance, and even the family, act as indirect/informal controls to delinquency and crime, and in some societies, the local rulers and their henchmen play vital roles in crime control and in redressing wrongdoing. Social services that deal with early intervention to help abused or wayward children, or that oversee individual well-being, family, and group harmony may influence the workings of the criminal justice system in unanticipated ways. When schools, churches, and social services are not quite effective in their involvement in the lives of youths, non-conforming behavior or conduct that is illegal may be exhibited, thereby prompting a stint with the criminal justice system. It is, therefore, necessary that in our study of the criminal justice system, we reach an understanding of how these informal mechanisms are utilized in other societies as measures of crime control, and how they affect the larger and formalized institutions that form the criminal justice system.

Before getting into a discussion of the various families of law, a brief explanation of the importance of learning about the criminal justice system of other countries is necessary. Below are some of the benefits.

Getting ideas on improvement: As we categorize and compare systems of justice, we realize the many benefits of such an endeavor. It is always necessary to study the system of a particular country in a larger context rather than in a limited context.

In the Philippines, for instance, the barangay captain (a locally elected leader) tries amicably to settle disputes. When mediation fails within 15 days, the captain chooses 10–20 community members (*lupon*) among whom the disputants select 3 to arbitrate their dispute. This informal dispute resolution is intended to preserve community harmony (Austin, 1987).

To increase knowledge: It is also necessary to compare systems of justice for knowledge sake. Even though there is plenty to know about one's country, there is a lot more to know about other countries and how their systems of justice work. Universities everywhere admit foreign students into their programs. These foreign students learn about the country in which they are studying. Wouldn't it be smart to also know about your classmates' country of origin? Being curious about what is on the other side of the mountain not only makes one academically adroit; it also enriches and changes one's perception of others for the better. Dammer and Albanese (2014) and Reichel (2008) explain that studying the justice systems of other countries help us ward off ethnocentrism. There is nothing wrong with pride of country, but that may be limiting if one's pride of country inhibits one's appreciation of the good things in other countries. While nothing beats experiencing the culture of a people firsthand, the next best thing is reading about it. Not knowing anything at all about others opens up room for ethnocentrism (see also, Time, 2006).

Studies on delinquency show a correlation between broken or single-family homes and delinquent behavior (Juby & Farrington 2001; Thornberry, Smith, Rivera, Huizinga, & Stouthamer-Loeber, 1999). In order to test this hypothesis in Cameroon, Ngale (2009) administered a questionnaire to 120 youths in the Batemba Correctional Centre in the Centre Province of the country. Ngale was unable to confirm this hypothesis since 66.1% of the youths came from families with both parents still married and living together. Ngale surmised that other factors such as absence of direct and steady involvement in the child's life (parents spend long hours away working low income jobs or doing farm work), relative fiscal deprivation, substandard living amenities due to overcrowding (too many extended family members living in a small space), and other factors contribute to children's delinquent behavior. So, in the Cameroonian context, just having both parents still in an intact union at home is not sufficient to contain children's delinquent behavior, a hands-on approach to raising the children, providing proper guidance, and instilling wholesome values are necessary to steer children in the right direction. This is just one example of how we can broaden our knowledge of an issue or a country.

To find ways of curbing transnational and international crimes: Crimes that transcend a country's borders are transnational crimes. Human trafficking for sexual and labor slavery, terrorism, cybercrimes, poaching of exotic animals, money laundering, drug trafficking, and a host of others, constitute transnational crimes. International crimes are those that are carried out within a country to subjugate or terrorize a class of people. Genocide, slavery, and torture are among crimes agreed upon by the community of nations as international crimes (Dammer & Albanese, 2014). These crimes, too, could be considered transnational crimes if their effects spill into other countries.

Today, many terrorist groups are sprouting, and travelers are ever more vigilant than hitherto. Security at airports is suffocating, as there is no telling where the next terrorist attack would take place, or who the next terrorist would be. In 2014, Boka Haram, a thug group creating havoc in Nigeria, kidnapped over 300 schoolgirls. ISIS, an extremist group, is also wreaking havoc in Syria and elsewhere, and Al-Qaeda has not been completely contained; it sporadically unleashes attacks in the Middle East and in Africa. An attack by gunmen on March 14, 2016, that killed 22 people in a resort beach in Cote D'Ivoire has been claimed by Al-Qaeda (CCTV News, Beijing, China, 3/14/2016). The United States, European countries, and some Middle Eastern countries' intent to find ways of ending terror have held bilateral and multilateral meetings, yet terrorism remains a real problem (Tolipov, 2006). Even when the terrorist attack occurs in one country, its effects are felt worldwide. As symbolic victims, everyone remains terrified and alert. Direct victims could be from a multitude of countries. Take the terrorist attack in the United States at the World Trade Center on September 11, 2001, for instance. Of the 2,753 killed (CNN.com, 2013/07/27), 372 were foreigners from 61 countries (Brilliant Maps.com, Sep. 11, 2015).

FAMILIES OF LAW

There are over 200 sovereign countries in the world today, each with its own system of justice and body of law. Studying and mastering each system of justice and law in every country may be too cumbersome and perhaps impossible for students whose curricula require that they take a course on comparative justice system in one semester. Fairchild (1993) notes that it is not only impossible for students to grasp details of each country's justice system, but that it may be needless in that such attempts only provide students with rudimentary knowledge when they could benefit more by studying in detail samples of countries from each family of law.

Families of law broadly explain the legal structure to which a country is premised, and which it practices. These families of law are divided into secular and religious, and some with a blend of both, while others blend both or one, and add traditional folkways into their laws. Secular systems emphasize and promote a system whereby man makes laws, and administers and enforces them with the predicate purpose of controlling human interactions. Religious systems are premised on divine laws, which cannot be changed nor modified by man. Traditional laws are based on beliefs and practices that over time become the norm. They are upheld and enforced by custodians of customs, chiefs, or a village ruler. The emphasis in traditional systems is group cohesion.

Early writers on comparative justice systems like David and Brierly (1968, 1985) glean three families of law globally: common law, socialist law, and Romano-Germanic law. To these Fairchild (1993) discusses the Napoleonic civil system apart from the Germanic civil law system, and adds Islamic law. In subsequent editions Fairchild and Dammer (2001) add the hybrid system of law. The countries from which these families of law originate form the model countries/systems: common law—England; Napoleonic civil law—France; Germanic civil law—Germany; Socialist law—Russia; Islamic law—Saudi Arabia; and hybrid system—Japan.

In order to understand the impact of each family of law on a country, the historical, political, and for some, religious leanings of a country, must be examined. This is important since the "model" countries spread their family of law to other countries through colonization, apartheid, or because of shared religion, tradition, beliefs, ideologies, language, race, and geography.

In this book we adopt the six families of law; instead of dwelling on the often-discussed model countries, we use the following sampled countries:

- Common Law: Singapore and Ghana
- Napoleonic civil law: Italy and Romania
- Germanic civil law: Brazil and Czech Republic
- Islamic law: Yemen and Iran
- Socialist law: Cuba and North Korea
- Hybrid system: Philippines and South Africa

We also added the Vatican City as a separate chapter based upon its uniqueness as the smallest independent state with canon law as its main system of law, and the Pope as its leader.

A little background information on the families of law and countries of origin is necessarily helpful.

COMMON LAW: ENGLAND

The common law system is a product of English law. The Middle Ages in Europe was marred by several wars, with causes ranging from the quest to spread a particular religion in the continent or to conquer and secure more territory, or to consolidate and solidify royal authority. When William the Conqueror, French nobility, conquered England in 1066 he sought to spread his influence and authority in the country. One way of accomplishing that was through the judicial system. In that endeavor, he established King's Courts also known as Curia Regis.

The system of dispute resolution at the time was through the writs system, which was basically a royal fiat that laid out specific outcomes for specific issues. This rigid system did not take into consideration the principle of individuality, which, in essence, notes that no two cases are exactly the same. So, to treat cases similarly when there were distinguishing factors smacked of equity or fairness. To right these apparent injustices, chancery courts or equity courts were established. These equity courts used Roman and natural laws to guide their decisions.

While the king's court and chancery courts operated separately, over time they each carved for themselves procedural and substantive standards unique to each. The king's court adhered to the common practice of having similar cases having similar results—a system of sticking with precedent, which eventually led to the concept of *stare decisis* (let that which has been decided stand), a system that advocates adherence to precedent when cases have similar facts. With compliance to precedence and laws uniformly applicable throughout the country came the existence of common law.

There are certain characteristics of common law that students of criminal justice must know:

1. Common law is not codified: Law is simply based on outcome of trials, and not on structured rules and statutes. The outcome of cases serves as guidelines for future cases with similar facts. This is what precedent is, and precedents are stored in court records/transcripts and law journals.

2. Common law systems are adversarial: This means that there are two opposing sides. The side that brings charges is the prosecutor on behalf of the direct victim, and the symbolic victim, the state (accusatorial side). The side fighting those charges is the defendant who is defended by an attorney. The judge is present as a detached and neutral person who acts as a referee or moderator to be sure that each side has adequate opportunity to present its case (Neubauer & Fradella, 2014).

3. Common law systems are based on a bench or a jury trial: An accused person may be tried by a judge alone (bench/court trial) or by a jury trial. The jury is composed of laypeople who represent all walks of life in the community. Modifications of the jury system can be seen in countries that apply the common law. Even when the jury makes a determination in a case, and recommends a sentence, the judge ultimately determines the sentence.

4. Common law systems proceed from the standpoint of "innocent until proved guilty": Throughout the process, regardless of how much evidence the state has against a defendant, the latter is considered innocent and only proclaimed guilty after the jury in a jury trial or a judge in a bench trial finds the defendant guilty at the conclusion of the case.

5. In the fact-finding process, both sides conduct direct and cross-examinations—a process that is intended to impeach the testimony of witnesses in hopes of having the truth prevail. This process is essential since it gives an opportunity for each side to present its case, and for the other side to reveal through cross-examination, weaknesses in the other side's case. This process better informs the court as the court tries to make a determination in the case, and more importantly, allows litigants' voices to be heard and considered (Sward, 1989).

6. The right to discovery: Discovery is a process whereby both sides to a case exchange information they have about the case. The process is intended to have both sides begin the adversarial process from a balanced position since each side would have knowledge of factual evidence that the other possesses. This process dates back to the Roman and Canon Law, but as Sward (1989) explains, it became more useful in the 19th century in England as a way of promoting equity.

NAPOLEONIC CIVIL LAW: FRANCE

Napoleon Bonaparte established the French civil code, or *Code Civil des Francais*, in 1804. When Napoleon became emperor of France, he embarked on making changes not only in the political and administrative arena, but in the judiciary as well. Notable of his reforms was the civil code, which has endured centuries after his death in 1815. When Napoleon was revising the laws of France, he engaged the services of legal experts who could put together an organized set of laws that eliminated the chaotic feudal and royal laws in existence at the time. Napoleon asked for a single code that would unify the various civil laws in the country and which reflected progressive ideals. The commission of four prominent jurists worked assiduously to compile the Napoleonic code or civil code, which consisted of 2,281 articles. Among some of the issues in the code were those that dealt with property rights, contracts, matrimonial issues, and a host of other civil issues (Merryman, 1985).

After harmonizing the civil code, Napoleon's next task was to put together a criminal code. The *Code Penale* of 1810 reflected his feelings of those who break the law, in that the code was deemed to be quite draconian (Fairchild & Dammer, 2001). The 1810 code replaced the

French penal code of 1791. The 1810 code was applicable in France until March 1, 1994, when a new penal code replaced it.

Characteristics of the French *Code Penale*:

1. It consists of codified laws: Rather than rely on precedents as obtained in common law, the French civil code is an exposition of criminal laws, classification and definition of crimes, and an outline of the corresponding punishment.
2. The trial process is inquisitorial rather than adversarial: The presiding judge plays a hands-on role in the criminal justice process. The judge supervises the search and gathering processes of evidence relevant to the case. He/she interrogates the defendant as well as witnesses on both sides of the case. In the process, attorneys on both sides question and cross-examine witnesses, but their role seems rather secondary as the judge assumes the lead in the process.
3. Accused is not presumed guilty: Even though a criminal defendant in the inquisitorial system is not presumed guilty, the fact that a case is only brought against a suspect when there is evidence showing involvement in a crime projects the impression that accused persons are presumed guilty. Worthy of note is the point that factual guilt is different from legal guilt, and this is the case in both an adversarial and an inquisitorial process.
4. Fact finders: Professional judges and lay judges who are known as assessors usually decide cases in inquisitorial trials.

GERMANIC CIVIL CODE: GERMANY

The German civil code, also called *Burgerliche Gesetzbuch*, came into existence about a century after the French civil code. Its origins are traced to feudal and territorial laws that developed in the 11th century. By the 13th century many of these laws were written in statute books. Both written and unscripted customary laws were applicable in the territory. Efforts at compiling and codifying the law in order to make it similarly applicable throughout the region occupied legal scholars and jurists.

At the same time that the Germans were putting together their laws, Italian scholars were modifying Roman law and spreading it to many European countries including Germany. It was easy for Roman law to spread in Germany because of the influence of Canon law and Germany's slow pace to unify their laws.

Giving several additions to the code, including aspects of substantive criminal law and criminal procedure, substantial progress to the German code was made. After the Napoleonic wars, Germany was intent on establishing a cohesive body of laws and a national identity fostered by a German code of laws. Otto von Bismarck was Chancellor of Germany from 1871–1890. During his tenure, he enacted a unified criminal code. With several tweaking and amending laws German scholars were able to come up with an acceptable civil code in 1896, which was finally adopted in 1900.

Differences Between the German and French Civil Codes

- The German code is lengthy and complex and intended to be used mainly by legal professionals. The code was not intended to unify or codify existing laws. Unlike the French code that reflects "assumptions" regarding human beings based on secular and natural law, German law is more of a reflection and collection of empirical data that situates the existing German legal system in its historical setting (Merryman & Perez-Perdomo, 2007).
- German code allows the flexibility of judges to interpret the code; but French judges adhere to a rigid application of the civil code.

Similarities Between the German and French Codes

- Statutes govern both. Both were developed to unify the nation. Parts of their origins are from Roman and canon law. Both stemmed from the era of industrialization and the spread of trade and commerce. They both spread their influences in colonized territories, and by modern states adopting the system of law.
- On November 13, 1998, a new version of the criminal code was promulgated which was subsequently amended (Criminal Code, Federal Law Gazette [*Bundesgesetzblatt*] 1, p. 3322). It was amended by Article 1 of the law of September 24, 2013 (Criminal Code, Federal Law Gazette 1, p. 3671), and with a follow-up text of Article 6 (18) of the Law of October 10, 2013 (Criminal Code, Federal Law Gazette 1, p. 3799). The Criminal Code outlines and defines crimes, and in essence explains substantive criminal law within its various sections, much akin to explanations of what one would find in an American textbook on substantive criminal law, except there are no cases, and no rulings, and no names of judges. The code is divided into different sections, which encompass definitions of offenses, parties to a crime, punishments for the various crimes, correctional measures, as well as juvenile justice.

- Court procedure is investigatory; the judge plays a major role in the investigation and in decisions made about the case.
- Judicial precedent is not applied to decide a case; rather judges apply statutes that are closely related to the issue.
- Higher courts correct any errors made by lower courts, just as obtained in most justice systems.

SOCIALIST TRADITION

Socialist law is a body of law used in communist countries. There are different versions of socialist law, Russian and Chinese being the most dominant. Origins of socialist law can be traced to 1917 when Russia found itself ruled by the Bolsheviks. The latter sought to have a society that was communist (Terrill, 1999). The prevalent ideas among jurists at the time was that socialist law was superior to laws applied in capitalist countries, since the goal of socialist law was to protect society's collective interest, unlike non-socialist law that was used in capitalist countries to economically exploit the masses.

Many credit Marxist-Leninist ideologies with the advent of real socialism (Reichel, 2008; Terrill, 1999) even though its roots can be traced to the Romano-Germanic tradition. In crafting their ideas, Karl Marx envisioned a society whereby the welfare of society trumps individual aspirations for competition (The Marx-Engels Reader, 1978). Vladimir Ulyanov, later known as Lenin (1870–1924) masterminded the Bolshevik Revolution in 1917 and became head of the Union of Soviet Socialist Republics (USSR). Lenin absorbed Marx's ideas and promoted them as he ruled over the Communist Party. Lenin was of the belief that in order to spread the communist ideals, citizens had to be attuned with, and accept socialist law (Terebilov, 1973).

Lenin's ideas were utopic and with the Soviet Union striving to establish trade relations with other countries, a new civil code with ideas drawn from the German, French, Swiss, and Russian codes was established. However, with Stalin's advent to power in the 1920s, the civil code gradually experienced changes that provided a distinctive body of law that was known as socialist law.

Characteristics of Socialist Law

- It is opposed to the notion that law is the pillar of society because it is simply a tool by which autocratic rulers assert power over their citizens.

- It is intended to protect the state, thereby making crimes against the state more serious than those against private property.
- Law is considered an educational tool, so crimes are a result of government's failure to properly educate its citizens (Neubauer & Meinhold, 2012).
- Trials mirror rules and procedures applicable in Romano-Germanic law systems. The procurator presents the state's case against the defendant. Judges and assessors ask questions relating to both physical and testimonial evidence.
- Economic crimes, that is, weakening or crippling of communal production (by means such as ineptitude, lackluster performance), may lead to criminal prosecution as opposed to dismissal or some administrative action.
- The prosecutor's role is more robust in that besides prosecuting cases, the prosecutor oversees police investigations to ascertain that they are in sync with the law. As well, the prosecutor oversees jails and prisons to be sure that they meet the standards set by law.

ISLAMIC LAW

Unlike other families of law that are secular, Islamic law is religion-based. In this regard, there is no difference between judicial or social controls placed on a person. Every aspect of life is governed and controlled by Islamic law. Islamic law is premised on the belief of Allaḥ (God), with Prophet Muhammad being the messenger. It is believed that throughout his life, Muhammad received several revelations from God—Allah—that were put together after his death to constitute the Qur'an (Moore, 2002). With no mediator or arbiter to resolve disputes among citizens, Allah's ways and Muhammad's response provide guidance. Such guidance that governs moral, personal, criminal, and civil issues constitutes Sharia, which in Arabic means "the right path."

Sharia, Islamic law, has two components: the Qur'an and the Sunna. The Qur'an lays out standards of behavior for Muslims, while the Sunna contains the teachings and actions of the Prophet Muhammad. Muhammad's teachings explain and highlight the meaning and intentions of the Qur'an. In essence, the two are used simultaneously. Besides the Qur'an and the Sunna that constitute Sharia or Islamic law, *Ijma* (which means consensus) and *Qiyas* (which means reasoning by analogy) represent other principles of Islamic law (Moore, 2002). Issues that may not have been addressed in the Qur'an or Sunna, or whose explanations are questionable, are addressed by a group of reputable legal thinkers by applying reason through drawing inferences or making assumptions based on how similar or different the situations are. The reliance on reputable lawyers to arrive at a unanimous decision (*Ijma*) based upon the application of precedent or a new and informed decision as the case may be (Qiyas), inform Islamic law as well.

Regions vary in their interpretation and application of Islamic law. Two main sects—Sunni and Shi'a—exist, and members of either sect decide which school of law they subscribe to. Five schools of law among several others are dominant: Hanafi, Maliki, Shafi'i, Hanbali, and Ja'afari (only Ja'afari relate to Shi'a Islam). Hanafi school is the oldest and has the largest number of followers. Followers of the Hanafi school endorse the teachings or guidance of the Qur'an, the Sunna, the ijma and the qiyas, and incorporate traditional folkways and reasoning in their beliefs (Reichel, 2008). The Maliki school strictly adheres to and applies all four sources of Islam. The emphasis of the Shafi'i school is the Qur'an and the Sunna; application of the ijma and qiyas takes second place. Similar to the Shafi'i school, the emphasis of the Hanbali is on the Qur'an and Sunna, seldom are the ijma and qiyas applied. The Ja'afari school is different from the others in that it subscribes to the Shi'a application of Islamic law. This school of thought was headed by Imam Ja'far ibn Muhammad al-Sadiq. Their belief rests on the fact that next to the authority of Muhammad is Imam, and those two are the only legitimate Muslim leaders ordained by God (see Bulletin of Affiliation).

Main Criminal Justice Facts Relating to Islamic Law

- There are three broad classifications of crimes (a) crimes against God (*Hudud);* (b) crimes against humans (*Qisas*); (c) crimes whose punishments are not specified in the Qur'an and the Hadiths (*Tazir*).
- Crimes against God are the most serious. They include apostasy, adultery, sexual offenses, drug and alcohol use, larceny and other acts of thievery including highway robbery.
- The Qur'an specifies the corresponding punishments for *hudud* crimes. These punishments including flogging, amputation, banishment, and death, and are non-negotiable (Souryal, Alobied, & Potts, 1996). Judges are bound to the mandates of the Qur'an in both the application and enforcement of the Qur'an.
- *Qisas* crimes are crimes against humans or crimes against another (Burki, 2013). They include assault and battery, and murder be it intentional or unintentional killing.
- The word *Qisas* means "equitable retribution" (Reichel, 2008). Accordingly, the victim has to be redressed equitably, unless the victim or family members choose to forgive or request a lesser punishment. The option to exercise leniency or forgiveness for *Qisas* offenses is stated in the Qur'an (Reichel, 2008; Souryal, Alobied, & Potts, 1996).

- *Tazir* crimes are less serious offenses. They are not included in the Qur'an; as a result judges decide through consensus (*ijma*) if an act is a *Tazir* offense, and based on the gravity of the offence determine punishments for *Tazir* crimes. A key focus of punishment for *Tazir* offenses is to rehabilitate the offender (Reichel, 2008).

THE HYBRID SYSTEM

This family of law represents a combination or mixture of other families of laws plus indigenous laws. Colonization, new states, and importation of laws have left many countries with legal structures that reflect a combination of civil law, common law, or Islamic families of law juxtaposed with home cultures and mores. This is evident in Asia, Africa, and South America where many countries have pluralistic systems of justice. This makes assigning countries to specific families of law tenuous. Orucu (2008) opines that it is necessary for some countries to re-assign their legal systems since their family of law occasionally vacillates. While Orucu (2008) prefers to use the terminology "mixed" systems, he also explains that the concept of mixed systems can occasionally be exaggerated or misconstrued, especially when an older system of law is subsumed by another system of law. In this regard, Orucu (2008) gives the example of Hong Kong where Chinese customary law was subordinate to the dominant English Common Law until 1990, but now, contemporary Chinese law is becoming more dominant law.

Ten Categories of Mixed Systems Have Been Deciphered Worldwide

Civil law and common law (3.47%); civil law and customary law (28.54%); Civil law and Muslim law (3.14%); Common law and Customary law (2.94%); common law and Muslim law (5.25%); civil law, Muslim law, and customary law (3.62%); common law, Muslim law, and customary law (19.17%); civil law, common law, and customary law (0.8%); common law, Muslim law, and civil law (0.23%); civil law, common law, and Talmudic law (0.09%) (Orucu, 2008, pp. 4–5).

Japan, as an example of a hybrid system, has a combination of Japanese indigenous law; Chinese influence; and French, German and United States' systems of law. Between 1603 and 1867, Japan closed itself off from outside influence. Before this time, the Chinese were the only external influence on the Japanese way of life and system of justice. It follows that the years from external influences allowed Japan to fully mold its culture and impart it on its citizens, and this cultural preservation has sustained despite subsequent external influences. During that time, Japan cultivated and retained a singular identity and language. The Meiji Restoration (Meiji name of then-emperor) denotes the period when Japan decided to embrace foreign ideas and influences after its isolationist policy. The Meiji era, which lasted from 1868–1912, was marked by enormous changes in political ideology, economic growth, and cultural modification (Reichel, 2008). Notable of its external influences during this period were Germany, Prussia, and China.

Japan's legal system from 1870, and revised in 1873, was heavily influenced by Chinese penal law—The New Code of Laws as the applicable legal document adopted in Japan at the time. With increased fascination with German and French ideas, Japan replaced its 1873 code in 1880 with one that closely mirrored French justice system, but then that too was eventually replaced in 1907 by a code that was influenced by German system of law. After the Second World War, Japan's judicial system drew many of its rules of criminal procedure and substantive criminal law from the United States, and that remains true today (Reichel, 2008). This period of occupation (1945–1952) was also marked by the enactment of a new constitution—The Showa Constitution, a constitution that mirrored English and American ideals. A parliamentary system styled in a purely British fashion, and a Bill of Rights that are a direct reflection of the U.S. Fourth, Fifth, Sixth, and Eighth Amendments of the U.S. Bill of Rights, were put in place (Terrill, 1999). Today, Japan's system of justice is a hodge-podge of French and German civil systems of law, Anglo-American common law influence, and an overlay of Japanese indigenous folkways and mores. In essence, hybrid systems constitute a mixture of borrowed laws and traditional laws, a pluralistic system of laws, so to speak.

CANON LAW

Canon law is law of the Catholic Church, and its teachings primarily influence the Holy See. As well, the Vatican City may revert to Italian civil law in matters not addressed by laws of the Vatican City. One may be tempted to attribute this state of affairs to a hybrid system, but that is not the case. The dominant practice of the Vatican City is reliance on Catholicism and canon law, and deference is only made to Italian law when there is absolute need to.

SUMMARY

This chapter explained the advantages of studying the various justice systems of the world. Among the advantages are to get ideas on improving one's own justice system and to look for ways to address cross-national and international crimes. In this chapter as well, a synopsis of the various families of law is made. With over 200 countries worldwide, it is quite tasking to master the justice system of each of the countries; consequently, in this chapter we acquaint readers on what to discover or glean when they read about the various families of law. In the book we use a sample of countries that have seldom made samples in other comparative justice books to discuss common law, Napoleonic civil law, Germanic civil law, Islamic law, Socialist law, hybrid system, and we added canon law as it relates to the Vatican City.

DISCUSSION QUESTIONS

1. Discuss three advantages of studying the justice system of other countries.
2. Explain what common law is. What are the differences between common law and Napoleonic civil law?
3. Distinguish Napoleonic civil law from Germanic civil law.
4. Explain Islamic law. How is Islamic law different from canon law?
5. If you had to replicate this study, list which two countries you would include in each family of law. Explain why.

REFERENCES

Austin, W. T. (1987). Conceptual confusion among rural Filipinos in adapting to modern procedures of amicable settlement. *International Journal of Comparative and Applied Criminal Justice*. Winter 1987, 11(2).

Brilliant Maps.com. (Sep. 11, 2015). Countries that lost citizens on 9/11. Retrieved from http://brilliantmaps.com/9-11-victims/

Bulletin of Affiliation. (1998). *Al-Madhbab Schools of Thought Statistic, 17*(4), 5.

Burki, S. (2013). *The politics of state intervention: Gender politics in Pakistan, Afghanistan, and Iran*. Lanham, MD: Lexington Books.

CNN.com (2013, July 27). September 11th terror attacks fast facts. Retrieved from Http://www.cnn.com/2013/07/27/us/september-11-anniversary-fast-facts/index.html

CCTV News. (2016, March 14). Beijing, China.

Dammer, H., & Albanese, J. (2014). *Comparative criminal justice systems* (5th ed.). Australia: Wadsworth/Cengage Learning.

David, R., & Brierly, J. (1968, 1985). *Major legal systems of the world today*. London: Stevens & Sons.

Fairchild, E. (1993). *Comparative criminal justice systems*. Belmont, CA: Wadsworth Publishing Company.

Fairchild E., & Dammer, H. (2001). *Comparative criminal justice systems* (2nd ed.). Australia: Wadsworth/Thomson Learning.

Juby, H., & Farrington, D. (2001). Disentangling the link between disrupted families and delinquency. *British Journal of Criminology, 41*, 22–40.

The Marx-Engels Reader. (1978). (2nd ed.). R. C. Tucker (Ed.). New York: W.W. Norton & Co.

Merryman, J. (1985). *The civil law tradition.* Stanford, CA: Stanford University Press.

Merryman, J., & Perez-Perdomo, R. (2007). *The civil law tradition: An introduction to the legal systems of Europe and Latin America* (3rd ed.). Stanford, CA: Stanford University Press.

Moore, K. (2002). Islamic law. In Krietzer, H. (Ed.), *Legal systems of the world: A political, social, and cultural encyclodepia.* (Vol. 11, pp. 752–755). Santa Barbara, CA: ABC/CLIO.

Neubauer, D., & Fradella, H. (2014). *America's courts and the criminal justice system.* Belmont, CA: Cengage Publishing.

Neubauer, D., & Meinhold, S. (2012). *Judicial process: Law, courts, and politics in the United States.* Boston: Cengage Learning.

Ngale, F. I. (2009). Family structure and juvenile delinquency: Correctional Centre Betamba, Centre Province of Cameroon. *Internet Journal of Criminology,* 1–19. Retrieved from www.Internetjournalofcriminology.com/ngale

Orucu, E. (2008). What is a mixed legal system: Exclusion or expansion? *Electronic Journal of Comparative Law, 12,* 1–18.

Reichel, P. (2008). *Comparative criminal justice systems: A topical approach* (5th ed.). Upper Saddle River, NJ: Pearson/Prentice Hall.

Souryal, S., Alobied, A., & Potts, D. (1996). The penalty of hand amputation for theft in Islamic justice. *Journal of Criminal Justice, 22*(1), 249–265.

Sward, E. (1989). Values, ideology, and the evolution of the adversary system. *Indiana Law Journal, 64*(1), 301–355.

Terebilov, V. (1973). *The Soviet Court.* (M. Saifulin, Trans.). Moscow: Progress Publishers.

Terrill, R. (1999). *World criminal justice systems: A survey.* Cincinnati, OH: Anderson Publishing, Co.

Thornberry, T., Smith, C., Rivera, C., Huizinga, D., & Stouthamer-Loeber, M. (1999). Family disruption and delinquency. *Juvenile Justice Bulletin,* 1–7.

Time, V. (2006). The benefits of on-site studies. *Journal of Academic Exchange, 10*(2), 260–264.

Tolipov, F. (2006). Multilateralism, bilateralism and unilateralism in fighting terrorism in the SCO area. *China and Eurasia Forum Quarterly, 4*(2), 153–169.

PART I

The Family of Common Law

CHAPTER 3

The Singapore Model

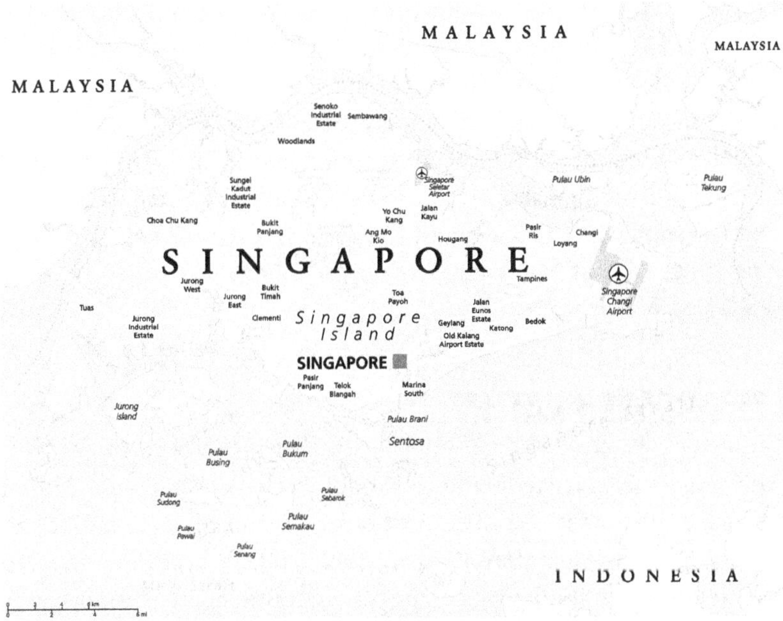

© Peter Hermes Furian/Shutterstock.com

INTRODUCTION

The Republic of Singapore is a diminutive island about three times the size of Washington, D.C., making it one of the smallest independent nations in the world. When Singapore makes the news, it is generally in regard to being on top, or near the top, of a list of nations that are safe, healthy, and successful—perhaps even happy (BBC News, 2013; Brodwin, 2015). It is true that when discussions turn to countries that seem to have solved their crime problem, Singapore must be in the conversation. The eyebrow-raising fact is generally remarked that Singapore takes seriously the old adage that if one spares the rod they will spoil the child. In Singapore, the rod, or rattan cane, is officially used in the administering of justice to adults as well as youth. We will often hear in the discussion that Singaporeans and visitors alike run the risk of the death penalty with no jury in sight if they are caught with specific amounts of illegal drugs. Next, we might hear that one cannot chew gum or litter the roads and walkways in Singapore without risk of punitive fees. All these characterizations have some truth in them, but they do not tell the complete story. We must go deeper into the culture to really understand what is happening in this small but dynamic nation. What really makes the island tick, particularly in regard to managing what appears to be one of the most effective programs of handling crime and justice in the world?

The Republic of Singapore is a strong example of the "common law" family that results from its close ties to the British legal system after 137 years of Great Britain's occupation of the island (i.e., 1826 to 1963). Adherence to the early English principle of relying on prior court decisions, or what had been common throughout the land to determine contemporary disputes (i.e., *stare decisis*) remains to the present day in Singapore. Although Singapore preserves its status as an independent nation, it stayed as a member of the Commonwealth of Nations comprised mainly of former British territories and headed by Great Britain. The influence of the British judicial system was noticeable until 1991 when the high courts of Singapore finally stopped wearing white wigs in court and using such expressions as "my lord" in addressing fellow judges (AP News Archive, 1991).

WHY OFF THE BEATEN PATH?

It is unclear why the social science literature would overlook the Republic of Singapore as a nation of emphasis in comparative justice textbooks. Of course, as noted, it has been in the conversation, but with a few exceptions (Austin, 1987; 2005; Mackey & Levan, 2013) remains often a sidenote to other criminological debates and cultural areas. The answer may lie in the remoteness of the island, hidden away between Malaysia and Indonesia and representing a population under six million, quite small in comparison to most nations. Also, over the past quarter century, the Singaporean society has been quietly minding its own business and has not come into major conflict with its neighbors, perhaps remaining somewhat out of sight and out of mind. Yet, over three decades have passed since Freda Adler presented her analysis of nations not obsessed with crime (Adler, 1983). Today, the small nation deserves closer attention.

GEO-DEMOGRAPHIC BACKDROP

If one wishes to create a low-crime nation, it is likely a good idea to begin with an island. Singapore starts with this advantage with its population contained, if not limited, from easily entering or leaving the island. For many decades only a single thoroughfare allowed citizens to depart the island by car, and this roadway bridge between Singapore and Malaysia remained highly regulated by on-site, personal inspection as well as constant video scrutiny. A second interisland expressway and checkpoint was added in 1998. From a purely ecological point of view, a car thief, or any offender for that matter, would be severely restricted in making a getaway. Similarly, the nation's authorities monitor the mobility of the population at the one major international airport, and at the single railway off the original bridge thoroughfare to Malaysia. The seaports are equally painstakingly controlled. Having said this, what is most remarkable about this island nation is that the population of 5.6 million citizens is squeezed onto a land space about 25 miles wide and 14 miles north to south. This fact makes Singapore the second most densely populated nation in the world following only the miniscule European Principality of Monaco. In 2016, the number of people residing in Singapore per square kilometer was 7,987. In comparison, Japan has 336 persons per square kilometer, the United Kingdom has 263 per square kilometer, the USA has 34.8, and Australia has 2.9 (CIA World Factbook, 2016).

It is notable that as Singapore contains such a crowded population while maintaining high levels of social harmony, it goes against established social science theory. The late 19th century social scientists discovered early on that urbanization should rather naturally lead to disharmony and conflict, not the opposite (Durkheim, 1893; Simmel, 1903). The question before us is not just how Singapore maintains such a low crime rate, but how it does so in severely congested conditions.

ONE-PARTY RULE IN SINGAPORE

In order to understand the justice system on the island, we must first understand the rather remarkable success and continuation of the nation's one-party government rule since its independence in 1959. It is true that the small nation receives its share of criticism from both within and without its boundaries from those who would argue that competition by opposing political parties would be a step in a positive direction and lead to a stronger society. Yet, the People's Action Party (PAP) has never lost a national election. It is true that a few fledgling opposition parties have emerged, and continue to persist over the past half-century, but none have gained enough headway to thwart the dominate ruling political party.

The island-state is subdivided into 28 political districts. Some of the districts elect a single minister to parliament and other districts with greater populations elect multiple ministers. As of 2016, a total of 89 ministers make up the parliament, all but six are members of the People's Action Party. Since 1959, no more than six provinces have won elections in opposition to the PAP. In such a scenario, it would be unthinkable that the dominant party would lose a vote on any contested issue, or for a national decision for electing the leader of government, either the Prime Minister or the President. Even with one-party political domination, following its early British heritage, the nation defines itself as a parliamentary democracy.

A number of reasons may account for the success of the People's Action Party and the lack of opposition. The island-state has experienced relatively low levels of inequality and most Singaporeans measure up rather well economically against other developed nations (Acemoglu & Robinson, 2005). Also, the citizenry were undoubtedly very content with their long-time Prime Minister, perhaps not unlike being under the leadership of a benevolent king. With available housing, a decent salary, and a relatively free-market economy, why change the status quo? Yet, when we look at the overall picture of the justice system, it may appear to most as a nation abundant with regulations (Austin, 1987; 2005).

THE NECESSITY OF MAINTAINING ORDER

What often goes unmentioned is the real possibility that the Singapore society has little choice in the matter of maintaining social harmony; they must either work to establish a well-ordered nation or else run the risk of decaying under its own weight. In other words, preserving high levels of social order may have survival value for the small island society with such an overcrowded population and with very few, if any, natural resources. Even finding fresh water became a perpetual dilemma that started with piping water supply from the neighboring mainland of Malaysia, an early dependency that has lessened only in recent years (Luan, 2010). With such crowded conditions, we can argue from hindsight that Singaporeans had to learn to stand in line rather than to scramble for goods and services, whether at the marketplace or on the street corner. One does not see throngs of people contesting for a taxi. Rather, it is a violation of a local ordinance to flag a cab outside of a taxi station where awaiting passengers are quietly and orderly standing in ques. Similarly, crowds gather in the Mass Rapid Transit (MRT) stations, but there is no pushing and shoving to enter the rail cars.

In recent years, in order to prevent chewing gum from being dropped into automatic door mechanisms, a regulation was enacted nationwide to outlaw chewing gum (Prystay, 2004; cf. Metz, 2015). Also, no eating is allowed on the MRT system, and public smoking is controlled. Such regulations might seem overly harsh in larger and less congested nations, but in Singapore they provide a necessary sense of order, if not concerns for public health and safety. Perhaps a clearer example is the regulation against pedestrians crossing the roadways (i.e., jaywalking) and bypassing the required walkway overpasses. Such antics can bring about sizeable fines. However, to allow random jaywalking could generate major traffic problems, especially with crowded sidewalks and busy streets.

These regulations might be regarded as situational but essential for maintaining order. For instance, with so little land space, not everyone can be expected to own an automobile. Thus, a regulation was enacted to disallow anyone from owning a car that is more than 10 years old, otherwise to pay a hefty tax almost as much as the original cost of the vehicle. A same rationale is endorsed to limit the number of births on the island with a goal of zero-population growth. Again, violations of such regulations have in the past resulted in heavy fines, more easily tolerated by the well-heeled. To counter overpopulation, benefits were put in place to appease citizens who agreed to terminate pregnancies. Importantly, such regulations became a matter of national law on the small island. Such rules might be considered as petty to the more well-to-do, but the fines can be problematic to the less affluent (Kuo & Wong, 1979; cf. McKillop, 2013). On the tiny island, any regulation can be rapidly disseminated to the public by the nationally controlled radio, television, and print media.

Nearby nations, perhaps even the world, watched in wonder when the sprawling seaport isle declared independence from Britain in 1963 and then Malaysia 2 years later, and with few assets, began shaping its economy and social institutions. The gamble of going independent was looked upon with curiosity and doubt as Mr. Lee Kuan Yew, a young British trained lawyer, took the wheels of government as Singapore's first Prime Minister in 1959, even before independence, and remained as Prime Minister until 1990, one of the longest continuous reins in such a governmental role in world history (Abdoolcarim & Chowdhury, 2015).

It is clear that the prime minister ran the Singapore city-state as a most successful business, developing trading partners throughout the world (Sandhu & Wheatley, 1989). Today, hundreds of cargo ships can be observed at any hour of the day or night waiting their turn to dock at Singapore's harbors to deliver goods and raw materials. Singapore became, and remains to this day, one of the very busiest of the world's seaports. In fact, if the island is too small, why not make it bigger? Thus, a successful effort continues to reclaim land at the water's edge and to literally expand the physical size of the island by 20%. This continues as a constant practice and provides additional space for expansion (Tan, 2015).

An immediate and ongoing issue was how to make available housing for millions of citizens packed into a small space. Prior to the 1960s, much of the populace resided in native Malay structures called *kampungs* (*or kampongs*), sometimes elevated on bamboo stilts above the swampy terrain and associated with a shantytown way of life. The solution was to transfer the population upward in high-rise housing blocks. This inaugurated what became one of the world's largest urban renewal and relocation programs. Not all residents were happy with the social movement that sometimes tore apart ethnically cohesive neighborhoods. The government saw the compulsory relocation of residents to high-rise housing blocks as vital for the overall well-being of the society, and by the mid-1980s the repositioning of the citizenry resulted in over 2,000 multistory apartment buildings soaring above the island's landscape.

Today, some of the taller housing blocks reach 50 stories high creating an imposing skyline. The important point is that everyone has a place, and individual flats are sold and sometimes rented based on ability to pay. Consequently, one does not find in Singapore what might be called in other nations hobo jungles, urban ghettos, or even homeless people wandering the streets. The relocation of the population, ultimately in an orderly fashion, even with some early difficulty, appears to have had survival value. Everyone has water, electricity, and gas for cooking, even if some of the earlier kampong spirit may be lost in the high-rises. The streets are swept clean by government regulated sanitation departments and the island quickly became touted as the "Mr. Clean of Asia" (*Time Magazine*, 1971). It is difficult to argue with success.

No society can be perfect, and even Singapore did witness periods of ethnic conflict as seen in riots in the late 1960s involving the diverse population of Chinese (74%), Malay (13%), and Indian (9%) citizens (Conceicao, 2007). Yet, the only other ethnically leaning skirmish occurred four decades later when 27 persons were arrested in 2013 after a traffic accident in the "Little India" section of Singapore (Singh, 2013). Otherwise, Singapore has remained notably peaceful with low rates of lawbreaking uncharacteristic of such a densely populated society.

INFORMAL POLICE PRESENCE

Even a diminutive nation that chooses independence must be able to protect itself. A strong military was established to include an army, navy, and air force with the latest high-tech advances to include modern fighter jets, quite unusual for such a tiny island nation. What is unique is that the requirement of conscription into the nation's armed forces can also be satisfied with service into Singapore's national police force. Each year thousands of young men and women choose police work in lieu of traditional military service. This activity has positive outcomes above providing a continuous supply of police recruits for the island's security.

Youth considering police service also reside in the high-rise neighborhood blocks and clearly must maintain a crime-free lifestyle if they wish to successfully enter police work when they come of age to fulfill their national obligation, indirectly helping to create social harmony in the housing blocks. In fact, those young men and women who choose any of the armed services must remain on reserve status for a decade after fulfilling their required obligation. This means that high-rise neighborhoods remain filled with youth aspiring for future police work, as well as citizenry living side-by-side with military and police personnel on reserve duty. This provides a rather automatic, even if unplanned, presence of neighbors readily available to intervene or to assist regular police in the unlikely event of social disorder on any of the many decks of a housing block.

NEIGHBORHOOD WATCH ZONES

Beginning in 1981, Singapore established a network of citizen volunteers to operate as neighborhood watch groups throughout the thousands of high-rise housing blocks (Neighborhood Watch Zones, 2016). Even at the start of the program, 100,000 citizens assisted in the organized watch activity. Typically, five households would participate on a particular floor of a housing block. The neighborhood watch functioned to safekeep each other's premises while maintaining close contact with other housing block organizations (residential committees) that oversaw issues affecting the entire housing block. Neighborhood watch networks also provided liaison with a neighborhood police post (NPP) commonly situated on the ground floor of a housing block. Indirectly, such groups functioned to uphold close comradery among neighbors with the added benefit of assisting with minor grievances that might arise on a particular floor of a housing block. Crime prevention, dissemination of information, and community spirit are supported and reinforced.

The more formal police agency maintains an awareness of any potential problems among the numerous decks of a typical high-rise housing block. Consequently, the thousands of residents of a single large housing block represent a community that is united under a combination of informal as well as formal controls. Patterned after the Japanese *Koban* system of neighborhood policing with uniformed officers residing in the neighborhoods, Singapore's Neighborhood Police Post system also requires officers to make regular contact with all residents of a housing block.

Singapore's small island existence with millions of residents forced to cohabit tight living quarters in high-rise housing blocks reflects a nation where it is difficult to draw clear distinctions between formal and informal policing. Yet, official, uniformed police do abound in Singapore and deserve closer attention.

FORMAL LAW ENFORCEMENT

The field of criminology has long accepted the idea that we can separate the formal from the informal systems of social control. We tend to think of formal law enforcement as police officers in uniform walking the streets with badge and gun, or driving around in their patrol cars while maintaining a noticeable distance from the people they are sworn to serve. Usually, we would suggest that formal control, or an official police organization, represents one administered by government whether at the local or national level. On the other hand, informal systems would represent those that are more non-governmental, community-based and controlled at the neighborhood level. Yet, such a separation may actually represent a false dichotomy. The formal and the informal structures can be seen as overlapping systems with one blending into the other so that it is sometimes difficult to draw distinctions. Singapore represents this kind of example.

With the densely populated island and with personal mobility kept to a minimum, citizens are rather compelled to exist in long-established extended families. Cohesive neighborhoods emerge, and from an ecological perspective, the citizenry cluster into natural areas whereby residents and neighborhoods generally find it has survival value to get along with each other—

to stand in line, for instance, rather than competing for a taxi as noted earlier. Maintaining peace makes more sense than conflict. In Singapore, the necessity of preserving social harmony might be seen as a logical outcome of living on a small, self-contained island. What is notable is that the early founders of the city-state seemed to recognize this and set out to build a government that both accepted natural informal controls of family and neighborhood, while setting in place government institutions that further encourage self-regulating communities. It is true that in Singapore, police and military personnel must also reside in the same communities and neighborhoods and this heightens the preservation of social harmony. However, as must be observed in all nations, the purely informal systems occasionally falter and must be augmented by a show of force by government sanctioned law enforcement. Singapore is no exception.

The Singapore Police organization is comprised of a workforce of about 41,000 members if one includes all the various part-time positions. Full-time police employees number slightly over 15,000 with approximately 8,000 making up the regular, sworn police officer force. These male and female officers are assigned throughout the island nation in a wide array of divisions and departments (See, for instance, www.police.gov.sg). Many of the departments are behind the scenes and out of public view in various administrative, planning, intelligence, and training capacities. The police force is under the Ministry of Home Affairs, one of the more heavily funded branches of government. The police force is headed by a Commissioner of Police, and follows a military model of organization with designations of rank displayed on blue uniforms. All police graduate from a rigorous academy requiring 6 months of training for junior level entry into the force, and 9 months for recruits with college degrees who seek entry into senior level police positions. Singaporean police carry firearms, a departure from British traditions.

Apart from the many staff level divisions of the police force (e.g., Administration, Finance, Planning, Internal Affairs, Intelligence, etc.), the more recognizable aspects of the police force, in public view on a daily basis, include numerous specialist or line units. These include such specialties as Traffic, Airport, Coast Guard, Training, Criminal Investigation, and what are referred to as the Land Divisions. The "Land Divisions" are six in number and are rather equally dispersed around the island. Each provides what might be regarded as the more regular or visible police functions with each Land Division providing services to a distinct geographic sector of the island. With the island's population approaching six million, each Land Division serves about a million people—some more, some less. Depending on the makeup of a particular geographic sector (i.e., central business district, shopping malls, residential districts, etc.), a specific Land Division contingency would be comprised of a headquarters building, a number of Neighborhood Police Centers (NPCs), and often up to a dozen or more Neighborhood Police Posts (NPPs). Thus, police officers are distributed rather evenly throughout the island and often into individual housing blocks.

It should be remembered that a housing block could hold several thousand residents that represents a contained or enclosed community. Over the years, policies were put in place to keep a small contingency of police in an office workplace located at the ground floor of a housing block. This provides immediate on-site access to residents in the event of some kind of disturbance or emergency. Police officers would "walk their beat" either by stairs or use of elevators from floor to floor and make personal contact with residents, a practice that came to be referred to as "vertical patrol." In recent years, the reliance on separate Neighborhood Police Posts at the base of housing blocks has been somewhat reduced, or found less essential, due to rapid cell phone communication between residents and police located only a short distance in the more centralized Neighborhood Police Centers. In any event, response time to the scene of any disorder remains swift (Austin, 2005).

OTHER SPECIALTY LINE UNITS

Traffic Police

It is likely a good guess that in most modern nations, a first encounter with police would be at the street level with a constable directing traffic. In the case of Singapore this might not be true. Four reasons account for this. First, one will not see aged jalopies on Singapore streets. Only the well-to-do will be able to afford the required newer automobile and maintain taxes. Consequently, automobile breakdowns are kept to a minimum making it less necessary for constant police presence. Second, pedestrian walkway-bridges cross over the busy streets. This works to keep traffic flowing smoothly and without numerous traffic signal lights. On the secondary roadways near the shopping districts, local citizens and tourists are more likely to cross streets en masse and a traffic constable is more probable. Third, video cameras are a common fixture at traffic intersections and roadways. Traffic violations detected on-camera are followed by a citation sent by mail. This keeps police officers off the streets and seldom with a need to pull over a motorist in traffic. Fourth, Singaporeans appear well aware of the regulations and penalties attached to violators. Again, on the small island, both minor and major regulations are easily and rapidly disseminated to citizenry.

Police Coast Guard

As added security, the island is under continuous police reconnaissance from the surrounding waters with the Marine Coastal Division of about 1,000 officers. This police operation takes over the roles normally provided in many nations by the military. Police duties include enforcement of law and order in Singapore's territorial waters, search and rescue operations, and investigation of illegal immigrant and/or smuggling activity. Officers assigned to the Police Coast Guard operate rapid response police cruisers, armed with cannon and machine guns, that patrol around the clock, simultaneously circumventing the island in both directions. The Police Coast Guard operate four coastal Neighborhood Police Centers situated north, south, east, and west on the coastal regions of the island. On the other hand, members of the Police Coast Guard may also be seen patrolling by bicycle when on the small islets situated just off the main island.

The Police Coast Guard represents one of the largest operational units of the force. With the concern of terrorism around the world over the past few decades, Singapore police have increased scrutiny of the hundreds of incoming cargo ships docking at all hours of the day and night. Officers receive specialized training to search for explosives, drugs, and fraudulent documents, and for boarding suspect vessels in the Singapore ports.

Gurkha Contingent

During the early years of Great Britain's occupation of India, Malaysia, and Singapore, the British overseers in Singapore recruited men from Nepal to assist with police operations on the island. The nation of Nepal, a landlocked country in the midst of the Himalayas, including Mt. Everest, holds a well-deserved reputation as a tough, robust, and resilient people, perhaps resulting from austere life in the high mountain altitudes. The Nepalese "Gurkha" soldiers, named after the "Gorkha" hill district of Nepal, had earlier proved to be fearsome guerilla fighters with the Indian and British armies. Today, Great Britain still recruits Gurkha soldiers into its military. A half century after Singapore's independence, the nation-state continues to recruit about 2,000 Gurkhas with what has become a long-standing unit of its police force, known for their fitness, combat, and survival skills.

The Gurkha contingency today in Singapore provides protection of dignitaries such as the President and Prime Minister, and at the more sensitive government locations on the island. As outsiders, they hold an enduring reputation for being impartial in dealing with Chinese, Malay, or Indian ethnic populations on the island. Although Singapore's major ethnic groups maintain relatively good relations, the prospect of a Singaporean police officer of Malay or Indian descent shooting a citizen of Chinese descent, or vice versa, could be problematic, a scenario that is avoided in the case of the non-citizen, Gurkha officers. The Gurkha members of the police force are relied upon in emergency police operations and more recently with any extremist- or terrorist-oriented plots on the island. The Gurkha unit also assists with training at the police academy of regular Singaporean police recruits (Liang, 2009).

Social life for the Gurkha officers, as non-citizens, remains rather awkward. Gurkha police are relegated to a camp centrally located on the island and outside the main business district. Close integration with Singaporean society is discouraged or, in some cases, disallowed. For instance, the Gurkhas are not permitted to marry Singaporean women. After an allotted period of years as Gurkha police, they are allowed to bring their spouse and children to Singapore. The children attend Singapore schools near the Gurkha camp, but must return to their homeland by age 21, or at the end of the Gurkha officer's tour of duty in Singapore. Only a very few Gurkha officers and families remain in Singapore on a permanent basis. Yet, this unit of the Singapore Police Force remains highly respected. They are distinctive in their dress uniform with unique hats cocked to one side with brims touching the right ear, and with each officer brandishing a foot-long, curved knife (*Kukri*) attached to their belt. The Gurkha units proudly take part in Singapore's national parades with their own band (Also, see discussion at Singapore's police website, 2018).

THE JUDICIAL SYSTEM

If the police system in Singapore represents a combination of informal and formal social controls, the same must be said about the judicial system. Concern here focuses on various agencies in Singapore available to manage disputes and violations of law either informally at the neighborhood level, or by mobilizing the court process after a formal arrest. We must presume that a nation such as Singapore, with one of the world's lowest rates of crime per capita, would experience low use of the court process. After all, crime rates are typically measured by how often the formal system of justice is put into action. Few arrests by police requiring fewer cases processed in court would result in a low crime nation. Logically, it would be possible to have a totally anarchic, lawless society with no police and no courts. But, crime could not be officially measured. In such a mythical case, we might anticipate dangerous streets. This is not the case in Singapore where official regulations are plentiful. Our point is that Singapore finds it unnecessary to make many arrests, in part due to a reliance on informal controls and an apparent realization by the citizenry that maintaining social order is essential with a crowded populace contained on a small island. The likelihood that strict punishments may deter citizens from breaking the law is also a real consideration.

However, if a crime occurs in Singapore that results in an arrest, numerous judicial processes can come into play. Basically, the judicial system is divided into the "High Court" and the "Subordinate Court" systems. The High Court acts as an appeals court, hearing cases not resolved by lower courts, but also will hear cases that are deemed too severe for the lower courts. These include cases involving the death penalty, cases that may result in more than 10 years in prison, or cases where a monetary fine exceeds 250,000 Singapore dollars. There are no juries in Singapore, with all cases being bench trials. As a final Court of Appeal, the High Court serves as a Supreme Court.

Subordinate Courts are sub-divided into an array of at least 10 specialized courts depending on a specific function, or on the severity of a case.

District Courts

Claims by litigants that involve more than 60,000 SGD (Singapore dollars) but less than 250,000 SGD in various kinds of civil disputes are heard before a District Court judge. District Courts may only sentence a person found guilty for up to a maximum of 10 years of incarceration. Other penalties for lawbreaking levied in the District Court may result in corporal punishment, probation, reformative training, or a combination of all of these.

Magistrates' Courts

A Magistrate Judge hears cases that result in lesser penalties than District Courts. Also, cases brought before the Magistrate Court pertain to civil disputes involving less than 60,000 SGD. At this judicial level, penalties cannot exceed 3 years imprisonment, generally in the range of 2 years, possibly in combination with corporal punishment, but less harsh than penalties imposed by the District Court. A fine of up to 2,000 SGD may also be mandated by the magistrate.

Juvenile Courts

A person under 14 years old is legally defined as a child in Singapore, as a "young person" at the ages of 14 and 15, and as a "youthful offender" at ages 16 to 18. Justice-related issues at these early ages fall under such categories as Beyond Parental Control; Child Care and Protection; and Juvenile Arrest cases. Regardless of the particular designation of juveniles, they are given multiple opportunities for counseling, rehabilitation, and court probation programs. If attempts at modifying a youth's behavior are unsuccessful in various home- or neighborhood-based agendas, young people can be sent to detention programs that include reformative training orders. Corporal punishment can also be ordered by the court.

Community Courts

Community courts were established in 2006 with more of a "problem-solving" orientation rather than a strict emphasis on determination of guilt. Such courts manage offenders with mental disabilities, neighborhood disputes, attempted suicide cases, family violence cases, abuse and cruelty to animals, and also cases involving "youthful offenders" (ages 16 to 18).

Family Court

Issues concerning adoptions, divorce, child custody, spousal and child maintenance, division of matrimonial property, and personal protection orders fall under the jurisdiction of the Family Court.

Syariah Court

About 15% of Singapore's five million population adhere to the Islamic faith (i.e., Primarily Sunni Muslim) and follow legal traditions outlined by the Qur'an. Even in the early days of Singapore independence, it was recognized that the special judicial arrangements were necessary to manage marriage and divorce disputes between parties who are either Muslim or have married according to requirements of Muslim law. Otherwise, Singapore citizens who happen to be Muslim and are involved in lawbreaking are heard by the regular judicial system (Djamour, 1966; cf. Syariah Court Singapore, www.syariahcourt.gov.sg).

Small Claims Tribunal

In 1985 Singapore established a government-sponsored agency to help citizens resolve conflicts arising from various monetary disputes. These may be private disputes between neighbors and unpaid debts, leasing disputes in the many housing blocks, and between displeased customers and/or suppliers of goods and services. The tribunal does not operate as formally as a court, and emphasizes mediation. Usually, the tribunal hears cases of monetary grievances less than 10,000 Singapore dollars. A person in dispute need not employ a lawyer, and if a case is not settled, an unsatisfied party may take a case to a Magistrate Court.

Singapore uses three other official court agencies: Traffic Court, Coroner's Court, and Night Court. All cases forwarded by the Traffic Police are processed through the Traffic Court. This relieves other Subordinate Courts of the important but sometimes routine duty of traffic mishaps and frees up District and Magistrate Courts for the non-transportation oriented lawbreaking. Any death that occurs in Singapore in a sudden or unnatural way, or by violence, is brought before the Coroner's Court. This would include suspected suicides, highway and industrial accidents, and any death occurring in a prison setting. Finally, the Night Court was established in 1992 to help manage the high volume of regulatory traffic cases in the highly urban city-state. It begins operation at 6 p.m. on weekdays, allowing for working folk to take care of court business without disrupting regular work duties.

ALTERNATE DISPUTE RESOLUTION

It is clear that Singapore consistently maintains a low crime rate relative to other countries of the world, but also upholds a generous assembly of regulatory judicial agencies. We must not forget that we are talking about a small island nation. Citizenry do not have to go very far to locate a judicial setting to air a dispute, or as discussed earlier, to find a police officer. Having said this, other than the High Court, and perhaps the District Courts, the variety of Subordinate Court settings emphasize the availability and advantages of resolving grievances in a peaceful manner without reliance on official judicial agencies. Calling upon the government court system is costly, time-consuming, and commonly results in a win-lose scenario. That is, after the court has made a decision in adversarial settings, only one party of the dispute will walk away pleased with the outcome, leaving the other disgruntled.

A decision to avoid entirely the official court system can take several forms. A personal grievance or dispute with a neighbor, for instance, need not go beyond the immediate housing block. All residential neighborhoods maintain citizen committees (i.e., residential committees or RC's) where issues can be aired and possibly resolved through negotiation or mediation with concerned residents of the immediate neighborhood. Such would not have to involve official contact with judicial or enforcement agencies. A second form of Alternative Dispute Resolution (ADR) can encompass what must be considered more of a semi-formal or quasi-official procedure. Over the past decade, Singapore realized the value of diverting civil cases from the Subordinate Courts and began mandating the use of ADR for a variety of disputes (i.e., non-injury motor accident claims; personal injury claims), and by 2012 the Subordinate Courts began to presume that civil disputes generally would first go before some aspect of alternate dispute resolution (State Courts Singapore, 2018).

Management of personal disagreements and basically any civil matter may go through the Alternative Dispute Resolution process and can comprise any of three levels of involvement. These are: Mediation, Neutral Evaluation, and Arbitration (See, for instance, State Courts Singapore, 2016). Mediation is a process whereby a neutral third party (a mediator) facilitates and guides the parties in negotiating a mutually acceptable settlement to a dispute. The mediator does not determine who is at fault in the dispute. Rather, the mediator helps the parties to focus on finding solutions that meet their concerns, without forcing a decision on either party. Such mediation is a service provided by the Singapore government.

Neutral Evaluation, on the other hand, is conducted by a neutral third party (an evaluator) who will review the case and provide an early assessment of the merits of the case. During Neutral Evaluation, the parties, with their respective lawyers, will present their case and the key evidence to the evaluator. The evaluator will then provide a best estimate of the parties' likelihood of success were the case to go to trial. Neutral Evaluation is a service provided by the Singapore government, and where a judge would be the evaluator.

Arbitration is a process where parties agree to resolve the dispute by bringing the matter before a neutral third party (an arbitrator) for final decision. During an arbitration hearing, both parties, with their respective lawyers, will present their case to the arbitrator. The arbitrator will make a binding decision (upheld in any higher court) based on the merits of the case. The parties must obey the arbitrator's decision. The Law Society of Singapore provides low-cost arbitration services.

PUNISHMENT AND INCARCERATION

As noted in earlier pages of this chapter, there is no question that Singapore upholds a long tradition of rather severe punitive actions against offenders of the laws. This is true whether the rather minor infraction is jaywalking, gum chewing, owning an outdated vehicle, or various traffic violations, or more major felony crimes. Smaller acts of lawbreaking will typically be met with fines against the perpetrator and payable at the lower courts. What makes the news more often is the rather provocative punishment of caning—what amounts to flogging with a rattan cane. This is possibly a holdover from the use of the cat-of-nine-tails common aboard ships at sea determined to maintained absolute discipline. Regardless, to this day one may read in Singapore's daily newspapers the number of episodes of caning that occurred the previous day, the number of strokes of the cane, and the crimes for which the caning was ordered by the court. The punishment is carried out behind closed doors in a prison environment. The rather gruesome scene has been characterized as intense and only anecdotal accounts have made their way into print. It is tempting to conclude that caning would have a deterrent effect, and along with the death penalty by hanging for major crimes, would be reasons for the long-standing low crime rates. However, with the heavy emphasis on informal controls, it is difficult to draw a clear cause and effect relationship between punishment and Singapore's low crime. It is safe to conclude that multiple factors are at play (Latif, 1994; Mathi & Andrianie, 1999; Sudderuddin, 2009).

SUMMARY

The Republic of Singapore was included as a nation of special focus in this book because the setting represents not only one of the smallest nations of the world, but also one of the most densely populated. How could such a crowded nation, and one reflecting mixed ethnicities of Chinese, Indian, and Malay peoples, manage such uninterrupted conditions of social harmony? Providing even partial answers to this question was our goal. As noted throughout the chapter, the answer apparently lies in a combination of the confining and controlling features of island life combined with early government appreciation of the advantages of informal controls at the most local neighborhood levels. That is, if petty offenses can be defused in the neighborhood, they will not fester to become major crimes later on. Additionally, even if we agree that Singapore remains a relatively new nation, barely half a century in age, we must conclude that it has been fortunate to have experienced highly popular elected leaders of government. Most notably, the long-reigning Prime Minister of Lee Kwan Yew, a beloved official who kept the best interests of the citizenry at heart from the beginning and built what has become for many a model nation uniting democratic rule with capitalism.

DISCUSSION QUESTIONS

- In regard to law and order in Singapore, what are some advantages of an island nation? What might be a few disadvantages?
- How does the Singapore example of a low-crime nation tend to counter traditional sociological theory, particularly in regard to population size and density?
- Why might we consider the Republic of Singapore to be "off the beaten path"?
- What are your thoughts about caning?
- How do you feel about a law regulating the chewing of gum?
- How might you argue that some of the regulations in Singapore are biased against the poor?
- How does the Singapore military system have indirect benefits for day-to-day management of law and order?
- What might you argue are a few features of Singaporean society that might be incorporated in other, perhaps Western, societies?

REFERENCES

Abdoolcarim, Z., & Chowdhury, N. (2015, March 22). Father of Singapore Lee Kuan Yew dies at 91. *Time Magazine*. Retrieved from http://www.time.com/3748684/lee-kuan-yew-obituary

Acemoglu, D., & Robinson, J. A. (2005). *Economic origins of dictatorship and democracy*. United Kingdom: Cambridge Press.

Adler, F. (1983). *Nations not obsessed with crime*. Littleton, CO: Fred B. Rothman & Company.

AP News Archive. (1991, January 7). Singapore judges doff wigs. Retrieved from: http://www.apnewsarchive.com/1991/singapore-judges-doff-wigs/id-a95788d639cc35d3

Austin, W. T. (1987). Crime and custom in an orderly society: The Singapore prototype. *Criminology, 25*, 279–294.

_____. (2005). Life on the atoll: Singapore ecology as a neglected dimension of social order. *International Journal of Offender Therapy and Comparative Criminology, 49*(5):478–490.

BBC News. (2013, October 24). Why does Singapore top so many tables? Retrieved from http://www.bbc.com/news/world-asia-24428567

Brodwin, E. (2015). The happiest countries in the world, according to neuroscientists, statisticians, and economists. *Business Insider*. (New World Happiness Report, April 23). Retrieved from http://www.businessinsider.com/new-world-happiness-report-2015-2015-4

CIA World Factbook. (2016). Langley, VA: Central Intelligence Agency.

Conceicao, J. (2007). *Singapore and the many-headed monster*. Singapore: Horizon Books.

Djamour, J. (1966). *The Muslim matrimonial court in Singapore*. New York: Bloomsbury Publishing.

Durkheim, E. (1893). *De la Division du Travail Social: Etude sur L'Organisation des Societes Superieues*. Paris: Felix Alcan. *The division of labor in society* (George Simpson, Trans.). New York: Macmillan, 1933.

Kuo, E. C. Y. and Wong, A. K. (1979). *The contemporary family in Singapore*. Singapore: The Singapore University Press.

Latif, A. (1994). *The flogging of Singapore: The Michael Fay affair*. Singapore: Times Books International.

Liang, C. Z. (2009). *The invisible force: Singapore Gurkhas*. Singapore: Ethos Books.

Luan, I. O. B. (2010). Singapore water management policies and practices. *International Journal of Water Resources Development, 26*(1):65–80.

Mackey, D. A., & Levan, K. (2013). *Crime prevention*. Burlington, MA: Jones & Bartlett.

Mathi, B., & Andrianie, S. (1999, April 11). Spare your child the rod? No. *The Sunday Times*. Singapore.

McKillop, A. (2013, October 21). Zero population growth: A forgotten fear. The Market Oracle Newsletter. Retrieved from www.marketoracle.co.uk/article42773.html

Metz, E. (2015, March 28). Why Singapore banned chewing gum? *BBC News Magazine*.

Neighborhood Watch Zones. (2016). Singapore Police Force. Ministry of Home Affairs. Singapore. Retrieved from www.police.gov.sg

Prystay, C. (2004, June 4). At long last, gum is legal in Singapore, but there are strings. *The Wall Street Journal*. New York.

Sandhu, K. S., & Wheatley, P. (1989). *Management of success: The molding of modern Singapore*. Singapore: Institute of Southeast Asian Studies.

Simmel, G. (1903). The metropolis and mental Life. In Kurt H. Wolff. 1950. (Editor and Translator). *The Sociology of Georg Simmel*, New York: The Free Press.

Singapore Police. (2018). www.police.gov.sg.

Singh, M. (2013, December 11). Chronology of a riot. *Business Times*. Singapore.

State Courts Singapore. (2018). Overview of alternative dispute resolution. Singapore Government Website. Retrieved from www.statecourts.gov.sg

Sudderuddin, S. (2009, January 13). To cane or not to cane. *The Straits Times.*

Syariah Court Singapore. (2016). Retrieved from www.syariahcourt.gov.sg

Tan, T. (2015, September 27). S'pore's largest reclamation project begins. Singapore: *The Straits Times.*

Time Magazine. (1971). *Asia's Mr. Clean,* 97(4):54. Time, Inc.

CHAPTER 4

The Ghana Model

© pavalena/Shutterstock.com

INTRODUCTION

The Republic of Ghana is a unitary constitutional democratic country with a president as head of government. It is a West African country with a population of about 26,327,649 people (World Fact Book, 2016). Ghana is bordered to the north by Burkina Faso, to the south by the Atlantic Ocean, to the west by Cote d'Ivoire, and to the east by Togo. Ghana's population includes several ethnic groups with estimates at 100 (Woodman, 2002). The main ethnic groups are the Akan, Ewe, Mole-Dagbane, Guan, and Ga-Adangbe. Villages, towns, and cities that align themselves to any particular group share commonalities in the local dialects, culture, and history. Group cohesiveness prior to and during colonization was necessary to fight for, or to lobby for, land to maintain trade routes, and as security against rival groups. Cultural differences still prevail in the country, but the several dialects unique to each tribe are spoken with English as the official language.

Previously known as the Gold Coast, Ghana was a British colony until its independence on March 6, 1957. Gold attracted merchants from Europe especially the British, the Portuguese, the Dutch, among others, to this coastal territory. With slave trade being a more lucrative venture in the 17th century, European merchants switched focus from gold mining to slave trade. Around the 19th century, cocoa growing became the focus and, until this day, cocoa beans remain a significant export commodity of Ghana.

While other European countries eventually limited their presence in Ghana, the British stayed on for the purposes of expanding their commercial stronghold, and to exert political control in the region. The British quest for political control led to constant clashes with the locales especially with the northern Asante confederacy. The war of 1873–1874 led to the formation by the British of the colony of the Gold Coast, which comprised the Southern territories. In order to establish absolute control, the British set up a Supreme Court, which was regulated by the Supreme Court Ordinance of 1876. This Ordinance that stayed in force until 1960 spelled out a provision that promoted the supremacy of British Rule and English law by declaring that applicable laws of the Supreme Court were to be those in force in England as of 1874, and were to prevail over any existing customary laws (Woodman, 2002). The Asante Confederacy remained defiant of British rule, but in 1896, the British were able to crush such resistance including the last act of defiance in 1900. In 1902, legislation was passed by the British, which brought the Asante confederacy and the colony of the Gold Coast under the leadership of the governor of the Gold Coast. Other northern territories and other parts that were not part of the Asante confederacy ultimately decided to be part of Ghana upon the independence of the country.

WHY GHANA IS PART OF THIS STUDY

Ghana is among the earliest countries in Africa to gain independence from colonial rule. The late President Kwame Nkrumah spearheaded this effort and, being a visionary, he declared that Ghana's "independence is meaningless unless it is linked up with the total liberation of the African continent" (Boateng, n.d.; Kachipande, 2013). Following Nkrumah's example in Ghana, over 30 African countries subsequently declared independence from their colonizers (Boateng, n.d.).

Next to Nelson Mandela who takes first place, Kwame Nkrumah has been hailed as the second "greatest African leader" (Top 10 Greatest African Leaders, n.d.), and again second to Mandela as the 100 greatest Africans of all time (Ankomah, 2004). Not only was he an avid campaigner of Pan-Africanism, he also was one of the original members of the Organization of African Unity (OAU). While these accolades go to President Nkrumah, one cannot underscore the fact that his voice was heard because he represented a country—Ghana.

Ghana has also produced Kofi Annan, hailed as "Africa's greatest diplomat of all time" (Ankomah, 2004). As a former Secretary General of the United Nations, Annan was known for his placid manner of tackling the world's issues, however grave they were. His method of diplomacy geared toward peaceful resolution of conflicts is consistent with the political atmosphere of his native land. Ghana, referred to as an "island of peace," is considered one of the most viable democracies in Africa (GhanaWeb, n.d.).

Despite Ghana's role in African and world politics, it hardly has been given much attention in comparative justice books. Now and then articles on aspects of Ghanaian politics or system of justice can be found in articles, but full attention to its criminal justice system is lacking even though it is among African countries that have tried (even if unsuccessful) to style its justice system in a western fashion.

LEGAL CONCEPTS

The constitution of Ghana declares the country as a unitary republic, with the president as head of state elected by the masses. There are three branches of government, the executive branch headed by the president; the legislative branch is overseen by a unicameral parliament; and an independent judiciary with The Supreme Court of Ghana having extensive judicial review powers. As the supreme law of the land, the Ghanaian Constitution sets forth the jurisdiction and functions of all branches of government including the judiciary, legislature, the people and their rights.

As in most, if not all, African countries, customary/traditional practices and laws play an integral role of the people. These traditional practices which are fluid depending on tribal practices over time (there are several tribes within each country) are protected and enforced by custodians of traditional practices who usually are chiefs, the elderly, or reputable people in the community. Traditional rulers are not included in official political roles. While a national house of chiefs exists, the functions of members are to oversee the roles of chiefs and to make decisions regarding customary laws (Woodman, 2002). Following provisions of the 1992 Constitution, judicial committees comprised of traditional leaders decide on issues relating to chieftaincy. Issues on appeal from this committee are reviewed by the Regional House of Chiefs, and if no satisfactory redress, the matter is forwarded to the National House of Chiefs, and ultimately, to the Supreme Court. As defined in Ghana's Constitution, customary law entails "rules of law which by custom are applicable to particular communities in Ghana" (Constitution of Ghana 11 (3)). While customary courts handle cases relating to customary practices, in the event of disagreement on procedural or substantive issues, deference is made to the legislation. In situations where customary law contradicts common law, the court looks at the intentions of the parties, or to the *lex fori*—law of the place where a contract, for instance, was entered into.

Officially, Ghana is a common-law country—a heritage of British rule. The 1876 Ordinance put in place by the British transplanted both English statutory and case law, and these were applicable in Ghana in their entirety. As Woodman (2002) reports, Ghanaian statutes have substituted all but nine of these imported laws; and the nine unchanged laws form Art. 459 of the 1993 Courts Act. According to Ghana's Constitution 11 (2), common law as applied in the country also includes the doctrine of equity and customary law. Common-law practice requires the application of precedent. In that regard, cases with similar facts are cited to buttress case outcomes. It is, thus, not uncommon to find English cases cited in judicial rulings in Ghanaian courts (Woodman, 2002). The adversarial process is applied, whereby both sides produce witnesses, argue out the case in court with the prosecutor having the burden of proof (see Chapters 1–2). While Ghana still retains the death penalty as the ultimate punishment, it is reported that the last known year when any execution took place was 1993 (Cornell Law School, 2012). According to the Constitution 19 (2) (a) (i), in all death penalty cases, the jury verdict has to be unanimous, (ii) for cases to which a prison term of life may be imposed, a majority verdict as prescribed by Parliament is required.

Ghana still has jury trials, but there are calls to abolish the jury system. According to Graphic Online (2011), among those requesting that Parliament abolish the jury system is Justice Efo Kosi-Kaglo, of the High Court in Koforidua, in the Eastern Region of the country, who is of the opinion that jurors lack the requisite knowledge to adequately comprehend the intricacies of a criminal case, and that has led to some defendants wrongfully convicted.

Other concepts of the adversarial system that Ghana has adopted are found in the Constitution Article 19 titled Fair Trial. Some of the provisions are presumption of innocence 19 (2) (c); defendant be informed of the charges against him/her 19 (2) (d); defendant has the right to self-represent or to be defended by an attorney 19 (2) (f); the right to be present during court proceedings 19 (3) among many others.

LAW ENFORCEMENT IN GHANA

Law enforcement practices and structure in Ghana have evolved significantly over time. Prior to colonization, when Ghana was still known as the Gold Coast, a group of merchants recruited men to protect their forts and castles, and traditional kings and chiefs were responsible for deploying local men (known as messengers) to perform various unremunerated functions and errands pertaining to matters of law and order, and crime control.

A more formal law enforcement force was put in place by the British colonizers in 1821 (Web.archive.org, n.d.). In 1844, the colonizers named the force the "Gold Coast Militia and Police" with responsibilities to guard the forts and castles, while others were deputized to serve summonses and to do investigatory functions for the courts. An 1894 Ordinance gave impetus to the civil force. In 1902, the police force was overhauled and four entities were created—General, Escort, Mines, and Railway. This division was given legal force by the Police Ordinance of 1904. Tweaking of the police force continued. The following were subsequent reforms:

- 1921–1922: Establishment of Criminal Investigation and Finger Print Department
- 1942: Establishment of Customs Excise and Preventive Service
- 1948: Creation of the Police Reserves
- 1950: The Wireless and Communications Unit was created
- 1952: With more Ghanaians recruited to the force, a women's branch was established to oversee juvenile and female offenders
- 1958: The first Ghanaian Police Commissioner was appointed

Following the enactment of Act 350 of the Police Service Act, 1970, the following functions of Ghanaian police were established:

- Crime detection and prevention
- Apprehension (arrest) and prosecution of offenders
- Maintenance of law and order
- Due enforcement of the law (Web.archive.org, n.d.)

ELIGIBILITY TO BECOME A POLICE OFFICER IN GHANA

In order to be a police officer in Ghana, the applicant must be a born citizen; he or she must be between the ages of 18–25, and must have a clean bill of health. The applicant must be physically fit, must not have a criminal record, and must comply with educational specifications put forth by the Appointment and Recruitment Board of the Ghana Police Service. Height restrictions are also in place—male applicants must be at least 5.8 ft, and women, 5.4 ft. Applicants are to take aptitude tests, and must agree to medical screenings (Ghana Police Service Recruitment—General Eligibility—Regluv., n.d.). Ability to speak English is essential, and at least a high school or secondary education, and those aspiring for rank positions must have a university degree (books.google.com, n.d.).

TRAINING

Rank-and-file officers are usually trained as entry-level employees at either a police center as an example in Winneba, or designated regional centers (Books.google.com, n.d.). Successful applicants undergo 9 months training comprising physical exercises and drill, use of weapons, conflict negotiation, first aid services, and patrol and escort services (Books.google.com, n.d.). Officers in advanced placement receive training in "criminal law and criminal procedure, methods of investigation, current affairs, and social sciences" (Books.google.com, n.d.).

Cadet Officers who attend Police College take a variety of courses including criminal law, criminal procedure, criminal investigation, evidence, police management, ethics, psychology, and many others. As well, seminars and symposiums, and intermittent guest lectures constitute other forms of formal training. Informal training entails field training in musketry and visits to relevant sites. Courses are also tailored to meet the needs of Junior Commanders, Chief Superintendents, Superintendents and their deputies, and Commissioners and their deputies. Such courses are offered with assistance from the Ghana Institute of Management of Public Administration (GIMPA) (Ghana Police Service, n.d.).

ORGANIZATION OF GHANAIAN POLICE FORCE

The Ghanaian police force serves 13 regions, with each divided into 51 divisions, with further subdivisions of 179 districts and 651 stations (Ghana police service (n.d.).

The police force in Ghana is divided in two broad categories: superior officers and subordinate police officers. Ranked from highest to lowest:

1. **Superior Officers** are: Inspector General of Police, Deputy Inspector General, Commissioner, Deputy Commissioner, Assistant Commissioner, Chief Superintendent, Superintendent, Deputy Superintendent, and Assistant Superintendent.
2. **Subordinate Police Officers** are: Chief Inspector, Inspector, Sergeant, Corporal, Lance Corporal, and Constable The Police Service [Amendment] Regulations, 1974 (LI 880). The National Headquarters is in Accra, and all divisions and subdivisions must report to the National Headquarters.

Functions of Ghanaian Police Officers

The structure and functions of the police are laid out in Section 3 of the Police Service Act.

- **Inspector General**: This is the highest ranked police officer. He/she is appointed by the President of Ghana following counsel by the Council of State. He/she is vested with responsibility of leading the police force, and for the "operational control and the administration of the police service" (Books.google.com, n.d.). Directors for auditing, criminal investigations, and so forth, report to the Inspector General. The Inspector General also has power to hire special constables when and where needed.
- **Deputy Inspector General**: Based on the Police Service Act, the deputy inspector general performs any duties assigned to him/her by the inspector general that may include operations and administrative services, as well as welfare and strategic planning.
- **Commissioners**: These are also directors promoted from the rank of deputy commissioners. They supervise specified units within the police department.
- **Deputy Commissioner**: They assist the commissioner in the duty of supervising units of the police department.
- **Chief, Deputies, Assistant, and Superintendents**: They supervise subdivisions or command units including, but not limited to, crime and court appearances, public relations, traffic, and arms (books.google.com, n.d.).
- **Chief Inspector and Inspector:** These are subsidiary officers with powers to recruit a constable in problem-ridden or potential trouble areas.
- **Volunteer Police:** There are also volunteer reserve officers that include chief inspectors, inspectors, sergeant majors, sergeants, corporals, and constables (the Inspector General still has powers over these officers) (books.google.com, n.d.).

PROMOTION OF GHANAIAN OFFICERS TO HIGHER RANKS

Officers can be promoted based on experience and longevity of service. As well, education of the officer, rank, and specialization at which he/she was hired may determine level of promotion. In this regard, those hired under the category of "superior officers," for instance, may only be promoted at a higher level within that category; in like manner, those hired under the category of "subordinate officers" may only seek promotion in that category.

Based on constitutional requirements, the president, with advice from the Police Council, decide on promotions of officers from one rank to the other (books.google.com, n.d.).

THE LEGAL PROFESSION IN GHANA

Prior to independence, the majority of lawyers in Ghana studied in England, and most were called to the English bar. Postindependence, many pursue their education in Ghana. The requirement to be a practicing attorney is a bachelor degree in law, and then two years study at the Ghana School of Law (Woodman, 2002). Bar exams are not taken after completion from the Ghana School of Law. Persons who already have a law degree and are qualified to practice law in a country whose system is common law, are required to take just 6 months of course work (conversion course, as it is known) in Ghana, and then called to the bar. With regard to the tribunals, it is not mandatory that members be lawyers; however, chairpersons are expected to be lawyers.

The Ghanaian constitution outlines the process of becoming a judge in the country. Requirements for judgeship in the circuit or district court requires years of service as a licensed lawyer, and with an excellent record of legal practice. Criteria for judgeship, retention, and dismissal are spelt out in the Constitution. The Judicial Council advises the Chief Justice who is vested with powers to appoint judges. The president of the country also can appoint judges. With regard to the position of a chief justice and justices of the Supreme Court, parliament has to approve the president's nominee. The Chief Justice is third in line to the President of the country (see Constitution of Ghana, Chapter 8).

STRUCTURE OF COURTS IN GHANA

The Courts Act of 1993 spells out the structure of courts in Ghana. Courts are hierarchically organized, from the lowest—Community Tribunals, motor courts that handle traffic violations—to the highest Court of the land, the Supreme Court.

- **Chieftaincy Tribunals**: These are traditional tribunals that arbitrate local chieftaincy disputes. These courts obtained jurisdiction through the 1992 Constitution. The Regional House of Chiefs reviews appeals from this court, and further appeals are heard by the National House of Chiefs, and ultimately by the Chieftaincy Tribunal.
- **Motor Courts**: These are courts designated by the Chief Justice to handle traffic offenses.
- **The Juvenile Court**: Juveniles under the age of 18 who offend are adjudicated in a juvenile court. Two district magistrates and two other officials including a social welfare officer serve during each hearing at a District Court assigned by the Chief Justice.

- **Family Tribunal**: The Family Tribunal is a District Court that is specialized in children's issues such as determining paternity, custody, and welfare of the child, and other related issues. Act 560 of the Children's Act 1998 governs such matters. The Chairman of the tribunal serves with two or more other officials with at least one who is a social worker.
- **District Courts**: The majority of courts in the country are District Courts, as each district has a minimum of one. This court of limited jurisdiction has several branches including family court, juvenile court, and motor court (Marful-Sau, n.d.). Its jurisdiction in criminal issues is limited to cases for which a prison sentence may not exceed 2 years; and for civil cases, such as tort or contractual obligations, for which fines do not exceed 5,000.00 cedi (Marful-Sau).
- **Circuit Tribunals and Circuit Courts**: These are regional courts presided over by judges. Theses courts handle misdemeanors and smaller felonies. They are also courts of original jurisdiction for civil cases whose claims do not exceed 5 million cedi (Woodman, 2002). As well, there are regional Circuit Courts that handle land and other civil disputes whose claims do not exceed 10 million cedi (Woodman). They are also vested with powers to adjudicate child custody cases, matrimonial issues, adoptions, and probate cases for which property values do not exceed 10,000.00 cedi (Marful-Sau, n.d.).
- **High Court**: The High Court is a court of original jurisdiction for gross misdemeanors and felonies, as well as for big civil matters. The High Court also has jurisdiction to review civil cases on appeal from community tribunals, as well as appeals on criminal and civil issues from District Courts. There are about 95 High Courts in Ghana (Marful-Sau, n.d.).

  Other duties of the High Court include exclusive powers to address encroachments on human rights stipulated in the 1992 Constitution of the country. It also has supervisory powers over all courts beneath it in ranking (Marful-Sau, n.d.). The Court has several specialized branches, including Commercial Court, Labor Court, Land Court, Family Court, Probate and Administration Court, Economic and Financial Crimes Court, and Fast Track Court.
- **Regional Tribunals**: Regional Tribunals have powers to try only criminal cases, and they have exclusive powers as per Court Act, 1993 to handle cases involving public property or fraud (Woodman, 2002). As well, cases involving jury decisions are deferred to the High Court. Based on legal prescription, the Regional Tribunal can only try cases against the state and public interest if Parliament so authorizes. When the

court sits, there are at least three members, with one serving as Chairman. Article 142 of the Constitution stipulates that the Chief Justice of the Supreme Court may establish a Regional Tribunal in each region if he/she deems necessary. As Marful-Sau (n.d.) notes, only Accra and Tamale have Regional Tribunals.

- **Court of Appeal**: The Court of Appeal does not have original jurisdiction to hear cases. It is simply a review court that reviews cases from the High Court, the Regional Tribunal, and the Circuit Courts (Woodman, 2002; Marful-Sau, n.d.). The Appellate Court has a Chief Justice, and at least 10 Justices (Marful-Sau). A panel of no less than three justices serves during any session (Marful-Sau).
- **Supreme Court of Ghana:** According to Article 128 (1) of Ghana's Constitution, the Supreme Court should consist of a Chief Justice and no less than nine other justices. This is the highest court of the land. It is the highest appellate court of the country, and has duties of interpreting and enforcing the country's Constitution.

CORRECTIONS IN GHANA

The prison system in Ghana is under the domain of the Ministry of the Interior. The seat of national prisons is in Accra. The Prisons Service Council and an advisory board play an integral role in running prisons and other holding facilities. The advisory board is also vested with responsibility of advising the President on prison issues be they organizational or maintenance. There are approximately 6,200 correctional officers and staff in the country (Ghana Prison System, n.d.). Even though there are 12 primary men's prisons and seven for women, there are dozens of correctional facilities and holding centers throughout the country.

Missions of Prisons

The goals of prisons are grouped into three broad categories:

1. Making sure inmates are safely housed and that prison conditions are humane.
2. Protecting the rights of inmates and their welfare by providing them with basic needs of sustenance such as meals, healthcare, recreation, and other amenities.
3. Providing rehabilitative programs that gear toward trade, educational, medical, and improvement of other life skills.

CLASSIFICATION OF PRISONS

Prisons in Ghana are classified like they are in most countries, from maximum security to minimum security. Maximum security prisons house death row inmates.

- **Central Prisons:** These prisons are, in a sense, maximum security prisons since they house long-term felons; however, because some of the inmates may eventually be released, prison programs are geared toward rehabilitation. In this regard, there are programs to teach inmates life skills and trade skills that may fetch them jobs upon release.
- **Local Prisons:** These are the equivalent of medium security prisons. As a consequence of poor funding, not much rehabilitative programs are offered. Inmates here, therefore, spend shorter prison sentences.
- **Open Camp Prisons:** These are minimum security prisons that at times act as transitional holding places for inmates nearing the expiration of their prison sentence. These prisons provide much flexibility to inmates to engage in agriculture, food production, and training of other inmates in contemporary farm and produce industry.
- **Agricultural Settlement Camps:** These are super minimum holding places, which typically are without fences. These camps house very low caliber offenders. These inmates engage in extensive agricultural activities; they produce crops for feeding inmates and for sale in order to generate revenue for prisons (Ghana Prison Service, n.d.).
- **The Senior Correctional Center:** This juvenile service center was formally known as Borstal Institute for Juveniles. This center is under the auspices of the Ghana Prisons Service, and governed by the Juvenile Justice Legislation Section 31 (6) of the 2003 Juvenile Act. Convicted delinquents under the age of 18 are housed in these centers. The goal of these centers is rehabilitation so as to enable juveniles to be fully reintegrated to society.

Problems of the Prison System

The predicate problem of prisons in Ghana is budget constraints. These problems include old dilapidated structures for prisons, overcrowding, insanitary conditions, diseases, limited rehabilitative programs, high rates of recidivism, and an unreceptive public of those tagged as ex-convicts (Ghana Prison System, n.d.).

INTERMEDIATE SENTENCES IN GHANA

Probationary Services in Ghana

The privilege of probation is provided in s.354(1) of COOPA. However, limited funding, and adults' unwillingness to abide by conditions of probation, make it such that adults are seldom sentenced to probation. Instead, probationary services in the country seem to be tailored to cater only for juvenile offenders (Fordjour, 2014). Probation officers are responsible for supervising juveniles who are not in holding facilities. According to Lawson (2013), the officers who are poorly trained are vested with supervisory powers, and "cognitive behaviour modification therapy" duties, conflict management abilities, substance abuse therapist roles, life-skill provider roles, and a plethora of other responsibilities. Lack of skills to carry these responsibilities in part is assumed to result in juvenile re-offending.

Parole System

Ghana's Constitution provides for a parole system as outlined in Chapter 16, Art. 208 (3f) (Constitution of the Republic of Ghana, 1992). There are Parole Boards that can decide on parole, conditions of parole and revocation, and can also decide on cases relating to probationers' revocation or reinstatement (Fordjour, 2014). However, as ASP James Annan of Ghana Prison Services' Kumasi Public Relations Office discusses in Aggrey (2015), hardly is the parole system used. Annan even contends that because of the absence of parole and probation, anyone found guilty in court gets sent to prison, thus the reason for prison overcrowding.

Community Payback

This is court-ordered community service which may entail between 30–400 hours. Offenders are to work between 3–4 days per week if jobless, and those who are employed may make arrangements as to payback work hours. There are different types of unpaid services that the offender may be ordered to do including wiping out graffiti, removing garbage, decorating public spaces, among others. Offenders on payback services must wear bright yellow/orange vests with the inscription of "Community Payback" at the back, and must be supervised by a payback officer.

Treatment and Programs

These are therapeutic programs intended to address issues that the offender has that prompted criminality. The other purpose for the programs is to prevent recidivism. The type of problem that the offender has determines the type of treatment or program to which he/she would be assigned. The various treatment and programs entail counseling services, drug testing, behavioral modification sessions, anger management, mental health services, basic reading, writing, and interviewing skills, among others. Failure to comply with terms of treatment, failing a drug test, or not completing a program may lead to a court action against the defaultant.

Restorative justice is also a program that may be ordered by the court. The intent is to have the offender meet with victim(s) of the crime, listen to their pain, apologize, and make any amends.

Conditions for all community services are stipulated by the court. These may include curfews, restrictions on places to visit like bars, constant reporting to the case worker or "offender manager" as they are known in Ghana, and other conditions as may suit the offender's circumstances (Fordjour, 2014).

SUMMARY

Ghana is a democratic country in the West Coast of Africa. It obtained independence from the British in 1957. It is one of Africa's peaceful democracies that has produced visionaries like Kwame Nkrumah and Kofi Annan.

As a unitary republic, the president is head of state and head of the executive branch. The Legislative branch is headed by a unicameral parliament, and the Supreme Court has extensive powers over the judiciary. Ghana also has a National House of Chiefs, which settles issues relating to chieftaincy.

The police force in Ghana serves 13 regions and the National Headquarters is in Accra. Among their many missions are to detect, apprehend, and prevent the commission of crime, and to maintain order.

Ghana is a common-law country that applies the adversarial system of justice. It also has customary courts that handle issues steeped in tradition. Formalized courts are structured in a hierarchy from district courts to the Supreme Court. Smaller courts like motor courts handle traffic offenses.

The correctional system is under the domain of the Ministry of the Interior. As stated in print, the focus of Ghanaian prisons is to house inmates in humane conditions, and to provide them rehabilitative programs. While intermediate sentences are available in Ghana, budgetary constraints hamper proper implementation of these programs.

DISCUSSION QUESTIONS

1. Ghana, like South Africa, applies customary laws. Why is Ghana classified under common-law countries and not under hybrid systems as South Africa is?
2. Do you think that it is necessary to have many categories of law enforcement officers in Ghana? Explain your response. If you were asked to give advice to the Inspector General of Police to streamline the police force, which ranks would you eliminate? Why?
3. What are the requirements to practice law in Ghana?
4. Some say that being locked up in prison is enough punishment. Do you have concerns with Ghana's Agricultural Settlement Camps?
5. Due to fiscal issues, having a viable probation and parole service in Ghana is untenable. What do you think about the absence of probation and parole in a country's correctional system?

REFERENCES

Africaranking.com. (n.d.). Top 10 greatest African leaders. Retrieved from http://www.africaranking.com/the-10-greatest-african-leaders/5/

Aggrey, P. (2015, January 30). We need parole and probation systems-prisons PRO. Retrieved from http://kessbentv.com/news/general/need-parole-probation-systems-prisons-pro/

Ankomah, B. (2004). 100 greatest Africans of all time. Retrieved from http://emeagwali.com/media/africa/100-greatest-africans-of-all-times.html.

Boateng, E. (n.d.). Ghana. Ghana/history/geography/Britannica.com. Retrieved from https://global.britannica.com/place/Ghana#toc55169

Books.google.com. (n.d.). The police, the people, the politics: Police accountability in Ghana. Retrieved from https://www.books.google.com/books?id=sOxAzVoEF

Constitution of Ghana. (1992). Wikisource, the free online library. Retrieved from https://en.m.wikisource.org/wiki/Constitution_of_Ghana

Constitution of the Republic of Ghana. (1992). Chapter 16, The Prison Service. Retrieved from http://www.ghanaweb.com/GhanaHomePage/republic/constitution.php?id=Gconst16.html

Cornell Law School. (2012). The death penalty in Ghana. Retrieved from http://www.deathpenaltyworldwide.org/country-search-post.cfm?country=Ghana

Fordjour, A. (2014, July 15). A death of Ghana's probation service? Justice Ghana. Retrieved from http://www.justiceghana.com/blog/law-justice/a-death-of-ghanas-probation-service

Ghana Police Service. (n.d.). Retrieved from http://web.archive.org/web/20071116093104/ and http://64.226.23.153/others/college.htm

Ghana Police Service Recruitment-General Eligibility-Regluv. (n.d.). Retrieved from http://regluv.com/ghana-police-service-recruitment-general-eligibility

Ghana Prison System. (n.d.). Retrieved from www.prisonministryghana.org

GhanaWeb. (n.d.). Background information about the country Ghana. Retrieved from http://mobile.ghanaweb.com/GhanaHomePage/country-information

Graphic Online. (2011). Abolish trial by jury—Kosi-Kaglo. Retrieved from http://www.modernghana.com/news/357554/1/abolish-trial-by-jury-kosi-kaglo.html

Kachipande, S. (2013, February 7). Ghana's dubious decolonization distinction—The first independent African country. Africa is Mine. Retrieved from https://africaismineblog.wordpress.com/2017/02/07/the-days-of-small-pig-innings/

Lawson, M.-C. (2013, November 1). When will probation officers in Ghana learn to offer offence-focused intervention programmes to address young offender's criminogenic needs? *Modern Ghana*. Retrieved from http://www.modernghana.com/news/500355/when-will- probation-officers-in-ghana-learn-to-offer-offenc.html

Marful-Sau, S. (n.d.). Two Days Seminar by the JTI/Ghana News Link for Journalist. The Courts Structure in Ghana, Justice of Appeal. Retrieved from http://slideplayer.com/slide/1720076

http://www.africaontheblog.com/ghanas-dubious-decolonization-distinction-the=first-independent-african-country. Retrieved, 7/15/2016.

The Police Service (Amendment) Regulations, 1974 (LI 880). Regional Police Establishments. Ghana Police Service. Archived from the original. Retrieved from http://en.m.wikipedia.org/wiki/Law_enforcement_in_Ghana#cite_ref-10.

Ghana police service (n.d.). Regional police establishments. Retrieved from https://archive.is/20130218115805/http://www.ghanapolice.info/regional.htm

Top 10 Greatest African Leaders. (n.d.). Retrieved from http://www.africaranking.com/the-10-greatest-african-leaders/5/

Web.archive.org. (n.d.). Brief facts about Ghana police service. Retrieved from http://web.archive.org/web/20070927212153/ and http://64.226.23.153/police_admin/history.htm

World Fact Book. (2016). Ghana. Retrieved from https://www.google.com/search?q=world+-fact+book+2016,+ghana&ie=UTF-8&0e=UTF-8&hl_en-us&client=safari

Woodman, G. (2002). Ghana. In Kritzer, Herbert, ed. (2002). *Legal Systems of the world: A Political, Social, and cultural Encyclopedia.* Santa Barbara, California: ABC-CLIO, Vol. 2: pp. 590–96.

PART II

The Napolenoic Civil Law System

CHAPTER 5

The Italy Model

© pavalena/Shutterstock.com

INTRODUCTION

Italy is a European country with a population of approximately 60,546,304 people in 2015 (Country Meters, n.d.). Strategically placed in the south of Europe, Italy's northern boundary is the Alps; with a southern peninsula that stretches into the Mediterranean Sea to the North East of Tunisia, Africa. It shares a border with six European countries: Austria, France, Vatican City, San Marino, Slovenia, and Switzerland. While Italian is the official language, it is not uncommon to hear German spoken in the northeastern parts of the Alto Adige, French in the northwestern part of Valle d'Aosta, and Slovene in Trieste and Gorizia (de Franciscis, 2002).

The majority of Italians are Christians (Roman Catholics), with Jewish, Islam and other smaller religions practiced throughout the country.

Italy became a unified state in 1861 with Victor Emmanuel (Vittorio Emanuele) as king. Prior to its unification, the French heavily influenced Italy, and that influence had far-reaching consequences in the political atmosphere in the country. On a lesser aspect, the Pope's influence in Italy was weakened, and on a larger point, foreign dominance precluded unification. At one point, Italy was partitioned into three. France annexed one third of the peninsula, another third became the kingdom of Italy, and the other third, the Kingdom of Naples (123HelpMe.com, 2015). The absence, too, of a unified language presented difficulties to those aiming at unification.

The Congress of Vienna (1815) was an eye-opener for Italians in the sense that they were able to grasp how little territory had been designated to native rule, and how much was under foreign dominance. This awareness sparked the Risorgimento (Rebirth), a movement so to speak, of national solidarity whereby all classes of Italians united to rid their territory of foreign dominance (de Franciscis, 2002).

In 1861, Italy became unified but then not much thought had been given to how the unified nation would be ruled. Very easily, the new rulers adopted existing codes used by hitherto French ruling government. In essence, the French Civil Code became applicable since translations had been made to Italian of not only the civil code, but of the penal and commercial codes as well. This French influence of law was also extended to how the courts were structured.

As Donati (2013) explains, the 1861 unification was not as seamless as some historians hold it out to be. The geographical barriers that had been in place prior to unification were still in place until 1866. During this time, there was the Brigands' war in the south, which precipitated high budgetary burdens to a segment of the country that already was marred by other financial difficulties.

Rome was made capital of Italy in 1871, and it became a bastion of the Catholic Church thereafter. Modern Italy has one of the largest economies in the world. It also has continued to assimilate diverse peoples and cultures. While the division between the very rich and poor is evident in just about every society, it is clear that Italy's immigrants from less developed countries are disproportionately left behind economically. While there are social welfare programs in place to cater for the poor, limits are in place, and as a member of the European Union, budgetary cuts are placed across borders.

Today, modern Italy is a republic (since June 2, 1946) with 20 regions and a constitution that was put in place on January 1, 1948. A president and a prime minister head the executive branch. The House of Parliament comprises a senate and the Chamber of Deputies. The judiciary will be the subject of a more elaborate discussion subsequently.

Like every industrialized country, Italy also has its own share of social problems. Crimes, including robberies and murder, abound. The mafia, reportedly, is instrumental to many crimes, and culprits stem from all walks of life, even from members of the judiciary and politicians (Culture of Italy, n.d.).

Italians continued to use the translated version of the Napoleonic civil code that entailed a division of judges into administrative and penal courts, and magistrates remained just law enforcers and not lawmakers. The purpose was to make sure that lawmaking remained in the hands of legislators. With the new codes of commerce, civil procedure, navigational, and criminal put in force between 1865–1870, it was clear that Italians were not parting ways with the French system (de Franciscis, 2002). The magistracy was restructured in 1907, but it still maintained vestiges of the French. Changes were eventually introduced to include crimes perpetrated against, or contrary to fascism. In 1946, the Constituent Assembly met to put in place constructive programs for nation-building. The focus was on ensuring separation of powers and promoting democracy. The Superior Council of Magistrates was established, Parliament was to interpret the spirit and intent of the law, and a constitutional court was to ensure the smooth running of separation of powers among the various entities (de Franciscis, 2002).

Following a national referendum in 1946, Italy became a parliamentary republic. The Constitution, which contains 139 articles, embodies Italy's laws. The president of the country who should be at least 50 years old when elected into office serves a term of 7 years. The president is vested with powers to appoint the prime minister, as well as the council of ministers. Following Article 134 of the Constitution, the president is responsible for appointing one third of judges who serve on the Constitutional Court. He also presides over the Superior Council of Magistrates (de Franciscis, 2002).

Parliament is bicameral and members are elected by universal suffrage. Parliament consists of The Senate of the Republic which is composed of 315 members, and The Chamber of Deputies which has 630 delegates (see Italy: Government in Italy, n.d.).

WHY ITALY IS PART OF THIS STUDY

Italy has consistently been ranked as one of the largest economies in the world (CNN Money: The new global economy; Economy watch.com: The World's Largest Economies, n.d.). Nonetheless, it continues to remain a shadow of other top nations in treatises on comparative justice. Granted, it borrowed much of its ideas on the justice system from France, but as a top nation now not only in Europe but worldwide, and with a legal system now unique to Italy, it deserves a spot in discussions in main treatises on comparative justice systems. Italy, more than any other country that assimilated the French/Napoleonic system of justice, also plays major roles in global current affairs. It is a member of the North Atlantic Treaty Organization (NATO), the European Union (EU), and the G8 nations; it is significantly involved with affairs in the Mediterranean region, and in its former colonies. Italy acts as a mediator in the Israeli–Palestinian conflict, has troops embedded in the Middle East, and in other regions of the world alongside those of its western allies. To those of the Christian faith, Italy is significant because its capital city, Rome, enjoys the role as seat of the Catholic faith (see Foreign Relations of Italy, n.d.). In 2015, Italy hosted the Milan Expo—Feeding the Planet, Energy for Life, a fair that examined ways by which approximately nine billion people could be helped by 2050 (see Italy, n.d.). With such active involvement in global affairs, it is only fair that students of comparative justice get a better understanding of Italy.

LEGAL CONCEPTS

Italians subscribe to the Napoleonic civil law system. Following the mandates of the Italian Constitution, the following rights are accorded to defendants:

1. As it relates to personal freedoms, no one can be searched or detained without any probable cause and without judicial sanction. However, when there is exigent circumstance, the police may act without judicial authorization, but must notify the judge within 48 hours of any such unilateral action. Failure to inform a judicial authority within 48 hours may invalidate any unauthorized police action (Art. 13).
2. "The right to a judicial defense" (Article 24). In essence, an accused has the right to present any defense that may justify, excuse, or mitigate the crime he/she is charged with. Embedded in this right as de Franciscis (2002) explains, is the right to face one's adversaries.

   As well, throughout the judicial process, an accused has the right to legal assistance. In this regard, Article 24 of the Constitution expressly states: "The indigent are assured, through appropriate institutions, the means for action and defense at all levels of jurisdiction."
3. Retroactive laws, that is, ex post facto laws are prohibited (Art. 25). No one should be subjected to adjudication for an act that was not a crime when the act was manifested.
4. Accused persons are presumed innocent until found guilty in a court of law (Art. 27). The article also forbids cruel and inhumane punishments, with the aim of punishment being rehabilitation.

Article 104 of the Italian Constitution addresses separation of powers among the three branches of government, and expressly states that as an autonomous organ, neither the executive nor legislative branches should meddle in the affairs of the judiciary. As de Franciscis (2002), explains, this judicial independence is affirmed by the Superior Council of Magistrates (*Consiglio Superiore della Magistratura*). What gives impetus to this is the fact that the president of the country presides over the Supreme Council of Magistrates, aided by the president of the Court of Cassation and the prosecutor general of the court. In addition, 30 elected citizens (20 of whom are judges elected by a body of other judges), 10 members who may be lawyers or law professors (elected by parliament), serve on the Supreme Council of Magistrates (see de Franciscis, 2002). It is this body of jurists that is responsible for hiring, promoting, transferring, and taking other actions on judges.

To ensure a fair, judicial process, and to be sure that sentences that are administered to those found guilty are proportionate to the crime, a sentence is reviewed by higher courts before it can be enforced. Appellate cases are tried de novo.

LAW ENFORCEMENT

There are two broad types of law enforcement officers in Italy: the police (*polizia*), and the *Carabinieri* (special branch of the army). The police force is under the jurisdiction of the Ministry of the Interior, while the *Carabinieri* is under the Ministry of Defense. The police (*polizia*) force has several branches on the national level, and two local police forces. Nationally, the police force is broken down into:

- State Police (*polizia di stato*)
- Finance Police (*guardio di finanza*)
- Military Police (*Arma dei Carabinieri*)
- Prison Police (*Polizia penitenziaria*)
- Forestry Police (*Corpo forestale dello Stato*)

Locally, the two police forces are:

- Provincial Police (*Polizia provinciale*)
- Municipal Police (*Polizia municipale*)

STATE POLICE (*POLIZIA DI STATO*)

The state police (*polizia di stato*) are responsible for patrolling, crime control, order maintenance, and law enforcement throughout the cities and towns. They are also responsible for crime control on all transportation and communication media. To this end, they have concurrent jurisdiction with the *carabinieri.*

The headquarters of the police force is in Rome. The police force in Italy, like that of other countries, is structured in a hierarchy. The police chief (*capo della polizia*) is the highest ranking officer, and also has an extended title of Director General of Public Security (*Direttore Generale della Pubblica Sicurezza*), as well as title of Honorary President of the National Association of State Police (*Associazione Nazionale della Polizia di Stato*). Three vice chiefs assist the chief of police (see, Organico della polizia di stato. Alte professionalita Vigili del Fuoco, n.d.).

Rank Qualifications for Promotion

- **Chief of Police (Capo della Polizia)**—Appointed by the President of the Republic following proposals from the Minister of Interior, and the Council of Ministers.
- **Assistant Chief (Assistente Capo)**—At least 5 yrs. of service and vigorous scrutiny of performance.
- **Assistant (Assistente)**—Promotion to this rank depends on service of at least 5 yrs. as senior officer, and intense scrutiny of performance.
- **Senior Officer (Agente Scelto)**—Promotion to this rank requires at least 5 yrs. of service as an officer and scrutiny of job performance.
- **Officer (Agente)**—Eligibility to become an officer depends on volunteer service in the Italian Armed Forces for 1–4 years (see Polizia di stato, n.d.; www.//en.m.wikipedia.org/wiki/polizia_di_stato, n.d.).

TRAINING OF ITALIAN POLICE OFFICERS

The Department of Public Security is responsible for police training. Its Central Directorate for Public Training Institute is directly in charge of police education and training. Programs are specialized depending on rank. First, the Police Training Institute provides elementary training for cadets, and for other lower technical operators. There are separate schools for police instructors, pilots, horseback officers, and canine handlers. There is also special training for officers involved in community policing. Community policing has special benefits. It emphasizes that partnerships between police and the community is vital and necessary for crime reduction.

The Police Academy established in 1982 is a higher-level educational institute responsible for teaching and training officers. As well, it is responsible for orientation and proficiency of senior officers (polise.osce.org, n.d.). In 1981, a Multi-Agency Police Academy was established to provide continuous training and refresher courses to officers (polise.osce.org). As of 2000, this Agency has expanded its functions to work collaboratively with other police departments throughout the European Union to effectuate uniform training (polise.osce.org).

MILITARY POLICE (*CARABINIERI*)

The *carabinieri* (named after a riffle "*carabina*" that officers used in the 1800s) are members of the military as well as police officers. The *carabinieri* was put together by King Victor Emmanuel in 1814 to guard the territory that was then known as Kingdom of Sardina (see Understanding Italy.com, n.d.). Their dual functions as members of the military and police officers expose them to military training and to a wide range of weaponry that they may use depending on the nature of their duty. Part of their function requires that they serve as peacekeeping troops in troubled places of the world, and their other function is to be law enforcers at home. The *carabinieri* are under the domain of the Ministry of Defense.

THE JUDICIARY AND JUDICIAL PROCESS

Those in the legal profession are divided into three groups: lawyers, magistrates, and notaries. Besides training, eligibility to practice in any of the three groups depends on affiliation; that is, one has to align oneself to the group that best represents one's calling. It is also required that the individual pass a state exam in order to become a practitioner. Further, to be eligible as a judge or a notary, one has to be a pupil under reputable lawyers or notaries who have established practices; two years of pupilage is expected, as well as a passing grade on the national bar examination. In some circumstances, the minister of justice may approve practice of a lawyer or notary based on redistricting (de Franciscis, 1986; 2002).

Upon an alleged commission of a crime by a suspect, the prosecutor sets in motion a criminal investigation. During this preliminary investigative period, the judge only intervenes if the suspect's rights are in jeopardy. A pre-trial hearing is held to determine if the accused should be kept in pre-trial detention. If the accused is a flight risk, risk to recidivate or to tamper or destroy evidence, precautionary measures to keep him in lock-up will be put in place. No investigative time frame is put in place; investigations last when the prosecutor thinks the evidence gathered is sufficient to build a case against the defendant. Prior to a preliminary hearing of the prosecutor's case, the defendant is apprised of the information against him, and also given 20 days within which to file a motion to contest the prosecutor's finding, or to seek approval to conduct the defendant's own investigation.

During the preliminary investigation, if the prosecutor is unable to prove probable cause, charges against the defendant are dropped. If the judge considers the evidence sufficient probable cause, charges are filed. At this point, the defendant may waive the right to trial, and request a sentence (a fast-track trial or *giudizio abbreviato*). This sentence generally should be one third less the prescribed sentence for that crime (Canestrinilex.com, 2016). This concession is made because the defendant gives up the right to a trial. Either the prosecutor or the defendant may appeal the sentence before the Court of Appeal.

Alternatively, a defendant may enter a plea bargain with the prosecutor for a reduced sentence. In order for the prosecutor to accept the plea bargain, the defendant must accept guilt. The judge is presented with the plea agreement, and upon examination of the defendant's dossier and the plea agreement, if the judge is not convinced of the defendant's guilt, he may refuse the plea agreement, and reinstate charges—an occurrence that hardly occurs (Canestrinilex.com, 2016). A judge also has discretion to ask for a trial should he determine that the prosecutor's sentence is too lenient (Canestrinilex.com). If the judge is in agreement with the plea bargain, that decision may be appealed to the cassation court. All that the court will examine at this point are matters of procedure and interpretation of law (Canestrinilex.com).

If the defendant does not outright enter a guilty plea, or get into a plea bargain, then a trial will take place. While investigations are of an inquisitorial nature, trials are of an adversarial nature in that both sides are given an opportunity to present their case, and to cross-examine witnesses. As well, guilt has to be proven beyond a reasonable doubt. For lesser offenses, the judge alone makes a determination of guilt or acquittal, which means there is no jury trial, but for serious crimes tried at the Assize Court, jurors (usually six) may be used (de Franciscis, 2002). Similar to what happens in adversarial systems, Italian judges are required to explain and have their decisions and reasoning published. In adversarial systems, while the presiding judge explains decisions and rationale of lower court cases, they remain in transcripts. Decisions that are published in law journals are those of appellate courts. Just as in adversarial systems, Italian judges are presumed to be impartial in the courtroom. In this regard, they are to make sure that the trial is fair, and that both sides are given reasonable opportunity to present their case (Art. 111, Italian Constitution). As well, accused have the right to a face-to-face confrontation in order to cross-examine their adversaries; consequently, evidence given without the benefit of cross-examination has very little weight or is discarded, and may not be used to convict a defendant (Art. 111 of Italian Constitution).

CRIMINAL COURT STRUCTURE

Courts are structured based upon a hierarchy. From the bottom to the top are: The justice of the Peace (*Guidice di Pace*), trial court (*Tribunale Ordinario*), Court of Appeal (*Corte di appello*), Court of Cassation (*corte di cassazione*). Cases of very serious nature are tried in three stages first by the Court of Assize (*Corte di Assise*), then reviewed by the Appeals Court of Assize, and final appeals are made to the Court of Cassation. This tripartite process for serious offenses is required as a means of ensuring that an accused is not given a disproportionate sentence, especially since the goal of punishment in Italy is rehabilitation. Courts for juvenile issues (Tribunale per i Minorenni) are separate from adult courts.

CORRECTIONS

History of Prisons in Italy Since Unification

The purpose of punishment under Italian law is rehabilitation (Canestrinilex.com, 2016). The idea is that while in prison, with the help of prison programs that enable inmates to obtain university credits and job skills, upon release inmates may become worthwhile persons in society again. The history of prisons in Italy has evolved since 1861 when the country was unified. In 1866, four prisons in Sardinia, Italy, adopted the Auburn system. The Auburn system, or Congregate system, was a system put in place in Auburn, New York, in 1817. In this system, prison structures had small cells with inmates under intense solitary confinement. While inmates could work in groups during the day, the requirement was that they had to remain silent throughout, and violators received lashings of a severe scale. At night, inmates slept in solitary confinement in hopes that they would ponder over their crimes (Samaha, 2006).

In 1870, two Italian prisons adopted the Pennsylvania system. The Pennsylvania system, as opposed to the Auburn system, required solitary confinement in cells as well as during work time, and silence at all times during the course of incarceration. In order to find a medium between the two systems, 52 prisons in Italy in 1870 were operated with blended policies from the Pennsylvania and Auburn systems (Roth, 2006). This blended system, as imperfect as it was, stayed in place because of lack of funding until 1931. In that year, Italy put in place a new penal code. The Palermo introduced the Institute for the Aid of Discharged Prisoners—an idea that was embraced in Rome, Milan, Florence, and Naples (Roth). This program opened up opportunities for ex-convicts to work in these institutes during the day and then return home at night. At this time, special skills or trade could be learned, and those former convicts could then receive remuneration, which generally was less than what non-convicts could earn (Roth). This, in essence, complied with what in the United States is the principle of less eligibility (a principle which states that inmates cannot earn the same amount of money for a similar job performed by one who has not committed a crime). As well, the "*All Aperto*" which means, "labor in the open" (Roth) was introduced in Sardinia and in the Tuscan region. This enabled inmates to work in agricultural fields. As well, a program was instituted that allowed inmates to go on work release during the day and get back to prison at night. Administrators disliked this program because the expense entailed for security was taking a toll on the budget.

The prevailing contemporary ideology is that prison work is not forced labor. When prisoners work, they have to be remunerated. Inmates are given the opportunity to work outside of prison grounds as long as they meet certain conditions including being low-risk offenders. Prisoners have the opportunity to earn credits toward university degrees, phone calls, and weekly visits.

PRISONS, JAILS, AND PRISONERS

More "modern" prison construction was completed in Rome in 1971. The Rebibbi Prison in Rome, a maximum-security prison for men, was styled to house 1,400 men. This prison was of a radial architectural style—a style that enables correctional officers to watch inmates from a central hub. As constructed in Rome, the prison was designed to accommodate single- as well as four-bed cells, with heavily monitored corridors.

Boom in Prison Population

Commentators on the prison boom in Italy have observed that there has been a steady rise in Italian prison population that far exceeds expected capacity. In 1995, Celestine Bohlen of *The New York Times* published an article titled "Bursting Population Overwhelms Italy's Prisons." When the article was written, Italy had a prison population of 54,000 inmates for a capacity of 29,000 (Ghosh, 2013). Prison crowding is not unique to Italy, although the problem there is worse than it is in many European countries. Prison capacity in many Italian prisons is 140% while the aggregate capacity in the majority countries in the European Union is below 100% (Ghosh).

Prison crowding has remained a problem in Italy. A decree in May 2000 focused on programs that would improve prison conditions within 3 years. This initiative led to improvements in inmate meals, lighting in cells, and opportunities for visitations and phone calls. Unfortunately, reports of overcrowding and other inhumane conditions in many Italian prisons have not stopped (Roth, 2006). In March 2010, the Italian government approved a budget of 350,000,000 Euros for the construction of more prisons. Reports as of July 2014 showed no positive results; that is, no new prisons had been built (Prison Observatory: Prison Conditions in Italy, 2016).

As of 2014, there were 53,623 inmates in Italy. According to data from the Ministry of Justice, prison population in 2015 including pretrial detainees was 52,636, excluding minors in juvenile institutions, while the capacity of the prison system was 49,605. That year, the prison population rate according to 100,000 of the national population was 87, and the national population was estimated at 60.81 million (Prisonstudies.org, 2016). The percentage of female prisoners in the same year was 4.1 excluding female minors. There were a total of 215 prisons in June 2015, 198 of them for adults and 17 for juveniles (Prisonstudies.org).

Reasons for overcrowding in Italian prisons, in particular, and in Europe, in general, have been listed as: (1) harsher sentences especially for drug-related crimes; (2) a system of justice that moves at a very slow pace; (3) limited funding for new prisons and jails (Ghosh, 2013). In recent years, foreigners are presumed to have surpassed the population of indigenous inmates. Reports indicate that one third of Italian prison population are immigrants (Ghosh). Those awaiting trial spend over half a year without their cases being called in court. It is stated that 42% of Italian inmates are persons awaiting trial (Ghosh).

Prison Administration

The Ministry of Justice is responsible for prisons, and in the lower levels the Prevention and Penalty Institute oversee its policies. The Warden is the highest-ranking prison official in charge of security, treatment, and budget.

Prison police are responsible for security throughout the prison even though they are not soldiers. They are union workers employed by the Ministry of Justice. They are also responsible for transferring inmates in and out of jail. They are accountable to the warden.

Educators such as psychologists are under split services between the Ministry of Justice and Ministry of Health. Physicians and other health care workers are directly under the supervision of the National Health Service, and the Ministry of Education supervises those who teach high school or college courses.

ALTERNATIVES TO INCARCERATION

Defendants sentenced to more than 3 years in Italy must serve that time in prison, but under certain circumstances, an inmate may apply for early release under some state supervision such as home detention, work release, parole, and so forth (Gualazzi, Mancuso, & Mangiaracina, 2012). Those that are sentenced to less than 3 years in prison may automatically have their sentences suspended based on provisions of Article 656 of the code of criminal procedure. Some kinds of offenders, based on their crimes, may not be amenable for this privilege (Gualazzi et al., 2012). Persons eligible for a suspended sentence or some alternative to incarceration have to apply within 30 days. Failure to apply within the required time frame vitiates any chances for a suspended sentence, and the defendant is remanded to prison to spend the duration of the sentence (Gualazzi et al., 2012).

Law no. 354 of July 26, 1975, governs alternatives to incarceration. Alternative sanctions serve the objectives of reducing prison crowding, keeping the public safe, and rehabilitating the offender, while still making it a punishment (Samaha, 2006). Alternative sanctions through privileges may be suspended or revoked upon violations of conditions. If suspended, the convict is remitted to prison pending an ultimate decision. The Surveillance judge forwards all relevant documents to the Tribunal that makes a final decision on the convict's fate. A time frame of 30 days is given from when the documents are forwarded to the Tribunal until when a decision is passed down. Failure to render a decision within 30 days will lead to the release of the convict to the program that he/she had initially been placed (Gualazzi et al., 2012). Following are alternatives to incarceration in Italy.

PROBATION

Probation is punishment in lieu of incarceration. In Italy, probation is under the domain of social services, and governed by Article 47 of Law on the Penitentiary System of July 26, 1975. Probation may be granted to offenders who are sentenced to less than 3 years, are low risk of flight, have evidence of stability in the community, and are less likely to recidivate (Gualazzi et al., 2012).

Several conditions attach to probation, including but not limited to refraining from recidivating, staying away from deviant and criminal friends, a ban on possession or use of weapons and other contraband, as well as maintaining a job or engaging in a worthwhile activity, and maintaining required contact with the probation officer. Violation of any of the conditions mentioned above, or those not mentioned herein, may lead to revocation of probation.

Upon violation of conditions of probation, or upon the commission of a new crime, the accused has a right to due process before the privilege can be revoked. The Surveillance Tribunal, which is the court vested with authority to make recalls on privileges accorded inmates, upon determination of misconducts weighty to revoke probation would revoke probation.

Home Detention (Article 47-*ter* of Law on the Penitentiary System [*legge penitenziaria*])

In order to be eligible for home detention, one has to be sentenced to no more than 2 years in prison. As well, inmates who have less than 2 years left on their sentence may apply, so are those who have no more than 4 years left of a longer sentence. Infirm persons, pregnant women, and custodial parents are also eligible for home detention (Gualazzi et al., 2012).

Persons on home detention have the privilege of going to work or school, to attend a religious ceremony, attend doctor's appointments or hospital visits, or some appointment related to his/her terms of home confinement (Gualazzi et al., 2012).

Reasons for revoking home detention include, but are not limited to, committing a new crime, use of drugs or possession of contraband, leaving the assigned residence without permission and for no just cause, or failure to abide by rules that promote efforts at rehabilitation (Gualazzi et al., 2012).

Day Release (Article 48-51, no. 354 of July, 26, 1975)

While on day release, the offender is still an inmate. The prisoner is allowed to leave prison confinement to attend school, work, or some other worthwhile activity, and return to prison at a specified time daily. The intent for letting prisoners go out in the community to work is to enable them to have a smooth transition to life in the community after the expiration of their prison term. Conditions attached to this privilege include refraining from committing crimes, and/or violating any instructions given by prison authorities, especially in regard to curfew (Gualazzi et al., 2012). Violators forfeit this privilege and are no longer eligible to spend their day outside of prison confines.

Automatic Remission (Article 54 law 1975/354)

The underlying purpose of automatic remission is to reward offenders who have fared well in custody by complying to prison rules, not engaging in deviant or criminal behavior, and engaging in prison programs geared toward rehabilitation. Remission, which is earning good time, requires that 45 days are deducted for every 6 months of the inmate's prison sentence (Gualazzi et al., 2012).

Parole

Parole in Italy is more commonly known as conditional release (*liberta condizionata*). Articles 176–177 of the Penal Code regulate parole. Only inmates who have spent at least 30 months of their incarceration, or at least 26 years for those spending life in prison, are eligible for parole. There will be no consideration of parole for inmates who have more than 5 years left of incarceration (Gualazzi et al., 2012).

Parole is the conditional release of an inmate from prison prior to the expiration of a prison sentence. The mission of parole is to rehabilitate the offender in the sense that the offender has the opportunity to exercise a smooth transition into the community. The offender is expected to engage in a useful activity, work, school, or some type of therapeutic activity. It is a punishment in the sense that the offender does not have unfettered freedom, and society is still protected because the offender is still monitored. The Surveillance Tribunal (*Tribunale di Sorveglianza*) oversees these early privileges.

Grounds for revocation of parole include (1) a new crime committed; (2) the offender violates any provisions of Article 230 c.p. that relate to conditions of parole, such as leaving the jurisdiction without permission from the parole officer, keeping miscreants as company, and other violations. As Gualazzi et al. (2012) explain, violations per se may not be sufficient reason for parole revocation based on the ruling of the Constitutional Court. Following recommendations by the Constitutional Court (*Corte Costituzionale*), it is incumbent on the Surveillance Tribunal to determine if the offender's violation is weighty enough to impede the offender's progress in reintegrating to society. Such enquiry must be thorough, and revocation of parole can only occur if the findings unequivocally reveal that the parolee's violation and behavior is egregious enough to stall any possibility of rehabilitation (Gualazzi et al).

The outcome of revocation is that the offender is taken back to prison, and he/she will have to once more prove that he/she may be trusted for early release in the community.

SUMMARY

Italy became unified in 1861 and adopted the French civil, penal, and commercial codes. The French, prior to unification, had a dominant influence in Italy, so it was just logical that its system of law already prevalent in the region be adopted, but modified to suit contemporary Italian realities.

Italy is included in the sample of nations in this book for a variety of reasons including its global involvement in world affairs and its prominence in the European Union.

There are two types of law enforcement officers in Italy: the police (*polizia*) and the special branch of the military (*carabinieri*). The police are under the auspices of the Ministry of Interior, while the *carabinieri* is under the domain of the Ministry of Defense.

Italy subscribes to the Napoleonic system of justice. Courts are based on a hierarchy from the justice of peace (*guidice di pace*) at the lowest level to the Court of Cassation (*corte di cassazione*) being the highest.

Defendants may plea-bargain if the prosecutor is willing to do so; if not, the case may be fully prosecuted. Investigations are of an inquisitorial nature, trials tend to take the form of an adversarial process in that both sides present their case and are subjected to cross-examination. For lesser offenses, the judge decides; for serious offenses, the Assize Court usually uses six jurors to decide the case.

The focus of incarceration in Italy is to rehabilitate. Yet, prison crowding seems to stall this goal. The prison system is under the sphere of the Ministry of Justice. Several alternatives to incarceration have been introduced in Italy to help alleviate prison crowding, and to help foster the rehabilitative process.

DISCUSSION QUESTIONS

1. Discuss four factors of the Italian Justice System that distinguishes it from that of a Common Law System like that of Singapore or Ghana.
2. Discuss the structure of Italian police, and explain the qualifications of getting to the top ranking position of police chief.
3. Summarize the arguments in favor of alternative sentencing. Does alternative sentencing lead to an offender's rehabilitation?

4. Given the problem of prison crowding in Italy, what policies would you recommend to abate the problem?

REFERENCES

123HelpMe.Com. (2015, December 31). Retrieved from http://www.123Helpme.com/view.ap?id=96780

Bohlen, C. (2015). Bursting Population Overwhelms Italy's Prisons. *The New York Times.* Retrieved from https://www.nytimes.com/1995/02/28/world/bursting-population-overwhelms-italy-s-prisons.html

Canestrinilex.com. (2016). The Italian criminal trial. Retrieved from http://www.canestrinilex.com/resources/trial/

CNN Money: The new global economy. Retrieved from http://money.com/news, economy/world-economies-gdp/index.html

Country Meters. (n.d.). Retrieved from countrymeters.info

Culture of Italy. Retrieved from http://www.everyculture.com/Ge-It/Italy.html

De Franciscis, M. (1986). Italy. In A. Katz (Ed.), *Legal traditions and systems: An international handbook* (pp. 149–168). Westport, CT: Greenwood Publishing Group.De Franciscis, M. (2002). Italy. In H. Kritzer (Ed.), *Legal systems of the world: A political, social, and cultural encyclopedia* (Vol. 11, pp. 761–766). Santa Barbara, CA: ABC-CLIO.Donati, S. (2013). *A political history of national citizenship and identity in Italy*, 1861–1950. Stanford, CA: Stanford University Press.

Economy watch.com: The world's largest economies. Retrieved from http://www.economywatch.com/economies-in-top

Foreign Relations of Italy. Retrieved from http:/en.m.wikipedia.org/wik/foreign_relations_of_Italy

Ghosh, P. (2013, June 18). Italy's overcrowded prisons: A growing tragedy of epic proportions. *International Business Times.* Retrieved from http://www.ibtimes.com/italys-overcrowded-prisons-growing-tragedy-epic-proportions-1310555

Gualazzi, A., Mancuso, C., & Mangiaracina, A. (2012). 'Back door sentencing' in Italy: Common reasons and main consequences for the recall of prisoners. *European Journal of Probation, (4)*1: 73–84.

Italy: Government in Italy. Retrieved from http://www.justlanded.com/English/Italy/Articles/Culture-in-italy.

Organico-della-polizia-di-stato-Alte-professionalita-Vigili-del-fuoco. Retrieved from http://www.apvvf.it/public/upload/VAPVF_A.pdf

Polise.Osce.org. Retrieved from http://www.polise.osce.org/countries/details?item_id=23

Polizia di Sato. Retrieved from www.//en.m.wikipedia.org/wiki/polizia_di_sato and www.poliziadistato.it/articolo/964-The-Public-Security-System-in-Italy

Prison Observatory: Prison Conditions in Italy. (2016). Retrieved from http://www.prisonobservatory.org/index.php?option=com_content&view=article&id=10:prison-conditions-in-italy&catid=13&ltemid=116

Prisonstudies.org. Italy/World Prison Brief. Retrieved from http://www.prisonstudies.org/country/italy

Roth, M. (2006). Italy. In *Prisons and prison systems: A global encyclopedia* (pp. 141–142). Westport, CT: Greenwood Press.

Samaha, J. (2006). *Criminal justice* (7th ed.). Australia: Thomson/Wadsworth.

Understanding Italy.com. Retrieved from http://www.understandingItaly.com/profile-content/Italian-police.html

CHAPTER 6

The Romania Model

© Peter Hermes Furian/Shutterstock.com

INTRODUCTION

Romania is in the southeastern part of Central Europe. It is located north of the Balkan Peninsula, and bordered by the Black Sea, with Bulgaria to its south, Yugoslavia to the southwest, Ukraine to the north, Hungary, Serbia to the west, and Moldova to the east. The capital of Romania is Bucharest, which is the sixth largest city in the European Union (see Geography of Romania). The River Danube, which is the second longest river in Europe, empties its waters in the Danube Delta in Romania.

The population of Romania based on the 2011 census is 20,121,641. Of this number, 88.9% are Romanians, while 6.5% are Hungarians, and Roma 3.3% (see Romanian 2011 Census Final Results). A July 2015 census places the population of Romania at 21,666,350 (see Search Yahoo.com).

Romanian is the official language and about 85.4% speak the language, 6.3% speak Hungarian, 1.2% speak Romany (Gypsy), and the rest speak other unspecified languages (see Romania People 2017; CIA World Factbook).

History has it that the earliest human fossil in Europe was found in Romania over 42,000 years ago (CIA World Factbook). Much of what is written about early life in Romania begins from 440 B.C. in the fourth book of Herodotus' Histories. There, he includes stories of the Getae tribe, which as contemporary history suggests constitutes the Thracians who lived in Dacia—a group of people considered to be part of Romania, Moldova, and North Bulgaria (CIA World Factbook). Included in the history of Romania is the point that Romanians by and large think of themselves as descendants of the Roman clan who under Emperor Trajan conquered Southern Transylvania (see Global Britannica.com). The intermarriages between the Dacians and the Romans precipitated the spread of both the Roman language and the Eastern Orthodox doctrine.

Between the fourth and fifth century when the Huns made their way into the territory until the 14th century when Walachia and Moldavia were established, hardly any recorded history exist about the Romanians (Global Britannica.com). It is reported that plagued by wars, and not being able to defend themselves, the Romanians fled. Walachia and Moldavia were united in 1859, and declared their independence from the Ottoman Empire in 1877 (Global Britannica.com). In 1878, Romania was accorded the status of an independent state by the Congress of Berlin.

During the Second World War, Romania fought on the side of the Germans. After the defeat of Germany, the Soviet Union spread its communist influence in Romania after ousting the Romanian King. From 1947–1989, Romania remained a communist country, but then reverted to its old system of civil law. Despite its checkered history, Romania's legal system today is civil patterned after Roman law.

Romania is a republic with a president and prime minister. The current Constitution of Romania, adopted in 1991, has eight titles which among several provisions are those relating to human rights and freedoms, the economy and public finance, and a host of other provisions. While the president is the commander in chief of the armed forces and the chair of the Supreme Council of National Defense, the prime minister is vested with powers of selecting cabinet members (see GlobalEDGE).

WHY ROMANIA IS PART OF THIS STUDY

Although Romania does not have the clout of many European countries, it has, despite its many struggles throughout history, played vital roles in Europe. When the Soviet Union invaded Czechoslovakia in 1968, Romania was the lone country among members of the Warsaw Pact to openly denounce the Soviets. Romania maintained diplomatic ties with Israel in 1967 after the Six-Day War. It established both diplomatic and economic relations with Germany, and its friendly ties with the Palestine Liberation Organization (PLO) enabled Romania to play a vital role in the peace process between Israel and Egypt, and Israel and the PLO (CIA World Factbook). Romania has been a member of NATO since 2004, and hosted the NATO 2008 summit. It became a member of the European Union in 2007. Its legal system has undergone a multitude of changes, incorporating a variety of legal doctrines over its history, and eliminating some—a process Mark Goodale states, "some commentators have referred to as a true case of legal pluralism" (2002, p. 1374).

Romania has produced several notable intellectuals including Georges Enesco (a composer), Eugene Lonesco (a playwright), Emile Cioran (philosopher), Mircea Eliade (religion historian), and George E. Palade (Nobel Laureate) (Global Britannica.com).

Its correctional system has undergone massive and persistent criticism by the European Court on Human Rights (ECtHR) especially because of the inhumane treatment of inmates, horrible structural facilities, overcrowding, and other issues. Despite attempts at resolving the issues, and issues relating to pretrial detention, reform is piecemeal and troubling as noted by the Council of Europe's anti-torture Committee (CPT) in 2015 (Prisons in Romania, 2015).

Romania is included in this book not because it has an exemplary criminal justice system, but because it has a system fraught with a checkered history and a substandard justice system based on European standards. Its addition here demonstrates why and how a country must continuously search for ways to improve its system of justice even when it is not classified as a developing country.

LEGAL HISTORY

The legal system of Romania is a hodgepodge of French, German, Italian, and Belgian systems of law and indigenous practices; it thus maintains this civil law heritage. This civil law leaning is traced to the 1600s when codifications of laws in the country went underway (Goodale, 2002). As reported, Vasile Lupu, ruler of Moldavia, set in motion attempts at drawing up a codified set of laws in Romania in 1646, which were known as *Pravila lui Vasile Lupu*. This was followed by Prince Matei Basarab's the *Pravila lui Mateiu Basarab* in 1652 (Goodale).

Even though many other codes such as the Byzantine and canon law existed in the country, the Romanian's, enamored by the French language and culture, chose to draw ideas from the French penal, civil, and commercial codes in the 1800s (Goodale). But, the Romanian system again underwent change during the 1940s, with integrations of Italian and German aspects of law. By the end of the Second World War, now a member of the Soviet Bloc countries, Romania embraced the Marxist-Leninist socialist ideology. For about 40 years, or a little over that, Romania's existing laws were glossed over by socialist laws, but between 1989–2001, Romania returned to its civil law heritage (Goodale).

LEGAL CONCEPTS

The laws that are applicable in the country are embodied in the constitution and statutes. Both the defense and prosecutor are involved in the investigatory process, as is the judge; therefore, the case law system and compliance to precedence are absent in the Romanian system of justice. Also absent in the judicial system are other vestiges of legal practices typical in adversarial systems such as jury trials, active direct and cross-examinations, among others. But, the Romanian criminal trial process promotes the presumption of innocence as a core principle just as common-law systems do.

Searches and seizures have to be effected in compliance with set procedural measures. The judge has exclusive powers to issue an arrest warrant, and any detention of an arrestee is limited to criminal investigations, and a prosecutor must be apprised of such detention with 24 hours. Pretrial detentions should not exceed 6 months; hence, the prosecutor has to file a request for any detentions over the 24 hours, and such extensions may not exceed 6 months (see Coe.int).

The constitution and statutory provisions grant everyone a fair judicial process and equal protection under the law. Accused persons are accorded rights to present their own side of the case and right to be defended by counsel. The right to legal assistance is guaranteed pursuant to the Criminal Procedure Code and the Civil Procedure Code, as well as Law no. 51/1995. While access to court and a fair judicial process are assured, alternative ways of resolving a dispute, such as mediation, have been introduced. Law no. 192/2006 put in force this legal alternative, which is under the domain of the Mediation Council (Coe.int; Luminita, 2013). Through this form of dispute settlement, parties who no longer want formal criminal adjudication, or parties who have reconciled amicably use a mediator to once and for all settle their dispute (Luminita).

Theoretically, there is judicial independence of courts in Romania. Following the mandates of the constitution, the Ministry of Justice is vested with powers to select and promote judges. However, the president makes the appointment of judges following recommendations by a panel of judges and prosecutors put together by parliament (see The Judicial System in

Romania). Further duties of the Ministry of Justice include overseeing that the justice system functions smoothly in compliance with the dictates of the rule of law. The Ministry also oversees the following agencies: The National Administration of Penitentiaries, Probation, The National Trade Register, and the National Institute of Forensics (see Coe.int).

The Superior Council of Magistracy is vested with managerial and disciplinary powers. In this regard, it appoints, evaluates, promotes, and decides on any disciplinary measures for judges and prosecutors. Because this Council answers to no one but to the law, there are Constitutional and statutory provisions that act as checks on its powers, and of that of the judiciary: Constitution of 1991, amended in 2003; Law no. 303/2004 amended by Law no. 247/2005; Law no. 304/2004 amended by Law no. 247/2005; Law no. 317/2004 amended by Law no. 247/2005. Besides being in charge of the National Institute of Magistracy, The Superior Council of Magistracy is also responsible for training of personnel in the National School for Clerks.

To become a member of this council, names of potential members are scrutinized by various entities including the Chamber of Deputies and the Senate with the two Chambers of parliament in a joint session ultimately voting.

In order to ease the responsibilities of the Ministry of Justice as supervisory organ of state marshals, notaries, and the national bar association, the ministry is divided into six directorates: civil courts, military courts, studies and legislation, personnel, administration, planning and accounting (see The Judicial System in Romania). Judicial reform has been at the forefront of reforms in Romania since the Treaty of Accession 2005 between Romania, Bulgaria, and the European Union. This treaty, which makes Romania a vital part of the European Union and its Constitution, has led Romania to prioritize judicial reform (see Ministry of Justice, Study on Romanian Court Rationalization).

While judges enjoy some degree of judicial independence, the Superior Council of Magistracy through its evaluative powers decides the fate of judges. Court rulings can only be reviewed on appeal by a higher court. Prosecutors are heavily involved in criminal investigations as a requirement by law; as well, they are obligated to supervise investigations done by police. While the Ministry of Justice oversees prosecutorial functions, it has no authority to interfere in the prosecutor's handling of criminal investigations (Coe.int).

The Constitutional Court (*Curtea Constitutionaia*) is separate from judicial courts; it nonetheless ensures that the rule of law is applied. It oversees parliamentary regulations, treaties, or covenants prior to their ratification by parliament upon the request of the President of the country, as well as decides disputes among public officials (Coe.int).

In order to be a judge, prosecutor, or defense lawyer (*avocat*) in Romania, one must attend 4 years of law school; upon completion spend 2 years of pupilage under a certified lawyer, take the bar exam thereafter, and upon passing, one becomes eligible to practice law, or to be appointed as a prosecutor or judge. Notaries too play important roles in the Romanian judicial system. They have to notarize documents in order to give them official binding force. Notaries are required to obtain a university degree and to pass the national exams for notaries.

On February 1, 2014, based upon Law no. 286/2009, a new Penal Code and a new Penal Procedure Code were put in place. The purposes of the new codes inter alia, were to make criminal trials simple and speedy, and to have provisions conform to those of other European nations as well as to the various international treaties to which Romania is a signatory. Even though several adjustments were made relating to sentence lengths, elimination of sentences for juveniles, and other adjustments, there is room for improvement in the country's justice process and system.

ROMANIAN POLICE

The Romanian police (*Politia Romana*) force is under the auspices of the Ministry of Administration and Interior. Among their many duties are to uphold the rights of citizens and keep them safe, order maintenance, and crime control.

The Romanian police force is organized in different units, with a very specialized squad known as the Independent Service of Special Interventions Operations. A General Inspector who also holds a cabinet rank of secretary of state heads the General Inspectorate, which is the central unit of the police force. The Prime Minister appoints him/her. The Central Unit is composed of several central directorates including that for fighting organized crime, criminal investigations, public safety police, and administrative police. Then, there are the territorial units.

Central Units

1. General Directorate for Countering Organized Crime: This unit has five subsections that include combat section for drugs; human trafficking; cybercrime; terrorism; and money laundering.
2. General Directorate for Criminal Investigations: There are three subsections including fraud investigations; criminal investigations; firearms explosives, and toxic substance.
3. General Directorate for Public Safety: This directorate includes three subunits—public order; traffic; and transport.
4. General Directorate for Administrative Police: This unit is divided into four central directorates: forensics; criminal records, statistics, and operational registry; logistics; and information technology and communications.

Territorial Units

Each of the 41 counties in Romania has its own police force and rapid response unit, as does the capital city of Bucharest.

Ranks

In June 2002, Romanian police changed their ranking system from a military style to a civilian style emulating the British and French ranking styles. The highest ranked police officer is the Commissioner or *Directeur des services actifs* (French) *Chestor-general de politie* (Romanian); while the lowest ranked is the Temporary or Probationary Inspector or *Lieutenant intern* (French) *Subinspector de polite* (Romanian). For non-commissioned ranks, the highest ranked is the Station Sergeant or Brigadier-Major (French) *Agent-sef principal de politie* (Romanian). The lowest ranked non-commissioned police are the Constables *Gardien de la paix stagiare* (French) (Romanian Police).

STRUCTURE OF COURTS IN ROMANIA

Following the 1992 law on the restructuring of the judiciary, a court system was created based on a hierarchy. Provisions on the restructuring of courts are found in the Constitution, and Law no. 304/2004 on judicial organization (Romanian Judicial System), subsequently supplanted the 1992 law. The lowest court is the Court of First Instance (*Judecatorii*), then the Tribunal (*Tribunale*), then the Court of Appeal (*Curti de Apel*), and then the Supreme Court of Justice (*Curtea Suprema de Justitie*). Below is the hierarchy of courts in Romania.

- **Supreme Court of Justice (Curtea Suprema de Justitie)/High Court of Cassation:** This is the highest appellate court. It reviews decisions from the Court of Appeal.
- **Court of Appeal (*Curti de Apel*):** The Court of Appeal reviews cases sent forward on appeal from the Tribunal, and under rare circumstances may act as Court of first instance for special cases (Goodale, 2002). There are 15 courts of appeals in the country (Coe.int, n.d.). Based on the Civil Procedure Code, just one appeal is allowed for simple offenses. For other issues, a second appeal may be allowed for challenges relating to issues of law.
- **Tribunal (*Tribunale*):** These courts have original jurisdiction over felonies, and over civil cases whose fines exceed 150 million lei, and for commercial cases for which property values exceed 10 million lei (Goodale, 2002). Tribunals also review appellate cases from the *judecatorii*.

- **Court of First Instance (*Judecatorii*):** These courts have jurisdiction over a wide variety of cases that encompass criminal, civil, administrative, commercial, and family issues. The jurisdiction of this court is limited only to cases whose fines do not exceed 10 million lei (Goodale, 2002).

CORRECTIONS IN ROMANIA

The Ministry of Justice is responsible for Corrections in Romania. Under the Ministry is the National Administration of Penitentiaries that had a staff of 12,657 in 2015 overseen by the Director General (Prisons in Romania, 2015). As of 2017, there are 45 prisons and holding places in the country (World Prison Brief, n.d.) with a prison population of 26,878. This constitutes a prison population rate of 137 per 100,000 of the country's population, and a 96.5% occupancy level (World Prison Brief, n.d.).

The primary goals of the National Association of Prisons in Romania are public safety and proper reintegration of inmates into society (Relu & Mihaela, n.d.). Since 2006 when Law no. 275/04.07.2006 was implemented, reforms have been ongoing, but problems of overcrowding, hygiene conditions, food, and access to work and educational programs have remained ongoing issues (Relu & Mihaela; ROMANIA926.PDF, n.d.). While the country has implemented some rehabilitative programs like educational activities, trade, crafts, gym, sports, and other recreational activities, these programs are few and some are not available in all prisons. It is for these inadequacies and the persistent overcrowding, inhumane treatment of inmates, and deplorable prison facilities that the European Court on Human Rights (ECtHR) constantly cites Romania for violation of Article 3 of the Convention (Prisons in Romania, 2015). Worthy of note, too, is that there is no death penalty in Romania.

TYPES OF PRISONS

There are 45 prisons/holding houses in Romania, all of which are run by the state. There are no private prisons in the country. Sixteen of the 45 prisons are maximum-security prisons, 19 of the prisons in the country are semi-open and open. There are two detention centers, two education centers, and six prison hospitals (Prisons in Romania, 2015). Following Article 68 of Law 254/2013, Romanian inmates have the privilege of receiving visitors in prison. Such visits have to be arranged through telephone calls or e-mails.

- **Maximum Security Prisons:** These prisons house the worst types of criminals, including murderers and armed robbers among others. Inmates in these prisons are accorded two visits per month from friends and family. Visits may last from 30 minutes to 2 hours. Inmates may also make phone calls of 30 minutes' duration per day to 10 people who have been pre-approved by prison administrators. Conditions in these prisons have notoriously been horrific: violence and inhumane conditions including overcrowding form some of the bases for criticisms (Prisons in Romania, 2015).

- **Medium Security:** Inmates here are felons whose crimes are not as egregious as those of maximum-security inmates. Inmates in medium security prisons have the privilege to receive three visits a month, and can make 30-minute calls each day to persons already approved by the prison authorities.
- **Minimum Security/Open and Semi-Open Regimen:** These prisons house non-violent and small-time offenders. They are accorded a visit each week, and can make phone calls that last up to an hour each day.

NON-CUSTODIAL PUNISHMENTS

Probation

Probation started in Romania between 1996–2000 (Durnescu & Haines, 2012). By 2007, the prison population had dropped from 45,309, when it was counted in 1995, to 39,031 in 2007 (Durnescu & Haines). During this time, incarcerations tanked while intermediate sanctions spiked from 445 in 2000 to 1,538 in 2004 (Durnescu & Haines). Probation and other intermediate sanctions appeared to be the panacea for overcrowded prisons. Following Law no. 252/2013, probation as an alternative to incarceration, and Law no. 253/2013 that regulates other non-custodial sanctions, were fully organized and integrated into the correctional system of Romania (Mutiu, 2014). Noteworthy is the fact that probation in Romania conforms to the recommendations of the Council of Europe (Mutiu; Durnescu & Haines).

The Ministry of Justice regulates the Directorate of Probation (Nichifor, 2013). Professionals trained by the National Probation Directorate supervise probationers. These professionals are responsible for ensuring that probationers comply with the terms of their probation and that they are fully reintegrated into society. In this regard, they are to monitor probationers so that they do not re-offend in order to ensure the community's safety, and evaluate therapeutic programs that probationers undergo (Mutiu, 2014). During the initial meeting between the probation officer and the probationer, the officer notifies the probationer of the conditions of probation, special activities or programs that the probationer must attend, and documents of evidence that the probationer fulfilled the requirements of the programs (Mutiu). The goals of probation are to decrease prison crowding, reduce costs entailed in incarceration, and to reintegrate probations in society as wholesome, productive citizens (Mutiu, Nichifor). For those with substance abuse problems, the "Stop! Think and Change" program has been developed to help reshape the thinking of alcohol and gambling addicts (Nichifor). A weekly session for 3 months is intended to help addicts find root causes of their problems and how to overcome them (Nichifor).

Parole

Circumstances under which parole may be granted to inmates differ based upon sentence length. Articles 99–100 of the Romanian Criminal Code provide conditions under which parole may be granted to inmates serving life sentences. An inmate spending life in prison may be eligible for parole after spending at least 20 years in prison. Further, the inmate must have displayed exemplary behavior throughout the prison sentence, and there is convincing fact that the inmate would do well upon release into society. Inmates owing restitution must also have paid off or at least proved inability to pay such restitution. Other conditions of parole and consequences for violating them are reiterated to the inmate.

For inmates spending sentences less than life, eligibility for parole depends on the inmate's completion of at least two thirds of the imposed sentence. This is the condition for inmates spending less than 10 years. For those sentenced to more than 10 to 20 years, the inmate must have spent at least three quarters of the sentence. The court must also be convinced that the inmate can be successfully reintegrated in society, and that whatever dues owed the victim have been paid. All other conditions of parole and consequences for violations are fully explained to the inmate prior to release.

Article 587 of the Criminal Procedure Code gives the court of first instance in the geographical area where the inmate is housed jurisdiction to make decisions on parole.

SUMMARY

Romania is a country in the Southeastern part of Central Europe. It is a republic with a president and prime minister. The 1991 Constitution, which is the most recent of the country has eight titles with a good number of them relating to human rights and freedoms. It is a European country that has played pivotal roles in world peace especially between Israel and Egypt, and between Israel and the Palestinian Liberation Organization (PLO).

While its justice system is not one for which compliments are due, the basis for its inclusion in this book is to compare systems of justice and to decide what to or what not to emulate from each country. The constitution and statutes embody laws applicable in the country. Romanian law enforcement has several units and all are under the auspices of the Ministry of Administration and Interior.

Law number 304/2004 imposed a restructuring of courts based on a hierarchy, and while in theory there is judicial independence, the Ministry of Justice elects and promotes judges with ultimate powers from the president. As well, the Superior Council of Magistracy checks the level of judicial independence.

Correction in Romania is under the domain of the Ministry of Justice. The goals of the National Association of Prisons in the country are safety and reintegration of inmates in society.

DISCUSSION QUESTIONS

1. Explain in detail why Romania is classified under the Napoleonic Civil Law.
2. Discuss the various law enforcement units in Romania. What are the criteria to become a police officer in Romania?
3. Explain the requirements to become: (a) a judge; (b) a prosecutor; and (c) a defense attorney in Romania.
4. Compare the Romanian system of justice to that of Italy.
5. What are some of the criticisms of the Romanian correctional system? What recommendations would you put forth to address the criticisms of the Romanian correctional system?

REFERENCES

CIA World Factbook. Romania/CIA World factbook. Retrieved from http://www.ciaworldfactbook.us/europe/romania.html

Coe.int. Retrieved from http://www.coe.int/dghl/cooperation/cepej/profiles/CourtSystemRomania_en.pdf

Durnescu, I., & Haines, K. (2012). Probation in Romania. *British Journal of Criminology*, 52, 889–907.

Geography of Romania. Retrieved from https://www.google.com/search?q=geography+of+romania&ie=UTF-8&hi=en&client=safari

Global Britannica.com. Retrieved from http://www.global.britannica.com/place/Romania

GlobalEDGE. (n.d.). Romania: Government of Romania—globalEdge. Retrieved from http://globaledge.msu.edu/global-resources/resource/5703

Goodale, M. (2002). Romania. In H. Kritzer (Ed.), *Legal systems of the world: A political, social, and cultural encyclopedia,* Vol. 11 (Vol. 3, pp. 1372–1377). Santa Barbara, CA: ABC-CLIO.

The Judicial System in Romania. Retrieved from http://www.dreptonline.ro/en_resources/en_judicial_system_romania.php

Luminita, D. (2013). Criminal mediation in the Romanian law system. *AGORA International Journal of Juridical Sciences, 2,* 91–94.

Ministry of Justice, Study on Romanian Court Rationalization. Pagina nu a fost gasita/Ministerul Justitiel. Retrieved from http://www.just.ro/files/Studii_si_analize/STUDY%20ON%20ROMANIAN%20COURT%20RATIONALIZATION.htm

Mutiu, F. (2014). Probation services and their role in the execution of criminal sanctions. *Journal of Eastern-European Criminal Law,* (1), 122–127.

Nichifor, E. (2013). The probation service in Romania: An overview. *Irish Probation Journal, 10,* 104–117.

Prisons in Romania. (2015). Retrieved from https://www.prison-insider.com/countryprofile/prisonsromania?sle.ssysteme-penitentiare#le-systeme-penitentiaire

Relu, M., & Mihaela, P. (n.d.). Preparing a draft strategy for the development of the prison system in Romania. Retrieved from http://content.ebscohost.com.proxy.lib.odu.edu/ContentServer.asp?

ROMANIA926.PDF. (n.d.). Retrieved from https://www.hrw.org/sites/default/files/reports/ROMANIA926.pdf

Romania People 2017. Retrieved from http://theodora.com/wfbcurrent/romania/romania_people.html

Romanian Police. Retrieved from http://www.en.m.wikipedia.org/wiki/Romanian_Police

Romanian 2011 Census Final Results. Retrieved from http://www.recensamantromania.ro/wp-content/uploads/2013/07/Resultate-definitive

Search.yahoo.com. Retrieved from https://search.yahooo.com/search=Romania&fr2=uh3_news_web_gs_12

World Prison Brief. (n.d.). Romania/World prison brief. Retrieved from http://www.prisonstudies.org/country/romania

PART III

Germanic Civil Law

CHAPTER 7

The Republica Federativa do Brazil Model

© pavalena/Shutterstock.com

INTRODUCTION

Brazil is a South American country with an estimated population of 205,823,665 as of July 2016 (CIA World Factbook). The majority of Brazilians speak Portuguese which is the country's official language, and less spoken languages include Spanish, German, Japanese, Italian, English, and others (CIA World Factbook). The ethnic population comprises close to 50% Whites, and almost 45% mixed White and Black, and then Blacks, Asians, and indigenous people. Brazil comprises 26 states, 5,570 municipalities, and the federal district of Brasilia. Each state is governed by a governor and assisted by a lieutenant governor, while local prefects and their deputies head the local municipalities. The president is head of the country.

Brazil was colonized by Portugal in 1808 following the action of the King of Portugal to move the throne from Portugal to Brazil due to Napoleon Bonaparte's invasion. The King of Brazil, Joao VI, eventually went back to Portugal but left his son, Dom Pedro, as regent. Brazil's independence was declared on September 7, 1822, and the country was ruled as a constitutional monarchy until 1889. Its first constitution was drawn up in 1824. The constitution is the supreme law of the land. While changes to the constitution have occurred over time, its last major overhaul was in 1988, and last amended in 2016. The 1988 version of the constitution provides for the election of a president every 5 years.

After a military takeover in 1891, the monarchy was dissolved and by 1895, a civilian government was established. The country established a federal system of government. Consequently, there are federal and state criminal justice institutions, somewhat akin to the United States.

Brazil acquired Roman civil law from the Portuguese and eventually promulgated its own civil code in 1917. Portuguese law itself was heavily influenced by the *Ordenacoes Filipinas,* a collection of laws that included canon law, the Visigothic Code, customary practices, rules, and legislations from Portugal (Rosenn, 2002). Mindful of the inadequacies of the existing laws in Brazil, the country strove to gradually and carefully draw from the writings of jurists, and from legislations of other nations, and put all in a code that would serve the people for a very long time. In that endeavor, several codes were put together including the civil code, the penal code, the code of civil procedure, the code of criminal procedure, and the commercial code (Rosenn). Even though Brazilian law was initially influenced by the Napoleonic Code, over time it became heavily influenced by the German Code, and aspects of it subsequently by the Italian Civil Code (The Brazilian Business, n.d.).

LEGAL CONCEPTS

As a federative republic, each state has its own constitution and laws, but they give deference to the Federal Constitution. As well, the various municipalities have their autonomy limited by both their various state constitutions and the federal constitution. The Federal Supreme Court, the Superior Court of Justice, the Regional Federal Courts and Federal Judges are core segments of the judicial branch of the country.

The legislature makes law. In event of a novel issue not addressed by the legislature, courts look to customs, established principles of law, and analogy for guidance. Such deference is made possible by the Law of Introduction to the Civil Code and the Code of Civil Procedure

(Rosenn, 2002). Criminal trials in civil law countries are non-adversarial, and that is the case with Brazil. Juries are not used in courts in civil law countries; consequently, only bench trials exist. However, a peculiar aspect of Brazilian judicial system is that it has Jury Tribunals (Rosenn). The Jury Tribunal decides cases such as intentional homicide, abortion, and suicide assistance, among others. A judge presides, and at least seven lay jurors make a determination in the case.

Trials in civil law countries typically hinge on the dictates of the Code and not on precedent. However, exceptions to this are carved out in Brazilian law: everyone is subject to decisions of the Supreme Federal Tribunal. Simply, courts fall back to decisions made by the Supreme Federal Tribunal in matters of constitutional uncertainties. Should change be the order, upon deciding on an issue, The Supreme Federal Tribunal furnishes the federal senate with its holding as a replacement to the status quo. Further, some decisions by higher courts, known as *sumula,* stay on as law until rescinded.

The process of plea bargain as practiced in the United States does not exist in Brazil. Instead, in order to ease court dockets, case dismissals are prevalent, as well, suspension of a trial, and withholding of a punishment may be exercised at the discretion of the judge (Academia.edu, n.d.).

In misdemeanor or felony cases, the judge may be advised by expert witnesses based on their professional opinion. Besides cases litigated in small claims courts where litigants may appear and lay out their side of the case, pleading stages in both misdemeanor and felony cases hinge on written documents (Rosenn, 2002). The judge alone asks questions to witnesses including those submitted by attorneys to the case. The adversarial process of cross-examination and recross-examination of witnesses done by attorneys in common-law countries does not exist in the Brazilian civil law process, the judge handles that (see Chapter 2). As Rosenn explains, a losing party to a case may appeal to have a de novo review of the case. The death penalty has been abolished in Brazil, but it could be administered to criminals accused of war crimes against the country (Academia.edu, n.d.). Maximum sentence for other crimes is 30 years, and this maximum is reserved for voluntary murder.

Federal courts in the country usually arbitrate cases for which:

1. The union has a patrimonial interest
2. The crime involves federal property or service
3. An international concern is present
4. Indian rights are disputed (Rosenn, 2002, p. 191).

In order to pursue a legal career in Brazil, the aspiring lawyer must first pass the vestibular which is an entrance exam into university. Every university administers the exam. Since 2009, students may also take a High School National Exam (ENEM) (The Brazilian Business, n.d.). Successful students attend a law school of their choosing. Every law school is accredited by the National Commission of Legal Education of the OAB Federal Council, and they are also subject to regulations by the Federal Ministry of Education (The Brazilian Business). Law students are encouraged to do internships. Upon completion of law school, candidates have to take the bar exam and join the Brazilian Bar Association—*Ordem dos Advogados do Brasil* (OAB). In order to become a judge, an attorney must have been practicing law for 2 years, and must pass both written and oral exams (Rosenn, 2002). Successful candidates then work in district courts and are eventually promoted to higher courts. Upon completion of 2 years as a judge, life tenure may be accorded. However, retirement age for judges is set at 70.

WHY BRAZIL IS PART OF THIS STUDY

One cannot overlook Brazil's significance both globally and regionally. As of 2015, Brazil has the seventh largest GDP in the world, and its official language, Portuguese, is the seventh most spoken language in the universe (Bethell, 2010). It has been lauded for its exemplary efforts to reduce poverty in the country in the last decade through sound policies that target health, agriculture, and other social programs (Barrientos & Amann, 2014), and for maintaining a peaceful democracy. As Barrientos and Amann state, developing countries ought to emulate Brazil's example. As a player in world affairs, Brazilians have served in prominent agencies such as the United Nation's Food and Agriculture Organization (FAO), the World Trade Organization (WTO), and the country has spread its economic interest in many African countries (COHA.org, 2013). As well, Brazil has sent troops on peacekeeping missions in trouble spots throughout the world.

Brazil covers 47.3% of South American territory. It borders all other South American countries but Ecuador and Chile. It is the fifth largest country in the world, with an extremely high literacy percentage. More than 91% of the population can read and write. Sao Paulo is the largest city in Brazil, and in 2016 it was determined to be the largest city in the Southern Hemisphere and the 12th largest in the world. It also has the second most number of airports in the world, and the world's second longest river, river Amazon. Brazil is a member of the Organization of American States (OAS); it is a member of the Rio Group of Latin American and Caribbean states, and member of the Community of Latin American and Caribbean States (Bethell, 2010). Its participation in the treaty of Asuncion in 1991 gave birth to the *Mercosur* trade bloc comprised of Brazil, Argentina, Uruguay, and Paraguay (Bethell). Argentina was eventually ousted as a member in 2017 (Wikipedia, 2017). The South America Community of Nations, including Guyana and Suriname, was established in 2004, and in 2008 at a conference in Brasilia this association changed its name to Union of South American Nations (Bethell).

Brazil was host to the 2016 world Olympic Games, and the soccer World Cup in 2014. Besides being known for producing some of the best soccer players like Pele, Ronaldinho, and Ronaldo, among others, Brazil is also known for its culture, art, music, and architecture.

In terms of criminal justice, Brazil is not exemplary in some aspects. The country unfortunately, has the fourth densest prison population after the United States, Russia, and China, and prisons notorious for overcrowding and gross human rights violations. Although crime receives extraordinary attention from the government, and the police force appear to receive adequate training, the philosophy of punishment appears to be geared toward retribution, which thus accounts for high rates of incarceration. Its peculiar history in terms of its civil law leaning makes the country a fascinating addition to this book. Over time Brazil has incorporated aspects of the Napoleonic, Germanic, Italian, and Portuguese Civil Codes into its Civil Code. The country's sheer size, its history, and its role in regional and global affairs, makes its inclusion in this book mandatory.

LAW ENFORCEMENT IN BRAZIL

Police missions in Brazil date back to the beginning of the 16th century. What is now a series of formalized police units started as minor security guard units with the function to ward off unauthorized persons at the country's borders. More investigative roles were eventually added to the watchman's role, and in 1566, the first investigator was hired in Rio de Janeiro (WOW.com, 2017). Further refinement of the functions of the police continued with order maintenance as an emphasis due to disorders that permeated the country caused by explorers seeking to get advantage in the gold mining business.

When the Portuguese monarchy moved to Brazil in the 1800s the king embarked on reshaping the police force. The General Police Intendancy (*Intendencia Geral de Policia*) was established, and piecemeal structuring of the force continued even after Brazil secured independence from Portugal. The Federal Railroad Police was the first federal police unit to be created in 1852, and almost two decades later following terms of law 2033, a distinction was established between judicial functions and police functions (WOW.com, 2017).

There are five law enforcement institutions in Brazil as mandated by the Federal Constitution. Given the country's federal system, there are both federal and state police officers. The federal police force includes the Federal Police, the Federal Highway Police, and the Federal Railway Police; while the state police force comprises the State Military Police and Fire Brigade, and the State Civil Police. The executive branch is in charge of law enforcement in the country. Brazilian police officers have two main functions: law enforcement and order maintenance.

Federal Law Enforcement

1. **The Federal Police (*Departamento de Policia Federal*):** This branch of the federal police is vested with the responsibility of investigating crimes perpetrated against the federal government or any governmental owned property or entity. In this regard, the federal police investigate crimes such as terrorism and immigration and border violations.

2. **The Federal Highway Police:** This faction of the federal police has the task of maintaining order, patrolling, and monitoring activities along and around federal highways.

3. **The Federal Railway Police:** This police force has surveillance responsibilities as well as order maintenance.

It is worthy of note that neither the Federal Highway Police nor the Federal Railway Police has investigative powers, so issues have to be deferred to the Federal Police.

State Law Enforcement

1. **The Military Police and Fire Brigade**: This police force is structured similarly to the military in that officers have military-style hierarchy, discipline, and the pomp and ceremony that go with the military. The force has order maintenance powers, arrest powers, and based on the type of crime committed the officer may hand over the suspect to the federal police or to the civil police. The fire brigade is part of the military police but does not do the typical kinds of functions ascribed to police officers like order maintenance.

2. **The Civil Police**: This is the legalistic branch of the state police. In this regard, the officers have investigative powers as well as powers to push for prosecution. These officers do not engage in street patrol, and generally do not wear uniforms.

There is also the National Public Security Force which is an amalgam of all police forces in the country that may be called to action in case of national emergency.

Qualifications to Be a Police Officer in Brazil

A would-be officer in Brazil, especially a military police officer, must pass a physical exam that includes endurance, agility, and physical stamina. The candidate must pass a written test, and must be cleared by a doctor to be of good health. After surpassing this hurdle, the candidate becomes eligible for consideration for further training courses as a Military Police officer in either the rank of an ordinary officer or a high-ranking officer.

With regard to age limits, an applicant must be at least 18 years old and, at the most, 30 years old. A high school certification is required for lower-level ranking officers. For applicants vying to become a police chief in the Civil Police Force, the candidate must have a law degree (WOW.com, 2017).

THE JUDICIARY AND STRUCTURE OF COURTS IN BRAZIL

The 1891 Constitution established a dual federal and state system of courts. Among the federal courts are The Supreme Federal Tribunal, Superior Tribunal of Justice, Federal Regional Tribunals, Federal Judges, Federal Small Claims Courts, Labor Courts, Electoral Courts, and the Federal Military Courts. The State Courts include Tribunals of Justice, Tribunals of Alcada, State Military Courts, Judges of First Instance, Jury Tribunals, Small Claims Courts, and Justices of the Peace.

FEDERAL COURTS

1. **The Supreme Federal Tribunal**: This is the highest court of the land. This court has both appellate review and original decision-making. As an appellate court, the Supreme Federal Tribunal reviews constitutional issues. As a court of original jurisdiction, the court has jurisdiction to decide constitutional challenges by groups of people, the government, or individuals. When such challenges are made, a quorum of at least eight is needed, and any decisions to make a procedure, practice, or law unconstitutional must be arrived at by at least six members of the court, and such decision replaces the contested one.

   There are 11 justices in this court appointed by the president of the country with senate confirmation. The position of chief justice or head of the court rotates based on seniority every 2 years. When court is in session, a designated member writes the court's decision and vote. The procurator general may sit in and opine, but may not vote as to outcomes.

2. **Superior Tribunal of Justice**: This is the second highest court in Brazil. The court comprises 33 judges nominated by the bar association, the court, and the public ministry and subsequently appointed by the president of the country. There are six chambers of the court with five judges overseeing each.

   The function of this court is exclusively appellate reviews. In this regard it reviews challenges of substantive or procedural applications of laws and treaties. It makes decisions on habeas corpus applications, challenges of lower court decisions, and any challenges of federal laws.

3. **Federal Regional Tribunals**: There are five of these tribunals. At any time, there are at least seven judges in each of the tribunals. The president of the country appoints the judges from a pool of lawyers, public ministry members who have served for over 10 years, and federal judges.

4. **Federal Judges**: These are courts of first instance presided over by federal judges. It is not uncommon for a state judge to decide cases in the federal judge court in judicial districts where there is a void in federal judges. These courts take on cases that involve federal matters.

5. **Federal Small Claims Courts**: These small claims courts came into existence following a law that was passed on July 12, 2001. The jurisdiction of this court is limited to cases for which the punishment does not exceed 2 years, and for which the fine is no more than "sixty times the minimum monthly wage" (Rosenn, 2002, p. 193).

6. **Labor Courts**: These courts handle only labor cases. Such labor disputes relate to collective bargaining, disputes between private persons in work capacity, and employer and employee relations.

7. **Electoral Courts**: These courts oversee elections to ensure that they are not rigged. There are no permanent judges in these courts; instead, judges and other staff members are summoned from other courts to serve 2–4 years terms. There are higher electoral courts—the Superior Electoral Court being the highest. Seven Judges selected by secret ballot preside in the Superior Electoral Court. There are Regional Electoral Tribunals as well, and each state capital has a Regional Electoral Tribunal.

8. **Federal Military Courts**: These are courts specialized in handling military matters and crimes committed by those in the military. There is a Superior Military Tribunal, which is the highest military court. The President of the country appoints the 15 judges who serve in the court for life.

STATE COURTS

1. **Tribunals of Justice**: These courts of justice are the highest courts in the country, and they are in each state. They are the highest state appellate courts in the country. Prior to the 2004 45th Constitutional Amendment, states like Sao Paulo and Minas Gerais had appellate courts (*Tribunal de Alcada*) different from Tribunals of Justice. That no longer is the case following Article 4 of the 45th Constitutional Amendment of 2004.

The state size determines how many judges serve in the Tribunals of Justice.

Besides their appellate functions, the tribunals of justice handle serious civil issues, and decide on the constitutionality of municipal statutes and issues relating to the functions of the civil registration and notary services.

2. **Trial Courts**: Every state is divided into judicial districts and then one or more municipalities. A judicial district based on size has at least a trial court which acts as a court of first instance for the majority of cases. These courts are not specialized with regard to types of issues brought to them. For instance, the courts may handle family matters, labor, civil issues, and criminal matters among others. There is usually one judge and a substitute. In this court, a judge alone makes the determination in all civil cases and in most criminal cases that are not expressly within the domain of the Jury Tribunal.

3. **Jury Tribunals**: These courts are presided over by a judge and seven jurors randomly selected. These jurors determine probable cause as well as guilt. Even though the jury is always sequestered, deliberation is not done in a group, and votes are cast independently in secret. Jury decisions that do not reflect the facts or evidence in a case may be set aside, and a de novo trial instituted (Rosenn, 2002).

4. **State Military Courts**: The military court of first instance adjudicates cases relating to military crimes committed by military police and military firefighters. These courts are usually staffed with seven judges.

5. **Small Claims Courts**: These courts handle petty criminal and civil offenses. Among the civil cases covered by these courts are tenancy issues, contractual obligations, automobile accident claims, and disputes relating to attorney fees, among others. Depending on the litigants, disputes can be settled by arbitration, by conciliation, or by a third party acting as an intermediary.

6. **Justices of the Peace**: These justices perform marriage rites and mediation services. The president of the Tribunal of Justice makes a list of three and from it the governor of the state chooses one. Justices of the peace are not constitutionally protected in that they do not have life tenure.

CORRECTIONS IN BRAZIL

At the top of the Brazilian correctional system is the Ministry of Justice, but the day-to-day running of the system is left to the National Penitentiary/Prison Department (*Departmento Penitenciario Nacional*). The Director General is head of prison administration. Following

2013 data, Brazil's prison population was surpassed by just those of the United States, Russia, and China (The Brazil Business, n.d.). There are 1,598 prisons and jails in Brazil, and each is overcrowded. Following a 2013 count, there were 581,000 inmates in Brazil, giving it a 163% occupancy level (The Brazil Business). The number of inmates has increased to 657,680 in 2017, but the occupancy level is still at 163.9% as of January 2017 (World Prison Brief, 2017). The prison population rate is 318 per 100,000 of the national population of a general population of 206.93 million (World Prison Brief). The recidivism level is also extremely high, placed at 70% (The Brazil Business).

Reasons for high levels of recidivism are varied. Foremost is lack of programs to reintegrate ex-convicts in society, and others include absence of rehabilitative programs in prisons to address substance abuse, and absence of life skills. Not to be ignored are problems that stem from gang and drug activities. It is reported that the Brazilian government has in place programs to facilitate a smooth transition of inmates from prison life to society life (The Brazil Business, n.d.). However, these programs seem not to be enough or effective. Reports show that lack of or limited psychotherapy programs and despicable prison conditions hamper therapeutic success (Taborda, Dias de Castro Bins, & de Borba Telles, 2017).

Similar to most countries, prisons in Brazil are divided into different levels based on the gravity of the offense and the caliber of the convict. While states have the responsibility to manage prisons, the federal government runs maximum security prisons. Prisons in Brazil are divided into maximum security, "closed regime" consistent with medium security, "open regime" which is the equivalent of minimum security prisons, psychiatric centers, and shelters.

- **Maximum Security Prisons**: The federal government manages the four to five maximum security prisons in the country. The most dangerous convicts, especially those convicted of organized crimes and atrocious murders, are housed in these prisons.
- **Penitentiaries (*Penitenciarias*)**: Inmates here live in secured locked-up premises. They may not be eligible for work release or temporary leave from prison unless discretionary measures are applied. Next to those in federal maximum security prisons, inmates in penitentiaries are dangerous criminals or habitual felons.
- **Agricultural and Industrial Colonies (*Colonias Agricolas e industriais*)**: These are semi-open prisons that give inmates the opportunity to get temporary leave for up to 7 days from their holding places. Following the Penal Law (*Lei de Execucao*), an inmate could apply for a 7-day leave from the prison confine, and such request could be renewed a maximum of four times a year. It is required that there is at least a 45-day span between requests for leave. Other restrictions include keeping the judge informed of the inmate's whereabouts/address while on temporary leave. The inmate

must be at that address at night, and the inmate must not go to restricted places like bars, nightclubs, and other places of loose living. Inmates may also seek temporary leave for educational or professional purposes.

Since 1984, employers may hire the services of inmates, but they are not obligated to provide remuneration to inmates commensurate to that of conforming persons in society, even for the same type of work.

Inmates' abuse of the privilege to temporary leave of absence is cause for concern. As reported in 2012, of the 47,537 granted temporary leave, 2,416 did not return (The Brazil Business, n.d.).

- **Public Prisons (*Cadeias Publicas*):** These are detention centers, more like jails in the United States. They are holding places for inmates pending trials.
- **Hospitals for Psychiatric Treatment (*Hospitais de Custodia e Tratamento Psiquiatrico*):** These are institutions that house mentally ill criminals, or those with severe mental retardation.
- **Shelters (*Casas do Albergado*):** These are holding places for people who have committed minor offenses. Security in shelters is lax.

PRIVATIZATION OF PRISONS IN BRAZIL

Prison overcrowding, inhumane prison conditions, and poor management of state-run prisons led the Brazilian government to reach out to private investors to invest in private prisons. In 2009, a conglomeration of five companies won a bidding to start housing inmates in private prisons. The first one was erected in Ribeirao das Neves in Minas Gerais state and the first inmates were brought in 2013 (The Brazil Business, n.d.). As Leeds (2016) reports, there are 21 private prisons in seven Brazilian states. Research as to the success or failure of private prisons is not yet out; what is known is that privatization is ad hoc since the Brazilian government intends to regain any private prisons subsequently (The Brazil Business).

Further, some like Patricia Mallen (a correspondent with the *International Business Times*) are apprehensive about relying on private prisons in Brazil as a panacea to prison crowding (Price, 2013). Her argument rests on the fact that private prisons are not financially tenable, and that prison crowding can better be solved by investments in education, healthcare, and other social programs.

INTERMEDIATE PUNISHMENTS IN BRAZIL

Probation

Brazilian notion of probation entails a suspension of proceedings against the defendant—*suspensao conditional de pena*; consequently, it is not exactly probation, as students in the United States or in many other countries know probation to be as there is no established probation department and no trained probation officers. Instead, in Brazil, the court looks at the defendant's conduct, his cooperation with authorities, admission of guilt, and contrition, among other factors and then decides if the punishment should be suspended. Type of crime and corresponding punishment determine if a defendant's sentence would be suspended. Sentences amenable for suspension may not be longer than 4 years. This process is more akin to a suspended sentence in the United States whereby the judge tells the defendant what the punishment for a crime is, but then decides not to enforce it on the proviso that the accused person stays away from committing further crimes. Violations may lead to revocation of the temporary privilege and the imposition of new sanctions.

Several conditions come with this privilege, including abstaining from criminal behavior and criminal companions, maintaining a job, remaining within the court's jurisdiction, promptly reporting any changes in lifestyle to a *delegado de policia*, among several other conditions (Academia.edu, n.d.).

Parole

Parole—*livramento condicional*—is conditional release from prison to serve the remainder of the prison sentence in the community. In order to be eligible for parole, the inmate must be serving a sentence of at least 2 years in prison, and must have served at least one third of their sentence or must have paid off any court-imposed restitution. Being out on parole is a privilege granted by the court. The court sets conditions of parole, which include abstention from criminal behavior, maintaining a job, among several others. The court determines which agency would be in charge of supervising the parolee.

SUMMARY

Brazil is the largest country in South America, and the fifth largest in the world. About 91% of the Brazilian population is literate. Brazil is a federative republic; each state has its own constitution but deference is given to the federal constitution. It is a civil law country which, over time, has incorporated aspects of Napoleonic, Germanic, Italian, and Portuguese Civil Codes in its own Code.

The Portuguese monarchy that relocated to Brazil in the 1800s reshaped the then-security force of the country, and that restructuring and reshaping continued even after the end of Portuguese rule in the country. Based on its federalist system of government, Brazil has both federal and state police with specialized units.

Besides criminal courts which are organized in a hierarchy, there are also labor, electoral, and military courts. As a federative republic, there are federal and state courts and that is the case with the correctional system. The peculiar thing about Brazilian prisons is that the federal government manages the maximum security prisons in the country.

DISCUSSION QUESTIONS

1. Explain the two main functions of Brazilian police. Distinguish functions of the federal police from those of the state police.
2. Discuss functions of the Supreme Federal Court. How does one become a Supreme Court Justice in Brazil?
3. Outline the various functions of state courts in Brazil.
4. Explain the different types of prisons in Brazil. Under what prison regimen, and why, do inmates get a leave of absence?
5. Explain your understanding of what probation is. Discuss the differences and similarities of probation in the United States or your home country, and that of Brazil.

REFERENCES

Academia.edu. (n.d.). The system of criminal justice of Brazil/Pedro Scuro. Retrieved from http://www.academia.edu/2365551/The_System_of_Criminal_Justice_of_Brazil

Barrientos, A., & Amann, E. (2014, April 17). Brazil: A role model for development? Global Development Network/The Guardian.com. Retrieved from https://www.theguardian.com/global-development-professionals-network/2014/apr/17/brazil-role-model-development-africa

Bethell, L. (2010, June 8). Brazil: Regional power, global power/openDemocracy. Retrieved from http://www.opendemocracy.net/leslie-bethell/brazil-regional-power-global-power

The Brazil Business. (n.d.). Prison System in Brazil. Retrieved from http://thebrazilbusiness.com/article/prison-system-in-brazil

The Brazilian Business. (n.d.). How to become a lawyer in Brazil. Retrieved from http://thebrazilbusiness.com/article/how-to-become-a-lawyer-in-brazil

CIA World Factbook. 2017. Retrieved from https://www.cia.gov/library/publications/the-world-factbook/geos/br.html

COHA.org. (2013, August 27). Brazil's foreign policy ambitions and global geopolitics. Retrieved from http://www.coha.org/brazils-foreign-policy-ambitions-and-global-geopolitics

Leeds, E. (2016). The Brazilian prison system: Challenges and prospects for reform. WOLA. Retrieved from https://www.wola.org/analysis/brazilian-prison-system-challenges-prospects-reform/

Price, B. (2013). Rejionder to 'Brazil's growing inmate population might require the privatization of prisons.' Retrieved from http://www.huffingtonpost.com/byron-e-price/brazil-flirts-with-prison_b-4512603.html

Rosenn, K. (2002). Brazil. In Herbert Kritzer (Ed.), *Legal systems of the world: A political, social, and cultural encyclopedia*, Vol. 1: A–D. Santa Barbara, CA: ABC-CLIO.

Taborda, J., Dias de Castro Bins, H., & de Borba Telles, L. E. (2017). Brazil, Corrections in. *The Encyclopedia of Corrections*, 1–8. Wiley online library. doi:10.1002/9781118845387.wbeoc103

Wikipedia. (2017). *Mercosur*. En.m.wikipedia.org. Retrieved from https://en.m.wikipedia.org/wiki/mercosur

World Prison Brief. (2017). Brazil/World prison brief. Retrieved from http://www.prisonstudies.org/county/Brazil

WOW.com. (2017, June 24). Law enforcement in Brazil-WOW.com. Retrieved from http://www.wow.com/wiki/Law_enforcement_in_Brazil

CHAPTER 8

The Czech Republic Model

© pavalena/Shutterstock.com

INTRODUCTION

The Czech Republic is a landlocked country in East Central Europe. It is bordered to the northwest by Germany, to the south by Austria, Slovakia to the east and southeast, and Poland to the north. Czech Republic comprises the provinces of Bohemia and Monrovia, and parts of Silesia. The country has also come to be known as Czechia, a short form of Czech Republic.

Czech Republic has a population of approximately 10,644,842 people, and an area of 78,867 square kilometers (CIA, World Factbook, n.d.). Its capital is Prague. The official language is Czech spoken by the majority of the population. Other prevalent languages are Romani, German, Polish, and Slovak. The majority of Czechs are non-religious and a tiny number belong to the Catholic faith.

HISTORY

Czech Republic's history can be traced to over 2,000 years (Maier, 2002). In its early history it was part of the Roman Empire under the auspices of the Bohemian monarchy. This was not destined to be forever. The Germans colonized the territory, and this brought plenty of disenchantment. With the Hussite revolution in Bohemia, religious tensions became entrenched in the 15th century. Czechs and Germans spearheaded a protestant uprising, which precipitated the Thirty Years War from 1618–1648 against the Catholic Habsburgs. With the triumph of the Habsburgs, German became the prevalent language for approximately two centuries. This state of affairs changed in part due to the industrial revolution and a cultural and linguistic renaissance, which swept throughout much of Europe in 1848.

When the Austro-Hungarian Empire collapsed at the end of the First World War the Czechs and Slovaks united as Czechoslovakia. The part of the country that was Czech was occupied by Germany during the Second World War, and was freed by the United States and the Soviets in 1945. Most of the inhabitants who spoke German left the country, and following an election in 1946, the Communist party of Czechoslovakia emerged victorious. In February 1948, a communist coup temporarily placed Czechoslovakia as a member of the Soviet bloc throughout the cold war. As the economy tanked under the leadership of Antonin Novotny, disillusion among the populace increased. The result was the replacement of Novotny, a staunch communist, with Alexander Dubcek, who pursued several liberal reforms that included freedom of religion, press, speech, and assembly (Maier, 2002). In 1968, worried about Dubcek's style of governing and the sweeping departure of his policies from core Soviet values, Soviet troops, backed by support of several members of the Warsaw Pact, launched an attack on Czechoslovakia. Dubcek was replaced. Communist ideals were reinstated including civil and criminal laws.

Following a spate of human rights violations in 1977, human rights activists signed Charter 77, which was a manifesto that levied several criticisms on the government for not respecting human rights that had been put together in a document. A civil forum was eventually formed with Vaclav Havel as leader, and under his leadership, the Velvet Revolution took place. The Velvet Revolution brought about the collapse of the Communist regime. Vaclav Havel was elected president on December 29, 1989. Dissension with the civil forum and emergence of other parties, and with the Slovaks requesting autonomy, a parting of ways between the Czechs and Slovaks was inevitable.

On January 1, 1993, Czech and Slovakia went their separate ways.

WHY CZECH REPUBLIC IS PART OF THIS STUDY

The Czech Republic is a former Communist country that transitioned into a parliamentary republic. In 1989, the Velvet Revolution ended communism in the Czech Republic, which at the time was Czechoslovakia. Shortly thereafter, in 1990, the country elected its first democratic president, and in 1993 an amicable split was effected between the Czech and the Slovaks. The country is exemplary in that its major transition from communism to democracy, and its breakup with Slovakia was peaceful, and it has maintained decorum since. Its peculiar history makes it a compelling addition to this study.

The capital of Czech Republic, Prague is considered to be "the handsomest city of Europe" (Hauner, et al., n.d.). Prague remains the epicenter of political, economic, and cultural success in Europe. Since its split with Slovakia, Czech Republic has played an integral role in European as well as global affairs. Czech Republic became a member of the North Atlantic Treaty Organization (NATO) in 1999, and the European Union (EU) in 2004. It is also a member of several organizations including The United Nations (UN), the Organization for Economic Cooperation and Development (OECD), the Organization for Security and Cooperation in Europe (OSCE), and the Council of Europe, among others. The United Nations Development Program (UNDP) ranks Czech Republic 14th in inequality-adjusted human development (Hauner et al.). It is ranked as the sixth "most peaceful country in its stance for democratic governance, and among the European member countries, it is deemed to have the lowest unemployment rate, and highly remunerates its employees" (en.m.wikipedia.org, n.d.). It is a welfare nation in that it provides universal healthcare, and free university education. It is ranked as the "27th most environmentally conscious country in the world in Environmental Performance Index" (en.m.wikipedia.org). The above facts are remarkable because such facts are associated with the well-known most industrialized countries, and that is not necessarily the case, yet a relatively small country like Czech Republic which provides universal healthcare and free university education does not make news headlines. Putting this in perspective in light of criminal justice, it is known that the more educated people are, the less likely they are to commit crimes (particularly, dangerous felonies), as well, the more a country provides for its citizens, the less likely are citizens to be disenchanted and rebellious.

There are other facts about Czech Republic that many do not know, as for instance, archaeologists have found some of the earliest human settlements dating back to the Paleolithic era in Czech Republic. As well, the oldest ceramic figurine—Venus of Dolni Vestonice—have been found in the Czech territory. The country is also known for some of its inventions. Czech Republic is famous for inventing contact lenses, sugar cubes, and was first to coin the word robot. Its capital, Prague, is the fifth-most tourist destination in Europe after London, Paris, Istanbul, and Rome (Bremer, 2015). While these facts do not provide gravitas for criminal justice inquiry, they, however, showcase the country as one of relevance.

Prague is the birthplace of famed writer Franz Kafka and poet Rainer Maria Rilke. Czech Republic is also birthplace of several famed scientists; for instance, Peter Grunberg, Nobel Prize laureate in physics, 2007; Gerty and Carl Cori, Nobel Prize laureates in Physiology or medicine, 1947; Gregor Mendel, father of genetics; and the list goes on and on. These facts are included to provide readers further incentive to read about the Czech Republic, and to understand its relevance in global history, civics, and justice issues.

LEGAL CONCEPTS

Czech's Constitution of 1993 is supreme law of the land. The Constitution stipulates separation of power among the executive, legislative, and judicial branches.

The executive branch is composed of the president, the prime minister, and a cabinet of ministers. The president, as commander-in-chief, serves for a term of 5 years and may only serve two terms.

The legislative branch is bicameral, comprising a senate and a chamber of deputies. There is a senate comprising 81 senators, who serve for 6-year terms. The chamber of deputies comprises 200 delegates who serve for 4-year terms. The government is welcoming to other political parties.

The judiciary is structured in a hierarchy. The Supreme Court is the highest Court of the land. There are Appellate Courts, High Courts, Regional and District Courts, Administrative, and Human Rights Courts.

The Constitution was adopted on December 16, 1992, and was put in force on January 1, 1993. Czech legal system is Civil Law following the Austro-Hungarian Codes derivatives of Germanic Code. There are no jury trials; however, in Courts of First Instance/District Courts, lay judges preside. The local council elects these lay judges by The Judges Act s. 64 and f. 2002. In these first instance trials, two lay judges sit in conjunction with a professional judge to pass judgment in non-specialized cases. The practice of case law is not applicable in Czech Republic, as the country follows the Germanic civil law. However, decisions of the Supreme Court and the Constitutional Court influence the justice system.

As a country that follows the code, it is informative to know a few of those codes:

1. **The Civil Code:** This is the main document that regulates court trials in criminal and private law. As discussed in Chapter 2, civil law trials revert to the civil law code in all issues during the trial. Unlike common-law countries that rely on precedent, civil law countries turn to the Civil code, which is enforced by law # 40/1964 Coll. [CIVC]. There has been a continuous interest in taking into consideration case law in the decision process by courts (Nyulawglobal.org, n.d.).

2. **The Criminal Code:** Even though the Civil Code governs criminal trials, the Criminal Code defines crimes and stipulates their corresponding punishments. The Criminal Code was put in place by Law # 140/1961 Coll. [CrimC].
3. **The Commercial Code:** This code regulates business transactions, rights, and obligations of undertakers and companies/businesses, from the inception of the venture to dissolution. This regulation is embodied in law # 513/1991 Coll. [ComC].

The Constitution and the Charter of Fundamental Rights and Freedoms mandate the rule of law. Among the rights granted by the Constitution are equality; free healthcare; equal protection of the law; and freedom of speech, religion, and assembly, among others. The Charter ensures that the rights of minorities and the preservation of their ethnic languages and culture stay intact. The charter upholds the right to due process; consequently, people are presumed innocent until found guilty in a court of law. Accused persons have the right to counsel, the right to appeal, and the right to an interpreter if Czech is not their language.

LAW ENFORCEMENT IN CZECH REPUBLIC

The Czech police force was established in 1991 with headquarters in Prague. It is under the auspices of the Ministry of Interior. There are approximately 40,500 law enforcement officers and employees (Wikipedia.org, n.d.). Their motto is to "help and to protect" (Wikipedia.org). The police are structured in a hierarchy from sergeant to general. Besides the State Police, there are military police, municipal police, and watchmen.

The State Police

The state police are responsible for investigating all types of crimes except those that fall under the jurisdiction of the military police, custom service, or some specified branch of government. They engage in search and rescue missions and in such ventures work collaboratively with the Mountain Rescue Service, and work with intelligence agencies to counter terrorism.

Police services are either national or regional. Nationwide jurisdiction encompasses duties like protecting state officials; anti-drug services; highway and border patrol; investigation of corruption, racketeering, organized crime; and many other criminal enterprises. Regional jurisdiction is split into 14 regional headquarters. Regional duties entail public order, patrolling, rapid response and SWAT team interventions, protection of railways, waterways, criminal investigations, and several other duties.

The rapid response team is highly skilled, and has three broad divisions: (1) rapid deployment (pyrotechnics); (2) special service (snipers, negotiators); (3) administrators and logistics service (lawyers and administrative staff). Eligibility to be a member of the rapid response team is that the officer must have served for at least 5 years as a Czech police, or must have a college degree. Training entails target shooting, self-defense, airborne medical assistant training, and so forth. They also practice and train with other European police.

Military Police

The military police was established in 1991 following Order CSFR MOD January 21, 1991. They represent about 1% of the Armed Forces of the Czech Republic. There are two main components of the military police: (1) security service; and (2) traffic control and law enforcement service. There is also a small subset of the military police that offers protection and escort services to dignitaries.

The main functions of the military police are order maintenance in military premises; investigation of crimes of military members; overseeing training of military drivers; ensuring the safety of military vehicles; helping protect military equipment, explosives, ammunition; and a host of other duties.

Military police officers could be recruited from the police force, and solicitations could be extended to civilians. Successful applicants must pass general knowledge tests (Home.mweb, n.d.).

Municipal Police

Municipal police are under the domain of the mayor or a designated official. Their main missions are order maintenance and collaboration with other departments to ensure safety of the people. They handle misdemeanor and petty offenses. They are not vested with investigative powers; what they do is to detain the suspect pending arrival of a state police officer. They bear arms and patrol the streets on foot, bike, or car. They work within the municipality where they are hired, and may only exceed their jurisdiction if they have been deputized.

Watchmen

Watchmen are civilians who are sworn in to help maintain order. Their authority is highly controlled; consequently, they can only do minimal things to control breach of the peace. They can stop people and ask them for identification, and can detain a person pending the arrival of the state police. Watchmen are usually unarmed. In order to bear arms, they have to undergo background checks like any civilian who wishes to bear arms. Upon approval, they may only carry concealed weapons. At times, watchmen may be tasked to be environmental watchmen, gamekeepers, forestry, and fishery watchmen.

Requirement to Become a Police Officer in Czech Republic

The requirements to become a police officer are outlined in the Police Service Act of 2005. It complies with the Strasbourg's European Code of Police Ethics. The main requirements are that the recruit must demonstrate sound judgment, maturity, positive and upbeat personality, good communications skills, good managerial and leadership skills, fair-mindedness, and an understanding of cultural differences.

Training

The Department of Police Education, Training, and Police Colleges is responsible for training police officers. This department oversees police colleges, training centers, and the police academy. Training comprises practical and academic training that consist of specialized courses. Recruits without a high school education may be offered courses toward that goal. The Police Department of Police Education oversees curriculum designed for high school diplomas. The high school level education provides general education without any, or with limited, specialization on police-related education (Pagon, et al., 1996). After the general pedagogy, graduates must undergo further police training before being given clearance to work as police officers. Basic police training may take from one day to one year, or even more (Pagon, Virjent-Novak, Djuric, & Lobnika, 1996). Such basic training may entail courses emphasizing traffic control, criminal procedure, general and administrative knowledge, including psychology, crime scene investigation, patrolling, and so forth. Skills like self-defense, use of equipment and computers, note-taking, handcuffing, and interpersonal relations are among many of the skills taught.

Czech police may also be required to undergo higher professional education with bachelor's or master's degrees conferred at the end. Such education is divided into different sections with different emphases. For instance, section one may entail advance courses in law and police-related issues, while section two may comprise criminalistics and criminology courses. Going through a higher level professional education section gives clearance to be a police officer with a rank higher than that of an entry officer. Police ranks range from sergeant, to warrant officer, to lieutenant, to captain, to colonel, to general. Promotion depends on education, longevity, and performance.

THE LEGAL PROFESSION IN CZECH REPUBLIC

There are four public law schools and no private law schools. There are, however, private schools that provide specialized legal education not the equivalent of a general law degree. There is also a judicial academy established in 2002 as an institution to provide refresher or continuous education for judges and prosecutors.

To be a lawyer, that is judge, prosecutor, or defense attorney, in the Czech Republic, one must undergo 5 years of legal studies ending with an MA (Magister or Mgr. as title). Advanced law degrees are the *juris utrisque doctor* (JUDr), which is considered a junior doctorate in law degree. In order to have this degree conferred, the candidate has to submit an essay/thesis after completing the MA. The title of JUDr is then placed before the candidate's name. In order to receive a PhD degree in law, the candidate must complete a dissertation—research approved by a committee. The title of PhD is then placed after the name of the recipient.

Public notaries and executors are also persons with a law degree who do a myriad of legal duties, like filing and endorsing legal documents (notary), or as an executor tasked with enforcing decisions in commercial and civil matters.

COURTROOM WORK GROUP

The Judge

In order to become a judge in the Czech Republic, a candidate must have a law degree, and must have at least 10 years of legal experience (Article 84 of the Constitution). In addition, the candidate must be a citizen of high moral repute, must be at least 30 years old as provided by Judges Act, 2002, s. 60 (1), and must be eligible to vote; in essence, must be a citizen of the Czech Republic (nyulawglobal.org, n.d.). The president of the country, with the approval of the senate, appoints judges. Judges have lifetime tenure except Constitutional Court Judges who have tenure limits of 10 years. Judges are to refrain from affiliating with any political parties and from making profit based upon their status as judges. Judges enjoy judicial independence and immunity from criminal prosecution. However, a judge may be removed from the bench if proven in court to have committed a felony, or if the majority of judges find a judge's behavior to be repulsive to necessitate expulsion from the bench.

The Prosecutor

Prosecutors undergo the regular 5 years of legal studies to be a magister, 3 years of training, and then take and pass a professional exam. Like in every country, the prosecutor brings criminal charges on behalf of the direct victim, and the symbolic victim—the state. Law no. 85/1996 Coll. governs the job of a prosecutor.

The Defense Attorney

A defense attorney must complete the requisite master's degree and thereafter undergo 3 years of pupilage under a senior attorney, and then take and pass a bar exam. The main functions of a defense attorney are to defend the rights of the defendant in court, counsel the defendant, and draw up legal documents necessary for adequate representation of a client.

Structure of Courts

Courts in the Czech Republic are hierarchical from the Supreme Court at the top, the High courts, which are appellate courts, then regional courts, and district courts. Courts are independent following Article 81 of the country's constitution. There are also Administrative and Constitutional Courts.

Supreme Court

The Supreme Court is the highest Appellate Court of the land and the Supreme Judicial Court for civil and criminal issues. It reviews new legislations in order to be sure that they are in sync with existing laws. As the highest appellate court, the court reviews cases with crucial issues relating to the interpretation or application of law. It also reviews issues of illegality in procedures in criminal cases, and the Minister of Justice files such requests for reviews.

High Courts of Appeals

The High Court reviews all appeals from the Regional Courts. Such appeals encompass criminal, civil, administrative, and labor matters.

Regional Courts

Regional Courts handle cases whose punishment is above 5 years. These courts also have jurisdiction over civil issues such as slander and libel, copyright, commercial, bankruptcy, and a host of others.

District Court/Court of First Instance

In all criminal matters, the court of first instance has jurisdiction.

Other Courts

Administrative Courts

These courts are responsible for administering justice in issues of administrative law and of individual rights. These courts are also responsible to intervene in the event of dissention in elections and all matters relating to elections.

The Constitutional Court

This court addresses only constitutional issues. Among the several issues it addresses are statutory law, issues regarding the ability of the country's president to govern and impeachment, election contentions, constitutional rights violations, and implementation of decisions made by international tribunals (Maier, 2002).

CORRECTIONS IN CZECH REPUBLIC

The Department of Corrections is under the domain of the Ministry of Justice. The Ministry of Justice is responsible for prisons and prison services. It also controls departments that are directly in charge of probation and mediation. As of 10/13/2017, the prison population was approximated at 22,446 (World Prison Brief, 2017). This number comprises inmates in prisons, pre-trial detainees, and remand prisoners. Women form 7.4% of the prison population, which is approximately 1,653 as of October 31, 2017, and juveniles comprise 0.4% of prison population (World Prison Brief). There were 35 correctional facilities in Czech Republic in 2016 (World Prison Brief).

Back in 1996 at a symposium in Prague, suggestions were made to the Czech government by some United States penologists led by Todd Clear to consider implementing intermediate sanctions, and to cater for the professional well-being of correctional officers/officials (see Blomberg, Maier-Katkin, & Yeisley, 1998). Unfortunately, the state of corrections/penology in Czech Republic continues to be rated poorly. Knowing precisely the state of affairs in Czech prisons is difficult. As Vane and Dirga (2016) acknowledge, getting access to study prison systems anywhere is difficult, and it is more difficult in Czech Republic.

In 2017, an open prison began operating in the city of Jirice. The concept of the open prisons was to provide low-level inmates smooth transition from regular prisons to these open prisons where inmates would take responsibility for their duties and activities without much supervision of guards. High walls surround the prison, but cells are open without walls separating cells. Inmates would have full-time jobs and would also do assigned prison jobs (Xinhuanet.com, 2017).

The Legislature made an Amendment to the Criminal Code in 2017 to abolish four types of prisons that until then existed in the country. The Amendment is yet to be signed into law to make it effective. Based on the terms of the legislation, only two levels of prisons will exist in the country—normal and maximum security. Persons with sentences over 8 years are to be sentenced to the maximum-security prison. The idea behind this is to reduce recidivism (Praguemonitor.com, 2016).

The four types of prisons prior to the passage of the 2017 Criminal Code are:

1. **Pre-trial Detention Centers:** These are jails and holding places for accused persons awaiting trial, and for those locked up for a very short period of time.
2. **Minimum Security Prisons:** These house very low-level criminals considered to be amenable for rehabilitation.
3. **Medium Security Prisons:** Like in most countries, these are prisons that house inmates who have to be supervised but not to the same extent as those in maximum security prisons. While rehabilitative programs are to be provided, the reality is that most prisoners have nothing to do (see radio.cz. 19-09-2005).
4. **Maximum Security Prisons:** These house murderers and other violent offenders and, based on the Criminal Code of 2017, maximum security prisons are to house inmates sentenced to terms of 8 or more years.

With not much known about Czech prisons, and hardly any scholarly articles written about the Czech prison system (Vane & Dirga, 2016; Dirga, Lochmannova, & Juricek, 2015), it is impossible to provide detailed information about what goes on in Czech prisons; however, here are some of the issues:

Prison Issues

1. **Overcrowding:** As of 2017, the occupancy capacity level on September 29, 2017, was 106.5%. The ombudswoman at the time—Anna Sabatova outlined issues with prisons in Czech Republic. Among them were overcrowding, poor living conditions, little or no rehabilitation programs, and prison staff overwork (Brno, 2016). Recidivism rate is high since 7 out of 10 inmates recidivate (Praguemonitor, 2016). Overcrowding has been a systemic problem, and it is because of that that in 2000 inmates across the country rioted against overcrowding and the mandated payment of 8 pounds per day required of each of them (see Connolly, 2000). Quoting Miroslav Krutina, attorney at the Legal Analysis Department of the Czech Committee at Helsinki, Czech prisons are "overcrowded, beds are in a terrible state, sheets are old and torn, windows are dark, prisoners have almost no walking space, and little time to spend in fresh air" (RadioPrague.cz, 2005).

2. **Understaffing of Correctional Officers:** The result of overcrowded prisons is the overworking of prison staff. Without budget to hire new staff, existing staffs are unable to monitor inmates adequately to be sure they are not in violation of cell requirements. As well, staffs are unable to work with inmates to enable them to realize the benefits of therapeutic programs. The stresses to staff and overcrowding have led authorities to contemplate privatization of prisons, but so far those thoughts have not been put into action (RadioPrague.cz, 2005).
3. **Hostile Prison Environment:** Prison issues such as power struggle among inmates, psychological manipulation to gain superiority through intimidation, assertion of superiority, economic gain (getting goods through intimidation), rape, and other forms of suppression can be found in Czech prisons (see Dirga, 2016).

Intermediate Prison Programs

Probation and Mediation Service: This is an alternative to incarceration. When the program was established in 2001, the goal was to promote rehabilitation, reduce recidivism, and reduce prison sentencing. However, these goals were hardly met as incarceration rates spiked, and by 2005, inmate population rose with an additional 1,161 inmates (RadioPrague.cz, 2005).

The probation service was beset with lack of staff. Despite the best efforts of probation officers, their shortage and capacity workload made their job tedious. As RadioPrague.cz (2005) explained, probation officials were less than 250 officials, 25% less than the required number to adequately work with the number of probationers. With hardly any programs aimed at rehabilitation and with re-offending on the rise, judges were thus forced to sentence criminals to short-term prison sentences thus leading to prison crowding.

Parole: The use of parole is quite sparing in Czech Republic. The first attempt at employing the parole system entailed just 55 convicts sentenced to parole. As Miroslav Krutina, attorney at the Legal Analysis Department of the Czech Helsinki Committee, noted, not "... enough personnel to deal with people on parole. This again means that there is no one who can work with them, influence them, and motivate them" (RadioPrague.cz, 2005).

SUMMARY

Czech Republic is a land-locked country in Europe. The country is a former communist country, which peacefully transitioned into a democratic republic, and peacefully split from Slovakia. The system of law practiced in Czech Republic is Germanic civil law. The country's constitution is supreme law of the land.

Czech Republic is a welfare state, and a major force in European and world peace, and of environmental consciousness. It respects the division of power among the three branches of government. Law enforcement in the country comprises state police, military power, and municipal police with a small division of watchmen.

In order to be eligible to be a legal practitioner, one has to attend one of the four public law schools and must undergo 5 years of legal studies ending with an MA (Magister or Mgr.). Courts are structured in a hierarchy from the lowest regional courts to the Supreme Court.

The department of corrections is under the domain of the Ministry of Justice. Its correctional facilities are segmented to house prisoners based on the level of their crimes. As in most countries, prisons in the Czech Republic suffer from prison crowding and understaffing.

LEGAL TERMS AND CONCEPTS

Administrative Courts: These courts are responsible for administration of justice in issues pertaining to administrative law.

Constitutional Courts: These are courts that address only constitutional issues, civil rights violations, and issues dealing with the limits of presidential power.

Military Police: These officers maintain order in military premises, oversee training of military drivers, and protect military property.

Municipal Police: These are low-level officers sworn in to maintain order. They bear arms, and only work within the jurisdiction in which they were hired.

Velvet Revolution: This was an uprising that ended communism in Czech Republic, which at the time was Czechoslovakia.

Watchmen: These are civilians sworn in to help maintain order.

DISCUSSION QUESTIONS

1. Briefly discuss the history of Czech Republic prior to its separation from Slovakia.
2. Discuss the various types of police officers in Czech Republic. If you were to be hired as a Czech police officer, which type of police officer would you want to be? Why?
3. Explain the requirements to become a judge in Czech Republic.
4. What are some of the problems you discern from the Czech correctional system? What recommendations would you advance to remedy some of the problems?

REFERENCES

Blomberg, T. Maier-Katkin, & Yeisley, M. (1998). Guest editorial. *Crime, Law, and Social Change, 28*, 189–193.

Bremner, C. (2015). Top 100 destinations ranking. *Euromonitor International*. Retrieved from https://blog.euromonitor.com/2015/01/top-100-city-destinations-ranking.html

Brno. (2016, March 23). Czech obmbudswoman calls for changes in prison system. Retrieved from http://www.praguemonitor.com/2016/03/24/czech-ombudswoman-calls-changes-prison-system

CIA The World Factbook. (n.d.). Retrieved from https://www.cia.gov/library/publications/the-world-factbook

Connolly, K. (2000, Jan.). Czech prisoners treated worse than dogs and made to pay 8 pounds a day. Retrieved from https://www.theguardian.com/world/2000/jan/16/kateconnolly/theobserver.com

Dirga, L. (2016). The structure of the inmate population in Czech prisons. *Sociologia, 47*(6), 559–578.

Dirga, L., Lochmannova, A., & Juricek, P. (2015). The structure of the inmate population in Czech Republic. *Sociologia, 47*(6), 559–578.

En.m.Wikipedia.org. (n.d.). Czech Republic- Wikipedia. Retrieved from https://en.m.wikipedia.org/wiki/Czech_Republic

Hauner, M., Blazek, M., Osborne, H. R., Zeman, Z. A. B., Carter, F. W., & Auty, R. (n.d.). Czech Republic/History-Geography/Britannica. Retrieved from http://www.britannica.com/place/Czech Republic

Home.mweb. (n.d.). Czech Republic Military Police. Retrieved from http://home.mweb.co.za/re/redcap/czech.htm

Maier, S. (2002). Czech Republic. In H. Kritzer (Ed.). *Legal Systems of the World: A Political, Social, and Cultural Encyclopedia* (Vol. 1: A–D, pp. 409–415). Santa Barbara, California: ABC-CLIO.

Nyulawglobal.org. (n.d.). An introduction to the Czech legal system and legal resources online. Retrieved from http://www.nyulawglobal.org/globalex/Czech_Republic.html

Pagon, M., Virjent-Novak, B., Djuric, M., & Lobnika, B. (1996). European systems of police education and training. Retrieved from https://www.ncjrs.gov/policing/eur551.htm/cas575.htm

Praguemonitor.com. (2016, March 24). Czech ombudswoman calls for changes in prison system. Retrieved from http://www.praguemonitor.com/2016/03/24/czech-ombudswoman-call-changes-prison-system

Praguemonitor.com. (2017, January 20). Czechs to have two types of prisons. Retrieved from http://praguemonitor.com/2017/01/20/czechs-have-two-types-prisons.

RadioPrague.cz. (2005, September 19). The Czech Republic's flawed prison system. Retrieved from http://www.radio.cz/en/section/talking/the-czech-republics-flawed-prison-system

Vane, J., & Dirga, L. (2016). The religiosity behind bars: Forms of inmate's religiosity in the Czech prison system. *Sociologia, 48*(6), 641–663.

Wikipedia.org. (n.d.). Police of the Czech Republic. Retrieved from https://en.m.wikipedia.org/wiki/police_of_the_Czech_Republic

World Prison Brief/Czech Republic. (2017). Retrieved from http://www.prisonstudies.org/country/czech-republic

Xinhuanet.com. (2017, October 17). First open prison launched in Czech Republic. Retrieved from http://news.xinhaunet.com/english/2017-10/17/c_136684368.htm

PART IV

Islamic Family of Law

CHAPTER 9

The Yemen Model

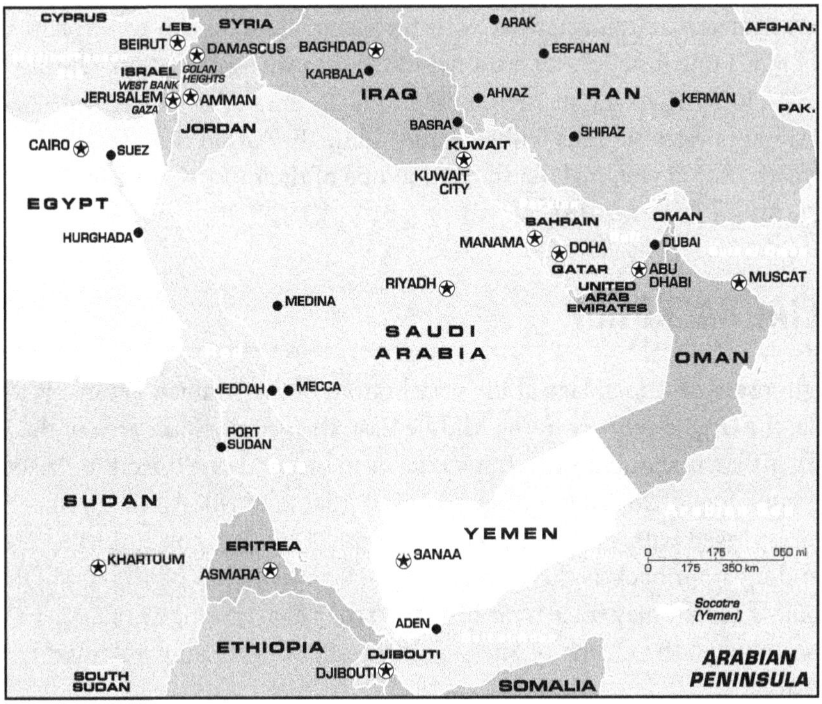

© Globe Turner/Shutterstock.com

INTRODUCTION

The decision to focus on Yemen was not an easy one. Our first thought was to delve into the Islamic nation of Brunei on the South Pacific island of Borneo. Surely it would qualify as off the beaten path. But, we realized that it held a similar world location adjacent to the Philippines and close to Singapore and decided to look elsewhere to elaborate on the Islamic legal system. Bahrain came to mind, but we concluded its similar Shia Muslim heritage would duplicate too much of the Iranian traditions. Saudi Arabia would be a worthy subject area, but much already appears in scholarly criminal justice literature. Finally, the Islamic nation fitting our objectives emerged—The Republic of Yemen. Also making Yemen rather distinctive as a chapter, and some might argue a disqualifier, is that Yemen presently finds itself engaged in heated conflict involving nations within and outside the Middle East. Consequently, with The Republic of Yemen we analyze how criminal justice institutions function in a nation during an extension of its ongoing civil conflict while at the same time undergoing military offensives from without.

Although other models of law covered in this book address justice systems in a wide variety of regions in diverse circumstances, with the Republic of Yemen we explain some of the intricacies of managing functions of criminal justice in a war-torn nation. During the last few months of 2017 into the spring of 2018, missile attacks entangled Yemen with Saudi Arabia, the United Arab Emirates, and the United States, while the nation simultaneously suffered the fragile aftermath of civil war, making the nation one of the most volatile world regions (UN/OCHA, 2018; *World Report*, 2018).

GEO-SOCIAL BACKDROP

Positioned almost as an appendage at the very bottom of the Arabian Peninsula and south of Saudi Arabia, the largest country in the Middle East, the geographical area of the Republic of Yemen is larger than one might expect. It stretches to one and one third the size of California and with a population of 28 million (CIA World Factbook, 2018). Although in contemporary times Yemen is linked with civil and political unrest, it holds a colorful, even if disordered, history extending as far back as the 11th century B.C.E. Noted in Biblical and Quranic texts, people of today's Yemen may trace their history to the Sabaean empire of ancient Yemen giving rise to accounts of the Queen of Sheba and her affairs with King Solomon of early Israel (Simpson, 2002).

Yemen, which may derive from the Arabic word "*yamn*" or "*yumn*" for blessed or fertile, retains to this day a most advantaged location as a convenient harbor and intersection point for ships crossing waters between the Indian Ocean and the horn of Africa (Bourrowes, 2010). Also, vessels seeking passage either on the Red Sea to the west of Yemen or the Persian Gulf to the east, logically find the southern coast of Yemen and the port city of Aden a most opportune stopping point. The favorable location for early sailing ships made Yemen a target for exploitation and even colonization by imperialistic-minded nations. And, the Yemen city of Mocha, the origin of coffee on the Red Sea coast, provided a lucrative marketing motivation for outside interventionism (Britannica Encyclopedia, 2010; Rippin, 2013).

The Ottoman empire, from what is today Turkey, occupied Yemen from the mid-18th century until the early 20th century. The valuable Yemen area was contested over the years by Romans, Egyptians, and Portuguese and by its neighbor to the North, Saudi Arabia. The

British, seeking a refueling station for coal in its expeditions to India for spices and silk, took control of southern Yemen as a protectorate from the late 19th century until 1967 (Gavin, 1975). For most of Yemen's recent history, the coastal country has consisted of two rather distinct regions, North Yemen, primarily Shia Muslim, and South Yemen, predominately Sunni Muslim. North Yemen became the Yemen Arab Republic between 1962 and 1990 and South Yemen became the People's Democratic Republic of Yemen between 1967 and 1990 (Bourrowes, 2010). Although the two areas reached agreement in 1990 to merge into the Republic of Yemen, the region remains today an uneasy union.

The Republic of Yemen is distinctive for another reason. The land represents a mix of hot, dry desert but with a fertile coast resulting in a combination of frequent droughts with occasional monsoons. The struggle for survival for plant and animal life in Yemen and its offshore islands has resulted in unusual, if not bizarre, adaptations—some stating the region to be one of the most alien looking places on earth with numerous species of plant and animal life appearing nowhere else (Habrova & Bucek, 2013; Scholte & De Geest, 2010).

WHY OFF THE BEATEN PATH?

It is somewhat of a contradiction that a nation such as Yemen would remain off the beaten path as it continues as a connection point between Africa and the Indian Ocean. We must conclude that the active hostilities of the region preclude all but the most strong-minded travelers into the region. The U.S. Embassy in Yemen issued the following severe warning:

> The U.S. Department of State warns U.S. citizens against all travel to Yemen because of the high security threat posed by ongoing conflict and terrorist activities. The Department of State is updating this travel warning to reflect concerns with detentions of U.S. citizens by armed groups in Sana'a (Yemen's capital city). The department continues to urge U.S. citizens to defer any and all travel to Yemen. We urge U.S. citizens currently living in Yemen to depart when they are able to do so. (U.S. Department of State, 2018)

The British government followed suit with its own warning stating it could not guarantee assistance to British nationals in Yemen (Gov.UK, 2018). Even with these directives, other reasons arise to discourage travelers from visiting this unique nation. The Republic of Yemen ranks as one of the world's poorest nations and one experiencing intermittent conflict involving Al-Qaeda and ISIL (Islamic State of Iraq and the Levant) insurgent groups that occupy and defend small segments of Yemen territory (USAID, 2017). Additionally, the number of airlines flying into and departing Yemen were reduced over the past few years and travel by land through Saudi Arabia or by sea remains cumbersome if not problematic to adventurist travelers.

SOCIAL-DEMOGRAPHIC PROFILE

War can impoverish a nation in multiple ways and Yemen is no exception. A civil war carried out simultaneously with outside conflicts since 2015 must result in insufferable outcomes. Estimates of war deaths reach 13,000 with 50,000 wounded and three million displaced persons, and some reporting many deaths were of civilians (Sherhan, 2016; cf., World Report, 2018). The social and economic impact of Yemen's war would be difficult to measure, but must contribute to its status as one of the world's most impoverished countries. War casualties led to a loss of skilled workers and apparently resulted in Yemen's worst-case scenario of resorting to the use child soldiers (Relano, 2017). The nation's health also suffers and is directly linked to poverty as bombing and missile attacks, purposeful or not, destroy agriculture production. Yemen suffers not only poor health but famine directly linked to the impact of the confrontation between the Shia population in the north and the Sunni in the south. Half of the nation's population goes hungry and without clean water with about one fifth of the citizens suffering starvation (Zouiten, 2017). Travel blockades by sea, air, and land deter supply lines for needed resources. In such a problematic condition, it is not surprising that the nation now reports a population median age of 19.5, the lowest of the world's nations, with unemployment at 34%, and a literacy rate of 70% (CIA Factbook, 2018). More than a million public employees have gone a year without salaries (Sharp, 2018).

Notwithstanding such dire circumstances, and with some outside humanitarian aid, Yemen strives to maintain social institutions necessary for existence, without which crime and disorder would be expected.

SOCIAL CONTROL OUTSIDE THE CRIMINAL JUSTICE SYSTEM

In near perfect environmental, economic, and social conditions we would predict low rates of lawbreaking. Adler (1983) addresses such circumstances in her analysis of nations not obsessed with crime, where social harmony persists and social control is maintained by informal institutions including family, religion, education, and economy. The formal institutions of police and courts become necessary only as a last resort. With Yemen we must assume the provision of social control through informal social institutions remains bleak or challenging at best. The family, as the most basic of the social institutions, must find its function of socializing young children for a confident and healthy future most depressing during a time of civil war and child-soldiers, compounded by poverty-stricken conditions.

To the extent that religion may also act as a control over errant behavior, we might also presume that Yemen, with its 99% Muslim majority, would reflect a relatively stable community of single-minded fellow-citizens. Yet, the political unrest involving Islamic factions at the national level appears to override the basic underlying moral principles of peace and harmony: the standard salutation among Yemenites being *As-sālamu ʿalaykum* (peace be upon you) (Abu-Nimer, 2000). We mention this only to underscore the apparent contradiction of what appears to be a persistence of street crimes and injustices in Yemeni society.

The restriction of a nation's citizenry in their ability to travel within, or to exit the country, and the ability to freely communicate also represents a style of control. It is not surprising that a poverty-stricken region such as Yemen, in war-ravaged times, experiences limited geographic mobility. Travel outside the capital of Sana'a requires a police permit. No rail service is available anywhere in the country, and there are only a few bus connections between some northern cities. Roads are in poor condition and most remain unpaved (CIA Factbook, 2018). Although telephone and Wi-Fi capability reaches about a third of the Yemini population, Internet use remains of low quality and highly regulated, as is the general reporting of news (Reporters Without Borders, 2016). Internet censorship is pervasive with suppression of nudity, gay and lesbian content, escort dating services, or any sites displaying provocative attire. Other censorship includes content pertaining to alcohol, gambling, drugs, religious proselytizing, or any recordings countering Sharia law or Yemeni political doctrine (Alsamawi, 2018).

MILITARY CONSCRIPTION

Other chapters in this book (e.g., Philippines, Singapore, Iran) have discussed the likelihood that compulsory service in the armed forces, to include conscription into the police agency, should provide incentives for youth to keep a clean record by avoiding run-ins with legal authorities during early school years. For the Yemen case study, we cannot find evidence to support this probability. Perhaps the opposite trend may be developing for Yemeni youth who predictably find discouragement in their vocational aspirations given extensive poverty, high unemployment, political internal unrest, and on-going conflict with outside nations. In 2001 Yemen abolished its compulsory military service only to reinstate it in 2007 to counter the high unemployment trends (Gaub, 2015). External reports emphasize extensive police corruption in Yemen undoubtedly linked to irregular or even absence of consistent police salaries and the general political unrest through the region (Sharp, 2018).

THE NATURE OF YEMENI CRIME

We underscore how suspicion must follow attempts to accurately survey the nature and quantity of crime throughout the world. The Republic of Yemen compiles no uniform crime report and much of what we presume to know about Yemen's crime and justice stems from inferences about the unusual behavioral directives in Sharia law often pertaining to behind-the-scenes victimizing of women. Also, when the United Nations reports of internally displaced persons, human trafficking for prostitution, child labor, and illegal drug markets, we assume considerable crime and injustices without precise counts (UN/OCHA, 2018; cf., USAID, 2017). Yemen's overcrowded prison system may provide a further indirect measure of the prevalence of crime, but also inexact with a lack of judicial due process. Many persons reportedly find themselves incarcerated after extrajudicial processes (Mangan & Gaston, 2015). Finally, with a nation overwhelmed with internal and external political conflicts, including terrorist activity, it is difficult to separate war-crimes from more traditional violations of law. Both war and street crime can result in violent death and sometimes overlap. Terrorist attacks against the United States from Yemen include the bombing of the Navy Destroyer USS Cole in October of 2000 killing 17 and injuring 39, and a bombing of the U.S. Embassy in Yemen in September of 2008 ending with 18 deaths and 16 injured (Country Reports on Terrorism, 2016).

While one journalist asks if Yemen is the worst place on earth (Cooke, 2008), travel warnings continue to advise tourists to avoid the nation even if sporadic transportation can be found (Gov.UK, 2018). When local safety issues include land mines, kidnapping, rebel violence, car snatching, and land squatting, all in a setting of poverty and unemployment, common street crime might be the least of worries to locals and visitors alike. Islamic Sharia moralities on public behavior derive from the Qur'an, including sayings and actions of the prophet Muhammad, regulate a variety of personal and social behaviors overlooked in most non-Islamic nations. Arrest and severe punishments may result from religious proselytizing, homosexuality, prostitution, alcohol, or illegal drug use. Importing pornography and pork products is forbidden, as is adultery. Common law relationships are forbidden and wives and children must gain approval of the husband before traveling. Holding hands in public remains outlawed, as does taking photographs of military or police activity, or tobacco smoking during Ramadan (UN/OCHA, 2018).

THE JUDICIARY

How disputes are resolved in the Republic of Yemen must begin with the way its people are dispersed around the nation. Only about 10 million of Yemen's 28 million population reside in cities. Stated differently, 39 of Yemen's cities are over 10,000 in population. The remaining 18 million people are spread throughout the hinterlands and desert in about 38,000 small villages, many only three or four hundred residents in size (Statistical Yearbook, 2014). The nation is divided into 21 governorates (comparable to provinces or counties) that are further subdivided into 333 districts. Districts are divided into cities, neighborhoods, and blocks. The thousands of villages in the rural area of the governorates are further subdivided into neighborhoods or *Mahallahs*. Due to poor road conditions and remoteness to urban courts across desert or mountain passes, much of the rural population relies on an informal system of dispute processing involving village leaders as decision-makers and adjudicators (Al-Zwaini, 2006).

The unique demography of Yemen, with the majority of citizenry residing in isolated villages, allows for a system of processing disputes that depends on tribal or customary rules rather than on the more formalized reliance on Islamic Sharia law more common in the urban court systems. Codes of conduct shared by Yemeni tribal peoples base their individual and interactional behavior on the sanctity of honor, keeping one's word, and protection of the disadvantaged. At the tribal or village level, disputes are more clearly based on mediation of conflicts with a goal of restitution and restoration and bringing back a sense of balance between persons or between tribal villages. At the tribal level, punishments pertain to restoring relationships among the collective rather than simply punitive action against an individual. That is, many wrongs in the rural village likely harm a tribe's honor. If compensation is required to be paid (i.e., blood money) for the wrongful action of an individual, the entire tribe may have to assume responsibility for the wrongful action (Al-Zwaini, 2006).

Disputes at the tribal or village level, depending on the severity of the infraction, fall into three categories or levels of local, male judicial authorities. Simple family conflicts and minor property losses are mediated by a lower level tribal leader. More severe cases involving highway robbery, aggravated assault, homicide, boundary disputes, and cases appealed from a lower-level authority will go before a higher ranking tribal leader. Disputes that involve intertribal conflicts, but still considered under customary or tribal jurisdiction, go before a third and the highest tribal position knowledgeable of all oral and written tribal customs. This uppermost local adjudicator of tribal laws remains a hereditary position of authority (Dresch, 1993; cf., Al-Zwaini, 2006). Disputes at the tribal level and under customary law generally apply to cases that fall outside behaviors proscribed by the Quran. Cases involving behaviors such as adultery, for instance, must go for arbitration before the more formal State court. Tribal cases not informally resolved by village leaders may be forwarded to the more formalized city courts that more strictly follow Islamic Sharia law.

State courts located in the more urban districts represent more formal or institutional judicial systems and follow strict Islamic principles of Sharia law. The courts reflect inquisitorial or non-adversarial procedures before a single male judge and without a jury (Al-Zwaini, 2006; Radwan, 2017). Defendants hold a presumption of innocence and may benefit from the presence of lawyers, but defendants are expected to speak for themselves. All judicial officeholders must represent Islam and its principles, resulting in an inherent prejudice against women (Country Profile, 2008; cf., Cooke, 2008). It should be underscored that about 70% of the Yemini people reside in the countryside and adhere to tribal or customary rule. Also, the more formalized city courts are said to acquiesce to customary rulings of tribal leaders should they appear in the State courts (Al-Zwaini, 2006).

Since unification of North and South Yemen, the country's national government adheres to a parliamentary democracy. A president is elected and limited to two, 7-year terms. The president appoints a prime minister who officiates over 300 representatives of the nation's districts. A strong majority of congressional members reflect the same political party, "The General People's Congress" (CIA Factbook, 2018).

LAW ENFORCEMENT

It should come as no surprise that a nation recovering from civil war and ongoing hostility from without, would also reveal sketchy systems of law enforcement. Coordination of effective police operations in the country must be impacted by the poor social conditions discussed in earlier paragraphs to include poor health, lack of basic resources, and high levels of poverty. Independent agencies report police corruption to be rampant with instances of torture during interrogation, forced extended detention without trial, and widespread bribery (UNHCR, 2017). Yemen's ongoing internal and external political conflicts likely hamper any attempts to systematically conduct research on policing operations in the country in recent years.

Keep in mind that about 70% of Yemen's population reside in small villages removed from urban centers. Just as disputes are managed informally by tribal leaders and outside the city courts, social control is undoubtedly managed informally as well. Formalized law enforcement would not make much sense in villages of only a few hundred residents. The limited available data on policing in the urban centers point out that the most feared internal security and intelligence operation is the "Political Security Organization" (PSO) numbering about 150,000 personnel (Country Profile, 2008). Reasons for the fear clearly result from the corruption attributed to the police force and the lack of due process provided during arrest and detention. Significantly, the PSO is a paramilitary organization, lacking effective training, resources, or consistent salaries. This major security organization reports to Yemen's politically elected president.

The Central Security Organization (CSO), a smaller policing network numbering with varying reports of its size (13,000 to 50,000 personnel), reports to the Minister of the Interior (INCSR, 2015; Knights, 2010). This organization appears to be more concerned with traditional police duties such as criminal investigation and police patrol compared to the PSO that concerns itself with monitoring and controlling counterterrorism activity, including political unrest such as crowd control and sabotage. Much of the policing efforts in Yemen's urban areas appears to involve security operations. These consist of providing escorts for visiting tourists, security at oil fields and gasoline transports, and monitoring public gatherings for political activism to include mosques (Global Security, 2015).

PUNISHMENT AND CORRECTIONS

Yemen appears to favor punitiveness and deterrence over rehabilitation and positivism. This becomes clear with the number of prisoners incarcerated, the unhealthy condition of the prisons, and the unprofessional conduct of prison personnel. Twenty-two prisons are spread throughout the 21 governorates of Yemen. These do not include four remand prisons to hold persons awaiting trial. The U.S. Institute of Peace conducted an extensive study of Yemen's prisons and reports an inmate count of approximately 9,000 detainees (Mangan & Gaston, 2015). How many years prisoners have been incarcerated or how many of the prisoners represent war captives makes such a count unclear. Because of the ongoing terrorist activity with enclaves of ISIS and Al-Qaeda rebel groups residing within Yemen's boundaries, up to 18 so-called "black sites" or hidden prisons have been reported to persist where dissident captives are routinely tortured (Fahim, 2017; Mayer, 2007). Human rights violations abound with perhaps the ultimate torture technique reported as the "grill" whereby an uncooperative captive is rotated on a spit over an open fire (Crider, 2017).

Supervision of Yemen's prison system technically falls under the Department of Interior. However, much of the prison networks, including the "black sites" remain administered by contract workers from the small neighboring nation of the United Arab Emirates. It is unclear why the prison function would fall to UAE workers. Likely, a shortage of Yemen's adult population during a time of war is a factor. Regardless, the lack of training of prison personnel is commonly reported with estimates that 2,000 prisoners disappeared into the clandestine prisons (Fahim, 2017; Michael, 2017).

The official Central Prisons spread throughout the governorates of Yemen are also reported as overcrowded with inadequate living conditions and torture-prone by the U.S. Institute of Peace (Mangan & Gaston, 2015). Female prisoners and juveniles remain incarcerated in separate sections of the same facilities as adult male prisoners. The Institute of Peace found most facilities lacked prisoner classification systems with little concern given to mixing prisoners of varied sentence length or pre-trial detainees with convicted inmates. On a positive note, the same report concluded that some of the inadequacies could be remedied with short-term training and at low cost.

The bulk of Yemen's prisons reflect an urban population. Some of the more rural prisons house only a few hundred inmates compared to the prison in the capital city of Sana'a with over 2,500 prisoners (Mangan & Gaston, 2015). This is not surprising in a sparse population with the more informal judicial systems common in the tribal, desert regions of Yemen where crimes would predictably be managed without formal institutions of law and order, to include prisons.

SUMMARY

This chapter reflects a second nation following the Islamic tradition of Sharia law. Citizens of the Republic of Yemen are 99% Muslim, though the nation is split between Sunni and Shia factions, with Sunni representing a majority. Nonetheless, these two factions have been in open conflict between the Shia northern region of Yemen and the Sunni Southern region until an uneasy unification in 1990. This chapter reveals a justice system operating over the past several decades amid lingering animosity between the northern and southern regions, but also with a number of external adversaries, including the United States. The presence of terrorist groups embedded in several regions of the nation compounds the ongoing political or religious factional difficulties. Perhaps, more severe outcomes of these combined conflicts include poverty, unemployment, and poor health. With these social problems as a backdrop, the criminal justice system lacks efficiency and professionalism. Corruption is widespread throughout policing operations, the court system, and various systems of incarceration. Importantly, Yemen illustrates a nation demarcated between extreme rural, tribal regions of the eastern desert, and the highly urbanized area along its Western, Red Sea coast. Clearly, the system of justice operates differently between these two extremes.

It is rather ironic that Yemen remains perhaps the world's poorest nation, with most of the adult population lost to war efforts after a long history of international conflicts. Yemen remains precariously situated between the Red Sea and the Persian Gulf and just a few miles from the horn of Africa, popular passage routes between the Middle East and Indian Ocean.

DISCUSSION QUESTIONS

1. How might Yemen's justice system be impacted by war?
2. How does Yemen's justice system differ between the tribal villages and the urban centers?
3. In what ways may Islamic Sharia law be explained as prejudicial toward women?
4. Why was Yemen considered a valuable region, or something to be fought over, even in early centuries?

REFERENCES

Abu-Nimer, M. (2000). A framework for nonviolence and peace building in Islam. *Journal of Law and Religion* (Muis Occasional Paper Series), January, 1–42.

Adler, F. (1983). *Nations not obsessed with crime.* Littleton, CO: Fred B. Rothman & Co.

Alsamawi, B. (2018). Caught in conflict, internet users in Yemen face blocking, shutdowns and slow speed. *Global Voices Advox.* Los Angeles: Creative Commons Attribution.

Al-Zwaini, L. (2006). *State and non-state justice in Yemen.* Paper for the Conference on the Relationship between State and Non-State Justice Systems in Afghanistan. Washington, DC: United States Institute of Peace.

Bourrowes, R. D. (2010). *Historical dictionary of Yemen.* Lanham, MD: Roman & Littlefield.

Britannica Encyclopedia. (2010). Mocha (Yemen). in *The Encyclopedia Britannica.* Chicago, IL.

CIA World Factbook. (2018). Langley, VA: Central Intelligence Agency.

Cooke, R. (2008, May 10). Is this the worst place on earth to be a woman? *The Guardian.* London: The Guardian Media Group.

Country Profile. (2008). *Yemen.* (Federal Research Division). Washington, DC: Library of Congress.

Country Reports on Terrorism. (2016). *National consortium for the study of terrorism and responses to terrorism: Annex to statistical information.* Bureau of Counterterrorism and Countering Violent Extremism. Washington, DC: U.S. Department of State.

Crider, C. (2017). The meaning of Yemen's secret prisons. (June 25). *The Atlantic.* Washington, D.C.: Hayley Romer, Publisher.

Dresch, P. (1993). *Tribes, government, and history in Yemen.* Oxford: Clarendon Press.

Fahim, K. (2017, June 22). Beatings, shocks, and the grill: Reports allege torture in secret prisons run by United Arab Emirates. *The Washington Post.* Washington, D.C.: WP Company.

Gaub, F. (2015). What ever happened to Yemen's army? *Brief Issues.* Paris, France: European Union Institute for Security Studies.

Gavin, R. J. (1975). *Aden under British rule,* 1839–1967. London: C. Hurst & Company.

Global Security. (2015). Yemen's intelligence agencies. Alexandria, VA: Global Security.org. Retrieved from https://:www.globalsecurity.org

Gov.UK. (2018). Foreign travel advise: Yemen. London: Foreign and Commonwealth Office.

Habrova, H., & Bucek, A. (2013). Overview of biotope of Socotra island. *Journal of Landscape Ecology. 6 (10).*

INCSR. (2015). Countries/jurisdictions of primary concern: Yemen. *International Narcotics Control Strategy Report.* Bureau of Narcotics and Law Enforcement Affairs: Washington, DC: U.S. Department of State.

Knights, M. (2010). Strengthening Yemeni counterterrorism forces. *Policy Watch Report #1616.* Washington DC: The Washington Institute.

Mangan, F., & Gaston, E. (2015). *Prisons in Yemen.* Washington, DC: U.S. Institute of Peace.

Mayer, J. (2007, August 13). The black sites: A rare look inside CIA's secret interrogation program. *The New Yorker.* New York: Advance Publications.

Michael, M. (2017, June 22). *In Yemen's secret prisons, UAE tortures and U.S interrogates.* New York: Associated Press. Retrieved from www.apnews.com

Radwan, T. (2017). Rethinking transitional justice in Yemen. *Menasource.* Washington, DC: Atlantic Council.

Relano, M. (2017, December 28). UNICEF: 2,100 child soldiers recruited in Yemen. London: Middle East Monitor.

Reporters Without Borders. (2016, November). Predators of press freedom. Paris: Reporters Without Borders.

Rippin, A. (2013). *The Islamic world.* Oxfordshire, UK: Routledge.

Scholte, P., & De Geest, P. (2010). The climate of Socotra Island (Yemen): A first-time assessment of the timing of the monsoon wind reversal and its influence on precipitations and vegetation patterns. *Journal of Arid Environments, 74*(11): 1507–1515.

Sharp, J. M. (2018, February 7). Yemen civil war and regional intervention. *Congressional Research Service.* CRS Report. Washington, DC: Library of Congress.

Sherhan, Y. (2016, August 30). The 10,000 civilians killed in Yemen. *The Atlantic.* Washington, DC: The Atlantic Monthly Group.

Simpson, J. D. (2002). *Queen of Sheba: Treasures from ancient Yemen.* London: British Museum Press.

Statistical Yearbook. (2014). *Yemen statistical yearbook.* Central Statistical Organization. New York: United Nations Development Program.

UNHCR. (2017). Yemen fact sheet. New York: United Nations High Commissioner for Refugees.

UN/OCHA. (2018). Yemen: Humanitarian response plan. United Nations Office for the Coordination of Humanitarian Affairs. New York: United Nations.

USAID. (2017). Yemen country study: A sociopolitical analysis of current conditions in Yemen. USAID Office of Transition Initiatives. Washington, DC: U. S. Agency for International Development.

U.S. Department of State. (2018). Travel advisories. Washington, DC: Bureau of Consular Affairs.

World Report. (2018). Yemen events 2017. New York: Human Rights Watch.

Zouiten, A. (2017). Yemen humanitarian response plan. Geneva, Switzerland: World Health Organization.

CHAPTER 10

The Iran Model

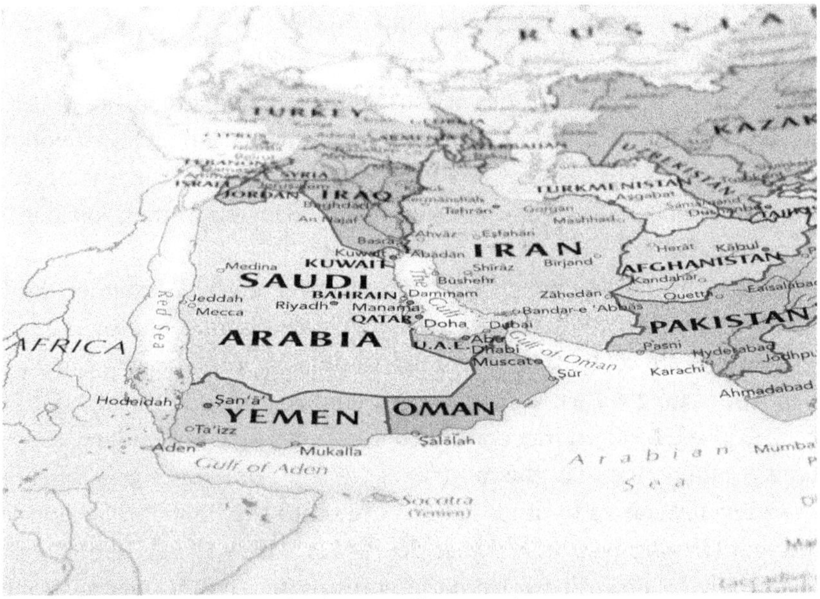

© Claudio Divizia/Shutterstock.com

INTRODUCTION

The Islamic Republic of Iran reflects one of four nations with a population majority following the Shi'a tradition of Muslim descent from the prophet Mohammad, other nations including Iraq, Azerbaijan, and Bahrain. The Shi'a nations comprise about 10 to 20% of the world's 1.8 billion Islamic followers with the majority following Sunni Muslim traditions who disbelieved Muslim leaders had to follow the bloodline of Mohammad (Lipka, 2017). Shi'a Islamic beliefs were introduced into Iran in 1501 A.C.E. (After Christian Era) with the rise of the Safavid dynasty into the Iran region from what today we know as the Azerbaijan area of the Middle East. Islamic faith was brought earlier to the area by Arabs around

642 A.C.E. after the death of the prophet Mohammad in 632 A.C.E. (Curtis & Hooglund, 2009; cf., Homan, 1980).

But, the narrative does not start or end here. The Islamic Republic of Iran (referred to as Persia before 1935) may justifiably boast of a storied past extending much earlier into the 3rd millennium B.C.E. (Before Christian Era). Notably, southwestern Iran borders the Tigris-Euphrates river basin (i.e., Mesopotamia), a most ancient region of the world, if not an origin of civilization itself. The region became the cross paths of major territorial and cultural revolutions over thousands of years culminating in the formation of the Persian Empire, what we know today as the Middle East, and today's modern Iran.

The nation of Iran must be viewed as a composite of this complex interplay of numerous empires, societies, and cultural identities. After conquering nomadic tribes of the region and establishing the first Persian empire, Cyrus the Great of the Achaemenian kingdom flourished from 550 to 330 B.C.E. A conqueror, yet a compassionate one, Cyrus was noted in Biblical scripts for his benevolence in freeing Jews from nearby Babylon in their journey to Palestine (Curtis & Hooglund, 2009, pp. 6–18).

By 330 B.C.E., the Middle Eastern regions were overrun by Alexander the Great from Macedon (modern-day Macedonia). Alexander's empire became one of the largest of the ancient world. By the 12th century A.C.E. and for about 100 years the area came under rule of Genghis Khan from Mongolia whose equally vast empire extended throughout Eurasia with Persia as a central point. Modern Iran continued to reflect a series of military coups and political revolutions resulting in one of the more dynamic and sometimes unstable regions of the world with varying allegiances to other nations even into the First and Second World Wars and to the present (Dowling, 2014; Mikaberidze, 2011). Likely the endurance of the Iranian region and its people results, in part, from the necessity to adapt to myriad empires voicing diverse ideologies. The 20th and 21st centuries continued to witness Iran in major conflicts with Russia, Great Britain, Iraq, Israel, and recently with the United States (Daryaee, 2012).

Iran appears as a region ranking somewhere in the middle of the world's nations regarding its crime problem. Iran remains a control oriented society yet still possesses its share of lawbreaking difficulties. Much of their crime complications stem from their nearly 1,000-kilometer boundary with Afghanistan, noted as the world's foremost growth of poppy fields with all its opium derivatives. Thus, Iran suffers the elements of illegal drug production, distribution, and consumption (CIA World Factbook, 2018). As well, Iran must contend with black markets specializing in illegal trafficking of alcohol, prohibited in modern Iran. In addition, Iran is a source, transit, and destination of women for purposes of sexual exploitation and involuntary servitude (U.S. Department of State, 2017). Without question, Iran is similar to other nations of the world suffering its share of crime resulting from social inequality and the embitterment associated with high unemployment and general lack of opportunity.

GEO-SOCIAL AND DEMOGRAPHIC BACKDROP

The Islamic Republic of Iran covers an area twice the size of Texas with a population of 82 million and with about 74% residing in urban areas (CIA World Factbook, 2018). For comparison, the population of Texas almost reaches 28 million with 84% urban. Based on population size, Iran is the 17th largest nation in the world bordering seven countries and two waterways. To the north includes Azerbaijan, Armenia, and Turkmenistan while Iraq and Turkey cover the entire western border. Afghanistan and Pakistan border Iran to the east, with the Persian Gulf forming the southern boundary. The landlocked Caspian Sea also extends for about 400 miles along the northern border.

Iranians tend to live to an average age of 74 which is higher than the world's average of 69 years. The average age of the Iranian citizen stands at 30 years matching the world's average age. As another measure of a nation's health, the annual number of infants dying per 1,000 births (infant mortality rate) for Iran is 15.9 compared to the world average of 34.1 (CIA World Factbook, 2018). Yet, on this measure, Iran ranks about the mid-point (99th) among the world's nations.

WHY OFF THE BEATEN PATH?

It is somewhat of a paradox that a nation at the crossroads of numerous civilizations would be off the beaten path regarding attention by comparative criminologists. Today, Iran remains in relative isolation from some of its immediate neighbors and from significant parts of the industrialized world. It is no exaggeration that Iran is geographically secluded with much of the population surrounded by high mountain ranges protecting a large central plateau. In earlier centuries, Iran was reachable by slow-moving caravans winding their way through the mountain passes. In modern times, the caravans have disappeared but access into the nation remains problematic. Even entry from the southern Persian Gulf is met with high mountain ranges.

Conducting research in Iran, especially ethnographic study by outsiders, would be difficult for other reasons. Travel visas to Iran are generally disallowed from Iraq, Afghanistan, Pakistan, and India, as well as Great Britain, Canada, and the USA, among others. Although Iran has been encouraging tourism the past few years, especially since the lifting of economic sanctions in 2016 by the USA and the United Nations, Iran remains hidden from view for much of the modern world and with travel warnings by the U.S. Department of State (Torbat, 2005). Even after the ease of economic sanctions, visiting Iran can witness complications with travel permits, when available, remaining slow, credit cards often disallowed, dress codes regulated for both men and women, and guides required to accompany U.S. citizens

(Glusac, 2016). Over recent decades, intermittent warfare on both the Western border with Iraq and the enduring conflicts in neighboring Afghanistan to the East only work to intensify the padlocked entry to Iran. Modern comparative texts are beginning to include Islamic states in their discussions, but often lack detail and cultural context of singular Muslim nations.

A CONTROL-ORIENTED SOCIETY

As shown in other chapters of this volume (i.e., Cuba, North Korea), nations that turn inward and remain relatively off the grid may resort to heavily regulated systems of control over the citizenry. Comparative data regarding crime rates must be viewed with caution even when it might be published. Regardless, Iran does not provide comprehensive accounts of crime statistics. Following the 1979 revolution, the regime has taken control of most newspapers and restricts content of television and radio to broadcasts favorable to the government (Curtis & Hooglund, 2009). The Islamic Republic of Iran represents a nation combining high levels of formal deterrence over its citizens (i.e., torture, incarceration, executions), while at the same time benefiting from other social institutions that may function as indirect forms of social order. Religion reflects a most notable, even if complex, example.

Religion as Control

Iran is one of very few nations of the world that wears religion on its sleeve as its official name reflects—the Islamic Republic of Iran. On the surface, one might presume that with a single overriding belief system throughout a nation, its citizenry would rather naturally coalesce into a relatively harmonious collective. On a most elementary level this may be logically concluded. Yet, with Iran fusing Islamic beliefs and customs into the political arena, and with religion holding ultimate priestly authority in government, the result appears to have given rise among the citizenry to periodic social discontent with street demonstrations over the past century. The dissatisfaction seems to be most clearly expressed by Iranian youth who, representing the information age, are more liberally minded than their elders with less rigid attachment to strict Islamic governance (Curtus & Hoogland, 2009).

Injecting Islamic culture, clerical dictates, and Muslim (*Sharia*) law into the political sphere appears to have become a double-edged sword for modern Iranians with the elderly segment of the society acquiescing to clergy control and the youthful segment arguably more willing to seek fortunes outside Iran (Armani, 2005). Notable examples of Sharia law include required modesty of women with compulsory wearing of the hair-covering *hijab* and allowing only skin of the face and hands to be exposed in public, or with the prohibition of alcohol consumption. Twenty-five percent of educated Iranians now reside outside the country in more developed nations with about 165,000 youth from Iran's educated classes seeking to emigrate the nation annually. This results in Iran ranking first in the world regarding depletion of educated citizenry or "brain drain" (Basmenji, 2005; NCRI News, 2014). The loss of educated citizenry contributes to Iran's unusually high 26% rate of unemployment and much of the country's social unrest (CIA World Factbook, 2018).

A date well known by contemporary Iranians is 1979, often simply noted regarding pre- or post-revolution time. This date signifies the exile of the Shah of Iran (Mohammad Reza Pahlavi) who had ruled the country since 1941. His departure from Iran signaled the end of a more secular society and the induction of Ayatollah Khomeini, an Islamic Imam as monarch. With the regime change also came more rigid adherence to Sharia law, including decrees of the Quran, as well as accounts of the Prophet's daily practices (*sunna*) and sayings (*hadith*) as obligatory behavioral guides.

Even with the discontent of more secularized youth, we must presume that the prevalence of dominant Muslim culture in Iran acts as an overriding deterrent to aberrant activity, or any behaviors deemed inappropriate for followers of the Prophet Muhammad. Simply stated, Iranians are expected to adhere to principles set forth in the Quran and sayings and actions of the Prophet, as well as obligations to obey all civil and criminal laws and regulations enacted by local governments. It is true that the mixing of religious and political requirements must complicate daily life while at the same time compelling the local citizenry to walk a narrow path regarding what is proper or improper. A similar illustration can be envisioned in a highly Christianized society with citizenry obligated to obey Biblical doctrines of proper behavior (i.e., commandments) while simultaneously following local government regulations. What is different in Iran, and in other intensely Islamic states, is that violation of Sharia requirements can necessitate severe punitive actions separate from, or in addition to, any government sanctions (Warren, 2008).

Examples of Sharia regulations frequent the news media because of the strict penalties that can be enacted upon conviction, and that S*haria* laws hold an inherent bias against females throughout Islamic nations (Otto, 2009). The Iranian government has historically upheld a patriarchal view of society and rulings of the Quran with some variation based on the sentiments of dissimilar monarchs. The edicts with clear prejudice against the female dictate not just how women must dress when in public, but also when and with whom they should speak, the nature of occupations available to them, and the value of their testimony in court compared to that of a male. A woman may have one husband compared to a husband allowed up to four wives. Testimonies of four men are required to prove rape of a female, but a woman who alleges rape without producing four male witnesses is guilty of adultery (Mohammedi, 2012) with a potential penalty of death.

Proscribed penalties of Sharia laws appear extreme to many. Criticizing the Quran, the Prophet Mohammad, or denying Allah is also punishable by death. Theft by either males or females after puberty may result in hand amputation (Otto, 2009; cf.: Souryal, Alobied, & Potts, 1994). Both males and females can be executed by hanging, or in some cases by stoning. The procedures for stoning of a convicted woman requires she be buried to the shoulders during the stoning, whereas the male is buried only to the waist. Should the convicted person free themselves, and subsequently confess their guilt, they may evade further stoning (Iran Penal Code, 2014). Our point is that religion acts as a prevailing control over daily behavior from the five daily prayer requirements to the proscriptions on behavior that can result in penalties deemed unforgiving by much of the non-Islamic world.

Military and Quasi-Military Organizations

As revealed in other world nations, compulsory service by citizenry in a country's armed forces logically contributes to social order distinct from other social institutions of religion, family, or formal justice agencies (For instance, also see chapters on Singapore or the Philippines, this volume). In the Islamic Republic of Iran, and from the early part of the 20th century until the 1979 revolution, all male and female able-bodied citizens were required to serve in the armed forces for up to 2 years. With the new regime of Ayatollah Khomeini in 1979, women were no longer conscripted into military service, though they could enter voluntarily. Males were drafted at about age 18 with length of service varying from 18 months to 2 years, depending on the nature and location of duty. Exemptions from required duty could extend to young men who had demonstrated excellence in academic achievement, or to those claiming sexual orientation that would arguably make accommodation to military life problematic, such as homosexuality or a transgender identity. Penalties could befall such irregular identity cases ranging from denial of driver's licenses or visas to travel outside Iran (Britt, 2009; cf.: CIA World Factbook, 2018). Conscripted males could be assigned to any of the military branches or to various law enforcement organizations around Iran. In the early 1980s, even those men exempted from military duty for educational alternatives were obliged to attend military summer camps (Derived from author's personal discussion with Iranian emigres to the United States).

Comprised of about one-half million personnel, the Iranian military is the eighth largest in the world with about half identified as male conscripts (Bengali & Mostaghim, 2017). The young men and those women who may wish to volunteer for the armed services must remain as reasonably upstanding youth and avoiding conflict with local agencies of law enforcement. The incentives for military service include being able to easily acquire passports, other government licenses, and to compete for higher status occupations after the tour of duty. For the time on active duty, the conscripts receive pay, and for some, training that may later lead to career opportunities.

Our point here is that youthful Iranian males must prepare at an early age how they will satisfy the conscription requirement, either exemption with scholastic excellence or by entering the armed services to include law enforcement. The argument is that this obligation places on the school-aged child a continuous reminder to stay out of trouble in order to make entry into the armed services as smooth as possible. With a troubled Iranian economy, the military provides consistent employment for many. It is also true that the ongoing social unrest between secular and Islamic motives, felt strongly among youth, may counter some of the deterrent effects of impending conscription.

Political Rule as Control

Considering the official name of Iran (i.e., Islamic Republic of Iran), a potential inconsistency emerges referred to by Curtis and Hooglund (2009) as "dual sovereignty." A republic is a state in which supreme power is held by the people and their elected representatives. Yet, in Iran, the Supreme Leader, who must be skilled and devout in Muslim affairs, holds the office for life. Once in office, the leader approves or appoints 12 members of the Guardian Council. The Council then approves 88 candidates for the Assembly of Experts who, only then, go before the citizenry in a general election. It is the Assembly of Experts who appoint the Supreme Leader. Consequently, the Supreme Leader is appointed by members of government who are themselves approved or appointed by the Supreme Leader. Whereas an Iranian president, similar to a prime minister, is elected to oversee the Assembly of Experts, it is the Islamic Supreme Leader who wields authority in major decisions including choosing heads of military, the legislature, and the judiciary; setting general policy; commanding armed forces; and declaring war or peace. The Supreme Leader also appoints members of the Supreme Court. Importantly, a parliament representing Iran's 30 or so provinces elects 290 representatives who must also receive the blessing of the Council of Guardians and therefore indirectly sanctioned by the Supreme Leader. Consequently, Iran combines some aspects of a republic contained within a theocracy, but with theocratic rule holding the upper hand in governmental matters (Ghobadzadeh & Rahim, 2016).

Since the 1979 Islamic revolution, only two Supreme Leaders have held office with the second Supreme Leader remaining in authority into 2018. With a prerequisite that the Supreme Leader hold Islamic beliefs and traditions in highest esteem, it is clear that the government understandably falls in line with Islam and Sharia law. The president of the Assembly of Experts (i.e., parliament) does, however, appoint ministers of 21 cabinet positions throughout government. As the second highest position in the administration, the president can impact daily operation of government, while remaining under ultimate rule of the Supreme Leader.

IRANIAN CRIMINAL JUSTICE SYSTEM

Law Enforcement

As found in many parts of the world, distinguishing between military and police proves difficult. Police organizations may be called upon to help protect the borders or even outside the nation during time of war, and the military may also support police with internal security. Prior to the 1979 revolution, establishing a new Supreme Leader and increasingly strict adherence to Islamic principles and codes of justice, policing functions in Iran were provided by a uniformed force of about 70,000 officers referred as the gendarmerie (French for "men of arms"). Today, the primary uniformed police force in Iran is named the Law Enforcement Force of the Islamic Republic of Iran, formed by a merger of the earlier gendarmerie with other revolutionary forces prevalent during the 1979 uprising.

In addition to traditional police patrol and criminal investigation, Iran's police force relies on multiple subunits (Special Unit Commands) emphasizing riot police, mounted police, border guards, hostage rescue, and an anti-terrorist special force. Police functions are under the control of the Minister of Interior. Including regular officers, conscripts, and reserves, the Iranian police force numbers about 500,000 providing services to the nation's expanding urban population of 98 cities, over 100,000 population throughout provinces. Also, the Law Enforcement Force of Iran manages passport, immigration, citizen identification card, and vehicle licensing issues. Just after the 1979 revolution, police operations included about 400 women officers, but in recent decades, no women were recruited into the regular police force (Bahramitash, 2003; Curtis & Hooglund, 2009).

Any conversation of Iranian law enforcement must include discussion of the Islamic Revolution Guard Corp (IRGC) as an irregular or quasi-military/police organization often working side by side with the regular police force or, as needed, with the military. The IRGC was first established to protect the new Islamic Republic after the abrupt exile of the Shaw of Iran in 1979. Understandably, fear of distrust of earlier police and military who might remain loyal to the deposed Shaw of Iran required a new organization of proven supporters of Ayatollah Khomeini, the new Supreme Leader. The new IRGC was concerned with counterrevolutionary movements still supporting the deposed regime. In recent years, the IRGC numbers about 125,000 members, ready for deployment for either internal or external duties.

A subunit of the Revolutionary Guard is the *Basij* (Persian for "mobilization") comprised of an occasionally uniformed force of civilian volunteers numbering about 90,000 regular paramilitaries, but with 300,000 reservists (Forozan, 2015). Known for their sometimes overly zealous allegiance to the Islamic regime, the *Basij* is a ground-up organization with local units in most cities throughout Iran that take orders from the Islamic Revolutionary Guard or from the Supreme Leader. Duties of the *Basij* can include neighborhood patrols, particularly around schools or places associated with potential resistance (MacFarquhar, 2009). Members may receive some benefits including a small stipend and ability to substitute *Basij* duty for military obligation. Regardless, the *Basij* and the Islamic Guard represent prominent auxiliaries to the regular police or military.

Judiciary

It is likely true that most of the world's justice systems pursue a blend of both punitive and rehabilitative processes in dealing with lawbreakers. Iran may be one of the exceptions by, but first and foremost, accepting a stringent deterrent philosophy. Punishments are doled out by a court system reliant on a judge trained in Islamic doctrine who interprets Muslim principles as practiced or uttered by the Prophet Mohammad, or scripted in the Quran (Souryal, Alobied, & Potts, 1994). Iranian courts do not use the jury system and most trials are administered by a single judge following an inquisitorial process of questions and answers rather than the sometimes-heated adversarial debate and argument common in European and American justice systems. With Iranian trials that may result in more severe sentences or death penalties, additional judges can be added to the bench comprising somewhat of a micro-jury although not denoted as such (Ginsburg & Mostafa, 2008).

Sharia moralities can appear quite harsh to many. We must conclude that rehabilitation for wrongdoings in Iran must take a backseat to extreme deterrent action that can include floggings and executions by stoning or hanging (Habid, 2017). A few examples of Islamic Sharia law sentences include up to 95 lashes as a penalty for consumption of alcohol, death by hanging for homosexuality, or death by stoning of a woman confirmed by a physician as a non-virgin prior to marriage (Alasti & Bronson, 2017; cf., Habid, 2017). A person accused of a crime may seek a defense attorney, but the attorneys themselves are under scrutiny to not overstep the rather absolute restraints placed on one charged with violation of Islamic moralities imbedded in Sharia laws. Overzealous defense lawyers may themselves be charged and disciplined (Ebadi, 2010).

Iran's judicial system operates diverse styles of courts. These include the Supreme Court, Revolutionary Courts, Public Courts, and diverse Special courts for crimes involving military and government workers. Additionally, a Special "Clerical" Court addresses wrongdoings by members of the clergy. Public Courts hear traditional criminal and civil cases, and Revolutionary Courts are reserved for trials involving attempts to subvert the government (i.e., *Mojahedine* groups). Principles of due process are said to be mixed across the different styles and locations of courts with the Revolutionary Courts reflecting the least due process values to defendants (Abrahamian, 1999). Judges are expected to hold the Shia status of *mojtahed*, an authority in Islamic jurisprudence (Curtis & Hooglund, 2009).

Incarceration

The concepts of rehabilitation and corrections remain relatively void in Iranian scholarly literature. Stated differently, the possibility of modifying behavior of a lawbreaker to allow successful return to society becomes secondary to swift and unforgiving styles of punishment not requiring incarceration. It is true that one can argue punitive measures such as severing of a hand for theft could technically be viewed as an unconventional interpretation of therapy. The offender, once undergoing limb loss, has basically been purged of the evil element and freed to re-enter society. Souryal, Alobied, and Potts (1994) provide an interesting rationale for this view in Saudi Arabia.

If statistical data is sketchy regarding overall crime rates in Iran, the same is true of the paucity of prison data. What appears true is that the prevalence of capital punishment in Iran, and other novel forms of torture, appear to fail in deterring the offender. We say this because the approximately 30 prisons spread throughout Iran also remain filled to overcapacity (Newman, 2010). Iran ranks at least in the top ten nations of the world in the number of offenders behind bars at 225,000, or ninth in the world with prisoners per capita (World Prison Brief, 2014). Evin prison, the largest and most notorious prison in Iran, situated in the capital city of Tehran, holds over 15,000 prisoners (Abrahamian, 1999; cf., Chiaramonte, 2013) compared, for instance, to the largest U.S. prison (Louisiana State Penitentiary) holding about 5,000 prisoners (Glaze & Kaeble, 2015). The United States, among other nations, has its own difficulty managing lawbreaking, and with high incarceration rates. The difference with Iran's prisons rests in the replete accounts of torture behind the prison walls portrayed in numerous personal accounts (Chiaramonte, 2013; U.N. Human Rights Council, 2017).

It is significant to recall that both males and females can be executed by hanging or by stoning according to the Iranian penal code, and both suffer similarly when incarcerated. Also, because Iranian youth are subject to the same penalties as adults, including execution. Young girls reach the age of responsibility for obeying Iranian laws at the age of 9, and boys at 15 years of age. Treatment of women and juveniles resulted in United Nations condemnation, notably with Iran leading the world in juvenile executions (U.N. Human Rights Council, 2017; cf., Death Penalty Database, 2014).

SUMMARY

The Islamic Republic of Iran and its justice system presents a challenge to summarize. As an off-shoot of the Persian empire, it represents a nation with a long and complex history, and a society fluctuating regarding its political structure and its relationship with neighboring countries. The criminal justice system reflects one of the clearest examples anywhere of how conflicting ideologies, or dual sovereignty, can confound a government and its people. Islamic traditions offer absolute doctrines proscribing individual and social behaviors that conflict with an ideology suggesting individual liberties, whether dictating how one should dress, what they can eat and drink, with whom they can socialize, or who they should worship. In Iran, or for that matter most anywhere in the modern world, and in an age of rapid communication and mobility, it is increasingly difficult to compel people to adhere to a single behavioral ideology. Modern-day Iran witnesses conflict among youth who may not share an absolute commitment to a singular ideology or creed.

Iran's system of government and laws are formulated to reflect Muslim comportment as revealed in the Quran or by the prophet Mohammad. The nation's leaders, and those who manage the justice system, must conform to Islamic doctrine and Sharia law as interpreted by the Supreme Leader serving a life-time term of office. Consequently, little room is left for non-Islamic rules and regulations. With absolute dogma as a baseline, it is not surprising that the Iranian justice system would follow a deterrent-based philosophy and with an inquisitorial judicial process. Moreover, convicted lawbreakers in Iran enter a system of punishment, incarceration, and execution based on deterring future offenders with little consideration paid to rehabilitation and reform.

DISCUSSION QUESTIONS

1. What appears distinctive about Iran's geographical location that has implications for its challenging socio-political circumstances and even its crime situation?
2. What is meant by Iran's "dual sovereignty," and how or why is this important to criminal justice?
3. Discuss Sharia law: What is it, and how might it differ from other systems of laws?
4. How is a deterrence and inquisitorial view of judicial processing relevant to crime and justice?
5. Compare and/or contrast the Islamic Republic of Iran to several other societies addressed in this volume.

REFERENCES

Abrahamian, E. (1999). *Tortured confessions.* Oakland, CA: University of California Press.

Alasti, S., & Bronson, E. (2017). *Corrections in Iran.* Hoboken, NJ: Wiley.

Armani, D. (2005). A book review of Baveh Basmenji's: *Tehran Blues: How Iranian Youth Rebelled against Iran's Founding Fathers* (London: Saqi Books). *American Journal of Islamic Studies, 25*(1), 108–110.

Bahramitash, R. (2003). Revolution, Islamization, and women's employment in Iran. *The Brown Journal of World Affairs, IX*(2), 229–241.

Basmenji, K. (2005). *Tehran blues: How Iranian youth rebelled against Iran's founding fathers.* London: Saqi Books.

Bengali, S., & Mostaghim, R. (2017, September 22). The trouble with conscripts in Iran's army. *Los Angeles Times.* Los Angeles: Ross Levinsohn.

Britt, J. (2009). Unwilling warriors: An examination of the power to conscript in peacetime. *Northwestern Journal of Law & Social Policy, 4*(2), 400–423.

Chiaramonte, P. (2013, January 28). Hell on earth: Inside Iran's brutal Evin prison. Fox News World. Retrieved from http://www.foxnews.com/world/2013/01/28/inside-evin-look-at-world-most-notorious-political-prison.amp.html

CIA World Factbook. (2018). Langley, VA: Central Intelligence Agency.

Curtis, G. E., & Hooglund, E. J. (2009). *Iran: A country study* (5th ed.). Area Handbook Series. Washington, DC: U.S. Government Printing Office.

Daryaee, T. (2012). *The Oxford handbook of Iranian history.* London: Oxford University Press.

Death Penalty Database. (2014). The death penalty in Iran. *Cornell Center on the Death Penalty Worldwide.* Ithaca, NY: Cornell Law School.

Dowling, T. C. (2014). *Russia at war: From the Mongol conquest to Afghanistan, Chechnya, and beyond.* Santa Barbara, CA: ABC-CLIO.

Ebadi, S. (2010, October 1). Iran lawyers defense work repaid with loss of freedom. *Human Rights Watch.* New York: Amnesty International.

Forozan, H. (2015). *The military in post-revolutionary Iran: The evolution and roles of the revolutionary guard.* London: Taylor and Francis.

Ghobadzadeh, N., & Rahim, L. Z. (2016). Electoral theocracy and hybrid sovereignty in Iran. *Contempory Politics, 22*(4), 450–518.

Ginsburg, T., & Mostafa, T. (2008). *Rule by law: The politics of courts in authoritarian regimes.* Cambridge, UK: Cambridge University Press.

Glaze, L. E., & Kaeble, D. (2015). *Correctional population in the United States.* Washington, DC: Bureau of Justice Statistics.

Glusac, E. (2016, February 8). Sanctions lifted: American tourists head to Iran. *The New York Times.* New York: The New York Times Company.

Habid, R. (2017). Iran: Wave of floggings, amputations and other vicious punishments. *Middle-East News*. Beirut, Lebanon: Amnesty International.

Homan, R. (1980). The origins of the Iranian revolution. *International Affairs, 56*(4), 673–677.

Iran Penal Code. (2014). Human Rights Documentation Center. (English translation of the 1991 Iran penal code with amendments to 2012). New Haven, CT: HRDC.

Lipka, M. (2017). Muslims and Islam: Key findings around the world. *Fact Tank: News in the Numbers*. Washington, DC: Pew Research Center.

MacFarquhar, N. (2009. June 18). "Shadowy Iranian vigilantes vow bolder action." *New York Times*. New York Times Company.

Mikaberidze, A. (2011). *Conflict and conquest in the Islamic world*. Santa Barbara, CA: ABC-CLIO.

Mohammedi, O. (2012). "Sharia-compliant wills: Principles, recognition, and enforcement." *New York Law School Law Review*. 57:259.

NCRI News. (2014, August 25). Iran ranking first in world in brain drain. Foreign Affairs Committee. Paris, France: National Council of Resistance of Iran.

Newman, G. R. (2010). *Crime and punishment around the world* (4 Volumes, p. 249). Santa Barbara, CA: ABC-CLIO.

Otto, J. M. (2009). *Sharia incorporated: A comparative overview of the legal systems of twelve Muslim countries in past and present* (pp. 615–616). Leiden: Leiden University Press.

Souryal, S. S., Alobied, A. I., & Potts, D. W. (1994). The penalty of hand amputation for theft in Islamic justice. *Journal of Criminal Justice, 22*(3), 249–265.

Torbat, A. E. (2005). Impacts of the U.S. trade and financial sanctions on Iran. *The World Economy, 28*(3), 407–434.

U.N. Human Rights Council. (2017). *Situation of human rights in the Islamic Republic of Iran* (Report of the Secretary-General). Twenty-Fourth Session of the Human Rights Council. New York: United Nations.

U.S. Department of State. (2017). *Trafficking in persons report*. Office to Monitor and Combat Trafficking in Persons. Washington, DC: U.S. Department of State.

Warren, C. S. (2008). "Lifting the veil: Women and Islamic law." *Cardozo Journal of Law and Gender, 15*, 33–65.

World Prison Brief. (2014). *Institute of criminal policy research*. School of Law. Birkbeck, England: University of London.

PART V

The Socialist Family of Law

CHAPTER 11

The Cuba Model

© Maximus256/Shutterstock.com

INTRODUCTION

It is rather ironic that a nation situated only 90 miles south of the shores of Key West, Florida, would warrant inclusion in this book. Yet, it makes sense. Although the Republic of Cuba holds a noteworthy place in the history of the United States, for most of Cuba's past, the two nations remained antagonistic toward each other, sometimes in heated conflict, but more often in a cold war-type relationship.

Christopher Columbus, in his epic voyage to what is now the Caribbean Sea or the West Indies claimed the island, among others, for Spain in 1492 disregarding the indigenous tribal peoples inhabiting the area. For the next four centuries, Cuba remained a Spanish colony. The growing population of the island, far across the Atlantic from Spain, carried out a number of rebellions against the island's suppressive government. In 1898, the neighboring USA sided with the Cuban people against the Spanish and sent a battleship, the USS Maine, into Cuban waters to protect American shipping interests. When the ship mysteriously exploded, killing 260 troops, the United States blamed Spain, resulting in a declaration of war and initiating the Spanish-American War. The conflict lasted less than 3 months with the United States as victors (see, for example, Bouvier, 2001; cf., Schoonover & LaFeber, 2005).

At the end of the intense but short-lived fighting, the war ended with the Treaty of Paris, an agreement that officially separated Cuba from Spain. The treaty yielded to the USA as booty of war the Spanish-held lands of Puerto Rico, Guam, and the Philippines. For three and a half years thereafter the Cuban territory remained a military protectorate of the USA and before the Cuban people received full independence in 1902. However, in 1903, an agreement between Cuba and the United States established that Guantanamo Bay, a parcel of land equaling 45 square miles of coastal harbor, would remain leased by binding contract to the USA, only to be broken by agreement of both sides. The existence of a foreign colony, even if small, within a sovereign nation must generate some animosity. For the subsequent century until the present day, the existence of the U.S.-occupied Guantanamo Bay, used now primarily as a prison camp, generated substantial political anxiety for both parties to the agreement (Gott, 2004).

Over the first half-century of its independence in 1902, Cuba underwent a series of regimes dominated by military and corrupt politicians (CIA Factbook, 2017). In 1959, a revolutionary force led by Fidel Castro succeeded in overthrowing the regime of Fulgencio Batista, also placed into power by a coup (Faria, 2002). Fidel Castro governed as Prime Minister from 1959 until 1976 and as President from 1976 until 2008 when replaced until present by his brother, Raul Castro. Significantly, Cuba developed an alliance with the Soviet Union during the Fidel Castro regime that included trade and funding amounting to $4 to $6 billion annually. Beginning in the 1920s and accelerated during the Castro years, Cuba recognized and established a socialist economic system with a communist government that persists into contemporary times, if only unevenly after the collapse of the USSR in 1991. The Republic of Cuba remains as one of the few nations of the world officially recognizing a communist ideology in its constitution (Worden, 2002; c.f., CIA Factbook, 2017).

WHY OFF THE BEATEN PATH?

Whereas it is true that some nations or cultural areas stay "off the beaten path" because they are geographically isolated, far removed from the outside world, it is obviously not always the case. The Republic of Cuba remains an example of a relatively secluded society even though located at the doorsteps of the United States, a most mobile and free nation. More significant perhaps than geographic isolation, is that the Cuban people find themselves somewhat in a state of political quarantine that works to constrain them from some of their neighbors. Various government, economic, and social restrictions placed on the Cuban people appear to have kept the culture in a frozen state . . . locked into an earlier time. This partially results from economic strife as well as an imposed absence of rapid mobility and communication with the outside world. To the extent that citizens lack freedom of movement to depart their homeland, or when outsiders find difficulty entering the country, an "off the beaten path" characterization emerges.

The lack of mobility of the population, especially in easily emigrating Cuba, but mainly with the inability of travel between Cuba and the United States, resulted in diverse modes of illegal trafficking of persons, primarily of those wishing to flee Cuba for the United States (Alexander, 2015). Although Cuba experienced an influx of tourism during the last half of the 20th century, the number of visitors from the USA remained abbreviated. Cuba, as a nation adhering to communist ideology, though to a lesser extent than North Korea (i.e., see chapter on North Korea in this volume), places the society under heavy government control and scrutiny. It makes common sense that a nation disallowing individual liberties would remain out of the mainstream.

Relationships between Cuba and the USA reached a most volatile point with the ill-fated attempt to overthrow the Castro regime in 1961, remembered as the "Bay of Pigs," a CIA-planned offensive during the Eisenhower administration but carried out during the Kennedy presidency (Gleijeses, 2010). Soon thereafter, the USSR conspired with Cuba to establish nuclear missiles on the island, an eminent threat to the USA. Now referred to as the "Cuban missile crisis," a thwarted threat of nuclear war between the USSR and the USA occurred in 1962 when American ships blocked the entry of nuclear weaponry into Cuban (Schlesinger, 2002). For the subsequent decades, the USA broke embassy contact with Cuba and established a trade embargo detrimental to the island nation. Travel between Cuba and the USA remained prohibited for half a century until some softening in the relationship during the Obama presidency (see Roberg & Kuttruff, 2007; cf., DeYoung, 2017).

GEO-SOCIAL AND DEMOGRAPHIC BACKDROP

As with other chapters in this volume, we must first examine a few of the social and population features to understand the Republic of Cuba. Only then does it make sense to focus on the specifics of the criminal justice system.

The physical size of Cuba, the largest island in the Caribbean, approximates that of the state of Pennsylvania. In fact, the population of Cuba and Pennsylvania hover at about the same number of residents with Cuba at about 11.5 million and with Pennsylvania about a million more citizens. As noted, Cuba is not a geographically isolated nation, being about 90 miles from Florida, about the same distance from the island of Hispaniola comprising the two nations of Haiti and the Dominican Republic, and only 125 miles from Mexico.

Unlike a number of other nations that may be "off the beaten path" such as the Philippines or North Korea, the Republic of Cuba remains reasonably healthy in regard to its population size and population-related social problems. It is not an overly crowded nation with the number of inhabitants for its land area about average compared to the rest of the world. Cuba's youthful population of 29% is slightly higher than that of the United States, and the median age of Cuba's populace stands at 41 compared to 38 for the USA (CIA Factbook, 2017). Cuba does reflect a low population growth of only .3% annually that places it toward the bottom of the nations of the world. This could be a long-range social dilemma, but not one generally associated with justice-related difficulties. In regard to the degree of urbanization, often associated with social ills, about 77% of Cuba's population resides in cities, slightly less than that of the United States at 81%, compared to the world's urbanization rate of about 50% (CIA World Factbook).

As seen in the following paragraphs, other sociodemographic features of the Republic of Cuba can be associated with social problems, at least theoretically, but fall outside the specific features of law and agencies of criminal justice. Yet, we argue these features work to provide a sense of social order and control apart from police, courts, and any official correctional or punitive systems.

ORDER AND CONTROL OUTSIDE THE CRIMINAL JUSTICE SYSTEM

Attempts to achieve low-crime status as a nation must address features outside the boundaries of police, courts, and corrections. With the possible exception of North Korea, low-crime nations do not typically rely upon strict deterrence by its justice agencies to achieve social harmony. Other sociocultural factors emerge that result in communal accord and make a reliance on formal justice less imperative (Adler, 1983; cf., Black, 1976). Although official data remains limited and inconclusive, it appears that Cuba represents a nation not obsessed with crime. Even with illegal activity associated with unlawful outmigration and human trafficking, index crimes, both violent and property, fall below crime rates experienced, for instance, a short distance away in Florida (World Health Organization, 2002). We conclude that a variety of interrelated features permitted the Republic of Cuba to preserve a relatively peaceful environment, apart from any specific consideration of its formal justice system.

Island Life

Although it is not a cure-all for a nation's crime problems, we agree with Fenwick (1982) that island nations possess a distinct advantage when insulated by sea compared to landlocked countries. A similar point arose with The Republic of Singapore highlighted in this book. We accept the quite rational assumption that island nations start with an advantage in providing security from others and in protecting its shores, at least compared to nations with contiguous borders with multiple countries.

Restricted Mobility and Communication

As suggested in earlier paragraphs, the Cuban society appears sealed in an earlier time, absent sleek, modern automobiles and generally tied to fixed-landline telephone systems, and without ready access to Wi-Fi networks and computers. To the extent that government regulations and laws disallow its citizenry rapid exchange of information and ideas, the society quietly remains passive and submissive. By its very nature, a culture embracing communist ideologies generally bans or at least discourages citizen contact with alternative ideologies outside its borders. Consequently, communist societies seeking a cohesive collective of like-minded citizenry would expectedly reflect lower rates of interpersonal conflict than a highly capitalistic society founded on open competition in the marketplace.

Religion and Familism

Eighty-five percent of Cuban people adhere to Roman Catholic traditions. With the society relatively sheltered from outside cultures, and low levels of mobility and cross-cultural communication, families on the island remain cohesive and localized. Maintaining a single religious belief system, along with the same language patterns and cultural identities, predictably reduces the number of normative struggles found in societies with multiple spiritual ideologies (i.e., mixed Muslim-Christian systems). However, Cuban society is not ethnically pure. With heavy acceptance of African slaves to work the sugar and coffee plantations in the 17th and 18th centuries, the resultant society is ethnically mixed with 9% Black, 29% mulatto or mixed, and 64% White (CIA World Factbook, 2018).

Education

To its credit, over the past half-century, the Republic of Cuba placed generous attention on its educational institutions. This may have partially resulted in a desire to ensure consistent indoctrination of its communist ideology in the early 1960s (Lakhani, 2010). As important, all education in Cuba remained free of charge including the university systems. For example, medical schools stayed cost-free resulting in one of the highest rates of physicians per capita anywhere (Carroll, 2007). Consequently, the literacy rate of the Cuban people remained high over the last half of the 20th century, as well as the rate of employment (CIA Factbook, 2017). We presume here that to the extent a society retains high educational levels, positive feedback results in overall social harmony. This high level of cost-free education could only persist with heavy subsidies from the Soviet Union, terminated in 1990 (Worden, 2002).

Economy and Social Stratification

The history of Cuba reveals perhaps more clearly than other nations the effects of socialism and communism on a society, before and after the fact. A socialist economy was rather abruptly set into place with the Fidel Castro rise to power in 1959 and lost much of its influence in 1990 after the collapse of the Soviet Union. With the beginning of the Castro regime, ownership of all lands and industry were collectivized, all property converted to social property, and with the government as the operational management (Balari, 1990). Suggested earlier in this chapter, we can from a theoretical perspective, logically predict that absent individual competition for goods and services, the level of conflict should expectedly subside. Conversely, highly capitalistic societies should see a rise in conflict. Our point here is simply that if a socialistic economy can remain ideologically vigorous, economic crimes should remain low. It is true that crimes in violation of communist regulations can replace those more purely economic crimes such as larceny and robbery. Nonetheless, adherence to a communist political ideology must remain as a societal feature that works to reduce crime levels separate from the impact of formal justice agencies. Conversely, when individual liberties and economic freedoms are encouraged, such as in the United States, higher overall rates of conflict and illegal behaviors expectedly emerge (Black, 1976; cf., Messner & Rosenfeld, 2007).

With the culmination of funding support by the former Soviet Union in the early 1990s, Cuba slowly began an acceptance of capitalism. Year by year an increasingly larger percentage of Cubans were able to own or improve their homes without government intervention and by 2010, 85% of Cubans owned their own homes (Cave, 2011). The shift to an acceptance of aspects of a capitalistic economy appears to have resulted out of necessity rather than a concerted effort of the political regime in authority at the time. With the termination of funding from the USSR, and lack of monetary support to maintain basic societal needs common in a socialistic economy, individual families took to the streets to fend for themselves, often in legal ways, and sometimes not. An era known in Cuba as the "Special Period in Peace Time" arose (Worden, 2002). The government acknowledged a difficulty sustaining an aging population with a reduced workforce, and trouble supporting early pension programs and social programs for the unemployed. When citizens found creative ways to make ends meet, whether selling items on a black market, or finding imaginative ways to profit from the tourist trade, the government had no choice but to turn a blind eye. Peters and Scarpaci (1998) report of Cuban professors selling books in an open market, or of an accountant selling a basket of fritters to help support her family as several of many emerging new work enterprises (i.e., *cuentapro-pistas*). A variety of private enterprises emerged frequently feeding off tourist dollars. With the advent of tourism and the increased allowance of a free-market economy in the first decades of the 21st century also came new regulations and subsequent opportunity for their violations.

Military as Informal Control

Military service is required for all able-bodied men since 1963. With the Cuban population at about 11.5 million, this means than a fourth of the island's population is actively associated in some way with the military institution. If all male and female citizens deemed fit for military service (i.e., 6 million) are included, over one half of the population could convert to the military establishment (CIA Factbook, 2017; English, 1985; Williams, 1988).

Our discussion here pertains to the major portion of the Cuban population undergoing important socialization during youthful years aimed at reaching adulthood while fit in all ways for a minimum of 2 years of conscripted military service. This includes reaching the conscription age of 17 to 28 years absent problems of behavior or physical adjustment. That is to say, all male children reared in Cuba must realize at a very early age that they must prepare themselves for eventual service in some aspect of the armed service. We are making the logical assumption that such youth undergo a rather natural conditioning process whereby future government service sits always in the back of their minds. Consequently, the prospect of a military draft system tends to act as a style of social control. Specifically, for instance, a youth preparing for military service cannot afford to engage in delinquent activity.

Historically, and of particular importance in regard to socialization of youth, is the Youth Labor Army. In earlier decades, male youth not deemed qualified for military conscription entered the Youth Labor Army (Military Units in Support of Production or *Unidades Militares de Ayuda a la Producción*—UMAP). Such labor camps were especially notorious in attempting to correct behavior of antisocial youth. Such units performed "economic tasks such as sugar-cane harvesting and construction work" (Worden, 2002, p. 129).

Considering the size of the military complex to the island's population, and including the Civil Defense Organization, Cuba became one of the most militarized nations in the world (See, for example, Williams, 1988). For further discussion on the impact that obligatory military service may have on societal social control, see the chapter on Singapore in this volume.

One-Party Government Rule

The Republic of Cuba has had its share of political conflict since its early origins. This includes coup d'états and regime upheavals. Yet, for most of its more recent history coinciding with the Fidel and Raul Castro presidencies to the present, the nation has advocated and sustained a one-party system—the Communist Party of Cuba (*Partido Comunista de Cuba* or PCC). Our point here is simply that maintaining a single ruling party avoids the clash and sometimes-fierce conflict associated with passionately opposed political campaigns. In fact, political campaigning, other than distribution of candidate biographies, remains generally disallowed in Cuba. The rather mild system of election of officers into the "National Assembly of People's Power," and with the single party communist system written into the constitution, circumvents some of the hotly contested election practices associated with a liberal democracy (See, for example, Roman, 1999).

To the contrary, grassroots democracies tend toward conflict occasionally expressed with street violence. As noted in earlier paragraphs, single party political systems such as North Korea should expect lower overall rates of lawbreaking.

CRIMINAL JUSTICE SYSTEMS

Policing

Even without considering formal agencies of police, we might correctly conclude that the island of Cuba reflects a relatively modest rate of crime and delinquency over the past half-century of communist rule. It must be noted that during the so-called "Special Period" when the outside funding abruptly ceased from the USSR, the nation entered a period of economic depression when out of necessity the Cuban government permitted a movement into some open markets and ownership of private property. A lessening of government provided salaries saw an increase in black markets and employee corruption as workers sought creative ways to make ends meet (Worden, 2002). Yet, the perception of Cuba as a dangerous place, or cities with crime-filled streets appears to remain absent. Newsprint from Miami, reporting of Cuban daily life by tourists tell of relatively safe streets with theft as only a minor problem, and kidnapping rarely mentioned (*Miami Herald,* 2015).

Formal law enforcement functions are today provided by the National Revolutionary Police Force (*Policia Nacional Revolucionaria*), or the PNR. The national police force numbered around 10,000 persons when first established in 1959, and now operates under the Ministry of the Interior. The Cuban government rarely releases demographic data of numbers of police personnel. Importantly, the conscription of all able-bodied males into the "armed services" of Cuba also includes the option of recruitment into service with the National Revolutionary

Police Force. Police tasks continue into contemporary times as a nationalized system throughout the island nation covering the country's 14 provinces, rural and urban. This is an important distinction. All police throughout the island nation are members of the same nationalized organization. This is similar to systems of policing in Singapore (see chapter in this volume), as well as Japan and Great Britain that also have nationalized systems of law enforcement. We would generally conclude that such nationalized systems lead to greater degrees of cooperation and coordination of all police operations compared, for instance, to the U.S. arrangement of rather splintered systems of separate law enforcement organizations at the federal, state, county, city, and town levels.

As noted in earlier pages of this chapter and in the Singapore chapter of this volume, the process of providing a choice of police service to all able-bodied men conscripted into the armed services provides collateral benefits. Large numbers of Cuban men, including women volunteers, reared throughout the nation furnish a cadre of youth who must maintain good character and conduct even in early school years to warrant entry into the National Revolutionary Police Force. These same youth residing in local communities, and prior to their conscription date, would expectedly remain loyal to any policing operations that might be ongoing at the neighborhood level.

Stated differently, the Cuban doctrine of "War of All the People" paralleled the rise of the Fidel Castro regime. The doctrine presumes that any crisis (i.e., military conflict, internal strife, or national disaster), must include all the citizenry. All capable citizens must take part in protecting the Cuban homeland. Such a principle necessarily supposes any domestic crisis generally under the jurisdiction of the National Revolutionary Police, would automatically involve a variety of quasi-military or security organizations. Of particular importance, include the Youth Labor Army and the Territorial Troops Militia (Worden, 2002). Youth not yet of age to serve in the armed services may still assist regular troop functions with agricultural and construction projects. The Territorial Troops Militia pertains to civilian volunteers comprised of a million citizens involving mainly women, elderly, and retirees pledging assistance to police and other armed services in any crisis, domestic or otherwise. Expenses of this extensive civilian force result from workplace contributions. This rather impressive participation of masses of citizenry provides a context for understanding the relative low rates of crime in Cuba, and a better understanding of traditional police functioning on the island.

The National Revolutionary Police represents the smaller and more traditional uniformed association of national officers sworn to uphold Cuban laws and to maintain domestic peace and order. These regular police forces assisted by canines also call upon a neighborhood-based, anti-crime group to help with security in tourist localities on the island. The citizen anti-crime group acts as a kind of vigilante or neighborhood watch program that supplements the other citizen involvement organizations (See, for example, Unified Prevention and Vigilante System or *Sistema Unificado de Prevención y Vigilancia*—"SUPV"; Worden, 2002).

Under the Ministry of the Interior, the National Revolutionary Police further subdivides into five categories or divisions including Uniform Policing, Criminal Investigation, Crime Prevention, Juvenile Delinquency, and Traffic Control. All of the approximately 60 Cuban cities over 20,000 in population maintain a police department with a police chief. The individual departments receive oversight from one of the 14 Cuban provinces where located and subsequently to the national Ministry of Interior. Police patrol in automobiles and on foot, have access to radio communication, and carry weapons limited to automatic pistols and a baton.

Judiciary

How crimes are managed in the Cuban court system requires acknowledgment of the historic and cultural context of the island nation. Three factors emerge. First, Cuba retains much of its character from its Spanish heritage, most notably its language and religion. Second, for most of its recent history Cuba accepted a communist political ideology and backing from the USSR and Russia. Third, and providing a key influence, pertains to the constant influence of the United States democratic rule just off its shores, accentuated by the large numbers of Cubans emigrating to American soil while maintaining contact with their homeland.

The contemporary judicial system of Cuba remains in a state of transition. For instance, the judiciary appears sandwiched between an inquisitorial system common in more authoritarian societies and adversarial processes found in more liberal democracies. Acts of lawbreaking are brought by the police to the court at the municipal or provincial levels where decisions are made if a trial is warranted. Decisions for trial must be made within 4 days and a state-appointed lawyer provided within 7 days. There are no jury trials in Cuba, and lawyers may not establish private offices to promote their services. Yet, private attorneys, assigned to defendants by the state, continue to appear in Cuban cities and may argue for their clients in court before the judges. The litigation process downplays American styled cross-examination, but defendants can have their case heard before adjudicators comprised of both professional and lay judges. Cuba does not plea-bargain its cases. Trials held at the lowest level in municipal courts reflect one professional judge and two lay judges. The bulk of minor street crimes in Cuba are processed at the municipal level and result in a penalty of a year or less of incarceration. Fines and probation are other alternatives. Higher courts, where penalties can be more severe, such as longer prison sentences and including the death penalty by firing squad, will have additional numbers of professional judges, but with lay judges representing the community remaining present (Worden, 2002). The involvement of lay judges in the decision process does soften the autocratic rule of the communist regime, even absent a jury procedure. The Cuban trial process appears similar to the judiciary of the Peoples Republic of China regarding involvement of the community and the participation of lawyers who may present findings to judges but without adversarial argument (See, for example, Jolley, 1994). Cases may be appealed to the Supreme Court that also includes both professional and lay judges.

Corrections

Any discussion of posttrial processes, whether of various systems of incarceration, work camps, or probation services, remains hampered by a lack of official reports by the Cuban government. This is not unusual for autocratic regimes. The actual number of prisoners reported has varied widely over the years from 19,000 in 1990 to between 100,000 and 200,000 in the mid-1990s. If the higher number is accepted, the rate of incarceration per capita would be among the highest in the Caribbean (Worden, 2002; cf., Gilsinan, 2016). One problem with attempts to count numbers of persons locked up is that it is unclear if persons held for trial are included. Also, because plea bargaining remains unacceptable in Cuba could account for a higher number of offenders jailed. Regardless, Cuba does appear to house its prisoners in a large number of facilities, including maximum- and minimum-security institutions and numerous work camps or farms.

It should not come as a surprise that communist regimes would place great emphasis on reforming offenders rather than simple punishment. In a one-party, one rule administration it becomes mandatory that citizenry walk to the beat of the same drum. The opposite is true, that in nations with open and free elections, and with multiple political parties, one would expect substantial conflict, intellectual or otherwise.

SUMMARY

This chapter presents a fresh view of crime and justice in a nation remaining off the beaten path while situated just south of the Florida Keys. As true with many chapters of this book, we find that to understand the character of the criminal justice system we must look beyond the daily operation of police, courts, and corrections to the sociocultural backdrop of the society and nation. A major conclusion reached about Cuba is that since its independence in 1902, it has remained in a rather constant state of turmoil and transition. This includes adapting to battlefield conflict with its powerful U.S. neighbor to the north, adjusting to multiple coup d'ėtats, and to acclimating itself to a socialist economy and communist rule funded by the then-powerful USSR. With the fall of the USSR and disruption of funds to support a socialist Cuban economy, the small island nation had to fend for itself with a mixed acceptance of private ownership and more liberal democratic principles. As a secluded society with limited mobility and communication for its citizenry, Cuba continues to struggle to compete in the modern world. Through all the transitions, the Cuban justice system has somehow managed to operate successfully by upholding what appears to be a nation characterized by high levels of social order and relatively low levels of crime. The social harmony likely benefits from the advantages of island security, high quality of health and education, single-party rule in national politics, and a dominate Catholic religious orientation of the citizenry. As Cuba moves into contemporary times, it enjoys a strong military, including a number of civilian security organizations that make reliance on a strong police force less necessary.

Cuba continues to struggle with the lure of democracy from the United States and with crimes associated with illegal attempts to escape the island and with crimes associated with tourism that has increased in the past few decades. With only a handful of nations of the world officially accepting communist rule, close attention to the Republic of Cuba is warranted and desirable.

DISCUSSION QUESTIONS

1. How does communism influence crime rates, and why would we conclude this?
2. In what ways does the proximity of Cuba and the USA influence illegal behavior between the two nations?
3. Why would we predict the military would act as an agency of social control within the boundaries of Cuba?

REFERENCES

Adler, F. (1983). *Nations not obsessed with crime.* Littleton, CO: Fred B. Rothman

Alexander, H. (2015, December 28). How more Cubans are fleeing for the US than ever. *The Telegraph.* London: Telegraph Media Grp.

Balari, E. (1990). Agricultural policy with social justice and development. In S. Halebsky and J. Kirk (Eds.). *Transformation and Struggle: Cuba Faces the 1990s.* Westport, CT: Greenwood Publishing Group.

Black, D. (1976). *The behavior of law.* New York: Academic Press.

Bouvier, V. M. (2001). *Whose America: The War of 1898 and the battles to define the nation.* Santa Barbara, CA: Praeger.

Carroll, R. (2007, September 12). First world results on a third world budget. *The Guardian.* London: The Guardian Media Group.

Cave, D. (2011), Cuba prepares for private property. (August 2), *The New York Times.*

CIA World Factbook. (2018). Langley, VA: Central Intelligence Agency.

DeYoung, K. (2017, June 15). Trump to revise parts of Obama's Cuba policy. *The Washington Post.*

English, A. J. (1985). The Cuban Revolutionary Armed Forces. In I. V. Hogg (Ed.), *Jane's Military Review.* London: Jane's Publishing Company.

Faria, M. A. (2002). *Cuba in revolution: Escape from a lost paradise.* Macon, GA: Hacienda Publishing Inc.

Fenwick, C. (1982). Crime and justice in Japan: Implications for the United States. *International Journal of Comparative and Applied Criminal Justice,* 6(1):61–71.

Gilsinan, K. (2016, November). Five years in a Cuban prison. *The Atlantic, 30,* 1–3. Washington, DC.

Gleijeses, P. (2010). Cuba and the cold war, 1959–1980. In M. P. Leffler and O. A. Westad (Eds.), *The Cambridge History of the Cold War, Volume II: Crises and Détente.* Cambridge: Cambridge University Press.

Gott, R. (2004). *Cuba: A New History.* New Haven, CT: Yale University Press

Jolley, J. C. (1994). Programs for criminal reform in the People's Republic of China. *Journal of Offender Rehabilitation, 20*(3), 1–20.

Lakhani, N. (2010, November 7). Latin lessons: What can we learn from the world's most ambitious literacy campaign? *The Independent.* London: Independent Print Limited.

Messner, S. F., & R. Rosenfeld. (2007). *Crime and the American Dream* (4th ed.). Belmont, CA: Wadsworth.

Miami Herald. (2015). Cuba: Police state or tourist haven? Depends who you talk to. (Special to the *Miami Herald*, January 16). http://www.miamiherald.com/news/nation-world/americas/cuba/article7039331.html

Peters, P., & J. L. Scarpaci. (1998). *Cuba's New Entrepreneurs: Five Years of Small-scale Capitalism.* Arlington, VA: Alexis de Tocqueville Institution.

Roberg, J. L., & Kuttruff, A. (2007). Cuba: Ideological Success or Ideological Failure. *Human Rights Quarterly, 29*(3):779–795.

Roman, P. (1999). *People's power: Cuba's experience with representative government.* Boulder, CO: Westview Press.

Schlesinger, A. M. Jr. (2002). *A Thousand Days: John F. Kennedy in the White House.* Boston, MA: Houghton Mifflin.

Schoonover, T. D., & and LaFeber, W. (2005). *Uncle Sam's War of 1898 and the origins of globalization.* Lexington, KY: University Press of Kentucky.

Williams, J. H. (1988, August). Cuba: Havana's military machine—On Castro's island, most of the population is under arms. Washington, DC: *The Atlantic Magazine.*

World Health Organization. (2008). Cuba's primary health care revolution: 30 years on. *Bulletin of the World Health Organization, 86*(5):321–416.

Worden, R. L. (2002). *Cuba: A country study.* Washington, DC: Library of Congress.

CHAPTER 12

The North Korea Model

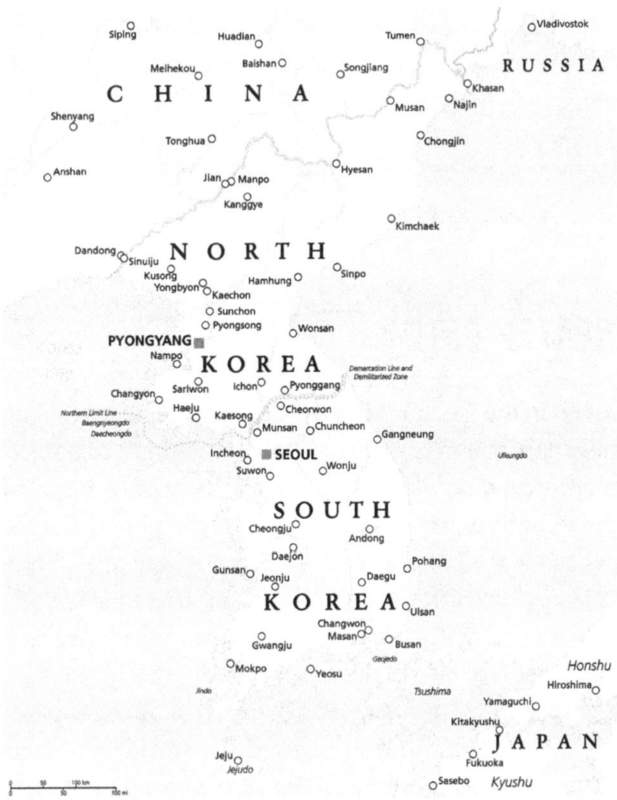

© Peter Hermes Furian/Shutterstock.com

INTRODUCTION

As a model of the socialist family of law, it comes as no easy decision to include in this book a chapter on North Korea (i.e., The Democratic People's Republic of Korea, or the DPRK). Two reasons account for this. First, North Korea appears in the national and international news on a near daily basis. The reasons for making the daily news appear provocative both in tempting its neighbors with nuclear threats, or with how North Korea appears to harshly manage rule-breaking at a more street level. It is understandable that one may have difficulty remaining impartial in any discussion about a nation that continuously frequents the news media for what seems to reflect inflammatory or ruthless motives. A second reason for reluctance to tackle North Korea as a book chapter pertains to the unavailability of data allowing an accurate portrayal of the inner workings of the DPRK. This is especially true when our subject matter pertains to penetrating topics of law and order, allusive crime rates, and even common social deviance.

Rather surprisingly, information on North Korea is quite abundant. However, the problem arises when the obtainable resources generally lack scientific rigor by independent, on-site researchers. Rather, most information necessarily flows from citizens or visitors who have fled the nation and are then willing to discuss or write about their experiences. It is unlikely that outside ethnographers, for instance, would find easy entry into North Korea with intent to explore the obscurities of a justice system kept comparatively isolated for decades.

WHY OFF THE BEATEN PATH?

The fact of being included in the "socialist family tradition" arguably isolates a society or nation from others. That is, the vast majority of the approximately 200 nations of the world fall outside the "socialist" tradition and family of law. Theoretically speaking, a nation that strives for socialism and widespread harmony through an autocratic regime would also hold a belief that outsiders would contaminate the system and be comparatively unwelcome. To the extent that a society represents a goal of leveling its wealth to result in a more purely communal style of life and a discouragement of adventurous capitalism, would likely see isolationism as the rule of the day. North Korea persists as one of the few nations of the world still adhering to a socialistic model and with communistic political tendencies. It should come as no surprise that the country chooses to remain distant from the rest of the world by maintaining a standoffish and unapproachable stance. Only about 24 (12%) of the world's nations maintain embassies in North Korea (Embassy Pages, 2017; cf., Wertz, Oh, & Kim, 2016). Having said this, we must admit that some of the more contemporary writers are beginning to report of sporadic capitalism emerging in the urban areas making a mixed bag of economic and governmental processes (Tudor & Pearson, 2015).

Political isolationism is associated with stringent social regulations and laws that restrict movement of visitors into North Korea, especially those from Western nations and particularly the United States. For example, the North Korean government permits only three Korean travel agencies to sponsor tourism into the nation. Government-approved guides must accompany all tourist groups and visitors must reside at a single government-approved site, the Yanggakdo hotel, in the capitol city of Pyongyang. The heavily safeguarded hotel is secluded on an island in the Taedong River that winds its way through the capitol city (Johnson, 2013). Visitor's converse with guides only at a minimum and with taking of photographs carefully monitored. Government guides also accompany tourists when outside the hotel. Photographs of statues of Kim Jong Un, North Korea's leader, must omit close-ups of his face and must include the whole body. Yet, North Korea has announced a desire to increase tourism in the next few years (Abrahamian, 2017).

Visitors must be cautious to obey all local regulations and this is particularly true for those without local embassy representation and safeguards, including the United States. The U.S. Department of State advises citizens to avoid travel to North Korea. Those choosing North Korea as a tourist destination remain warned to pay strict attention to passport and visa details. The expiration date must not be less than six months, and two blank pages must be available in the passport for additional visa stamps upon entry and exit. Entry for tourists is only through the People's Republic of China, and visitors must satisfy all visa requirements for the People's Republic of China as well as for North Korea. Failure to adhere to all regulations could result in fines, detainment, arrest, or imprisonment (U.S. Department of State, 2016).

In addition to isolationism resulting from political and legal regulations, North Korea remains relatively secluded in physical space that makes access to the nation most challenging. All three of the nations that border North Korea (People's Republic of China, the Russian Federation, and the Republic of Korea or South Korea) make North Korea geographically isolated. Most notable is the southern border with South Korea. The two nations are separated by a 2.4-mile-wide and 150-mile-long strip of unoccupied land referred to as the "Demilitarized Zone" or the "DMZ." Both sides of the DMZ have remained heavily fortified ever since the end of the Korean War (1950–1953) that ended with a ceasefire agreement with neither side declaring an official victory. The northern border of 880 miles separating North Korea with the People's Republic of China reflects fewer fortifications, but the natural mountain barrier and two rivers make illegal crossing problematic even if desired. The Chinese military monitors crossing between North Korea and The People's Republic of China. Four weakly but heavily monitored train crossings extend from Beijing to Pyongyang.

The far northeastern tip of the border between North Korea and Russia extends for less than 20 miles along the Tumen River with a single bridge connecting the two nations. With bridge crossing only by rail, there are no roadways into North Korea from Russia. Paris and Morris (2016), travel writers for the London *Telegraph,* refer to North Korea as the "world's most secretive country" and Kim (2010) refers to it as "the world's most repressive country."

SOCIO-DEMOGRAPHIC BACKDROP

Before we can delve into the structure and function of the criminal justice system, it makes sense first to consider a few aspects of the North Korean society in regard to the broad subject of social organization. Not only does North Korea remain an isolated nation, it also sits at the middle-range of all nations of the world in regard to its land mass and population size. Its population hovers slightly over 25 million in an area just larger than the State of Virginia and with 60% of its people residing in urban areas. Several statistics become noteworthy. First, the average age of death for North Koreans is 70.1 (186th in world rankings), with males on average at 66.2 years at death, placing inhabitants toward the bottom of the world's 200 or so nations (CIA Factbook, 2017). In comparison, South Korea reveals an average age at death as 82 years or 12th in the world and toward the top in rankings. In regard to the Infant Mortality Rate, North Korea comes in at 76th place in the world with a score of 26.1 infants dying per 1,000 births in the first year of life. Across the border into South Korea, the infant mortality is three per 1,000 births.

Economic vitality, as suggested by the unemployment rate, is also a telling indicator of individual achievement and a sense of well-being. North Korea's rate of unemployment hovers at 25.6% of the labor force, placing it at 178th and toward the bottom of the world's nations. This compares to South Korea's 4% unemployment or to the world average of 8.6% unemployed (CIA Factbook, 2017). It is hard to pinpoint why North Korea would have such a low score in regard to average age of death. The nation reports an improved water supply, but with a lower level of improved sanitation (81.9%) compared to 100% for its Korean neighbor to the south. Interestingly, North Korea reports a larger number of hospital beds per 1,000 population (13.2) than South Korea (10.2).

North Korea is racially homogeneous, and with very little variation in language and religion. This is not surprising given the strict border enforcement, natural or otherwise. The overwhelming majority of the population remains Korean with a very few number of Chinese and Japanese peoples. The national government of North Korea keeps mobility and communication with the outside world to a minimum. Television and radios leave the factory built to remain stationary at government broadcasting stations. Most telephone service remains with fixed wire lines and mobile service relatively rare placing North Korea at 146th among nations. North Korea reports eight Internet hosts, that puts them at the very bottom among countries of the world (CIA Factbook, 2017).

Our point here is that remaining in a relatively isolated and restrictive country and with a way of life resulting in poor health, high unemployment, and high mortality rates produces dysfunctional or negative features of social organization. Arguably, the citizenry indirectly suffer such negative features as much or perhaps more than any straightforwardly imposed controls by a formal criminal justice system.

EARLY IDEOLOGIES OF SOCIAL ORDER

North Korea represents an economically poor nation isolated from the world and a society held under the yoke of extreme social controls. Patterns of social control throughout the land extend far beyond the bounds of those imposed by traditional criminal justice systems of police, courts, and corrections. Before approaching such specific subject areas of justice, we must dig deeper into the sociocultural background that works to regulate the daily lives of the citizenry and only secondarily gives rise to a rigid system of criminal justice. The roots of an unforgiving climate of social order in modern-day North Korea extend as far back as the 14th century Joseon Kingdom that lasted until the end of the 19th century and just prior to the Japanese occupation between 1910 and 1945 (Ch'oe, Lee, & de Bary, 2000).

Four ideological patterns (e.g., *Yangban* or hierarchy, *Suryong* or obedience, *Juche* or sacrifice, and *Songbun* or worthiness) persist at various levels of influence in North Korea and act somewhat as an umbrella under which basic elements of police, courts, and corrections must function. The four patterns tend to overlap with each other, and with one aspect of the ideological culture morphing into the other. Each deserves brief but separate attention.

Yangban

As with other North Korean ideological concepts, *yangban* does not translate smoothly into English. We are using it here as closely aligned with "hierarchy," an ordering system into which a North Korean person may be born, as into a social class or status of family, or in some ways, a social class that one may aspire to, or may lose (Deuchler, 1995). One's *yangban* does not have the permanence of British royalty or nobility, nor that of a caste system of India. Rather, one may reap the benefits of the ruling class by working one's way into the higher position, rather traditionally associated with working one's way into and becoming part of the bureaucratic aristocracy and assigned to a government post. To compete for such highly valued government positions and to be part of the esteemed *yangban* status, one had to pass a rigorous civil-service examination. The finances and study time in preparation for the exams favor those in the upper classes, or children of families already among the *yangban*. Once a member of the *yangban*, one's family is also included at least for a period of three years. That is, one must continuously strive to remain in the esteemed work role or else the individual and the family would lose the *yangban* status. Such ruling classes would include military. Admittedly, this ideology has faded from its heyday in earlier centuries, but put in place a mindset of acceptance of a ruling class of persons who, with continued diligence, may remain in authority for generations. Even today, citizens occasionally boast of being members or descendants of the *yangban* (Deuchler; cf., Tudor & Pearson, 2015).

A published registry of citizens maintained at the provincial level reflects citizenry *yangban* status. Such a status designation arose, in part, with the recognition of generations of Confucian doctrines designating rather rigid social class differences as appropriate. These include such patriarchal distinctions as sovereign to subject; husband to wife; parent to child; and older brother to younger. The emergence of the *yangban* system of social order also logically parallels the expansion of a feudal system of land ownership and distribution in early Korea, obliging the peasantry to work for and sometimes defend the landed gentry. Not surprisingly, the landowners were often also of the ruling class and *yangban*. The primary point here is that five centuries of a *yangban* system of class designation worked to maintain an acceptance of a type of social order. To the extent that the *yangban* system generated a sense of social control, subsequent systems of formal justice would be less necessary (See, for instance, Ch'oe, Lee, & de Bary, 2000).

Suryong

Whereas the *yangban* tradition provided an expectation and acceptance of a long-lasting ruling class structure, even with family-based dynasties, the concept of *suryong* supplements and enhances *yangban* by a requirement mandating absolute obedience to the ruler. The *suryong* ideal of unconditional submission to the sovereign also derives from Confucian doctrines of *filial piety* as in the obedience of a child being pious or devout toward the head of the family. (This near religious ideal extends to the ruler who receives absolute devotion by the citizenry.) Thus, the ruler obtains the designation of "supreme" or "great" leader or "dear" leader (i.e., *suryong*).

Some leaders appear imbued with the label upon taking office and others may develop *suryong* through their personality and ability to capture the minds of the citizenry (Williamson, 2011). Following Confucian tradition, and analogous to a religious fervor, great *suryong* leaders are believed to receive their titles as mandates from heaven. North Korea's Kim family dynasty reflects such a case. Beginning with Kim Il-sung, president from 1948 to 1994, followed by his son Kim Jong-il, president from 1994 to 2011, and today's president, Kim Jong-un, replacing his father in 2011 and to the present. This ongoing family dynasty now extends into its seventh decade of rule. The grandfather, Kim Il-sung, was elevated to head of state of North Korea after leading a celebrated military campaign against the Japanese occupiers toward the end of WW II. The title of *suryong* accompanied the erecting of numerous statues and effigies that further venerated his reputation. After nearly half a century of Kim Il-sung's reign over the DPRK, the acceptance of the son, and then the grandson as *suryong* leaders was automatic, following *yangban* traditions.

Juche

In addition, difficult to translate easily into English, "*juche*" is an ideology of sacrifice of one's self, or one's life almost in a spiritual sense to a mastery of the works of the great *suryong* leader (Suh, 2012). If the citizenry at-large accept and abide by the *juche* philosophy, then the nation will result as a resilient social collective. This is the product of extreme acceptance of the Marxist tradition prevalent in pre-WWII Germany. All citizens must sacrifice for the good of the national collective or the state. Kim Il-sung's writings and speeches accentuated this philosophy (Armstrong, 2013). In a tradition of familism, with children worshiping every word of the father, the entire society emerges with a social unity analogous to a political religion. Stated differently, the *suryong* leader as portrayed by Kim Il-sung, when imbued with *juche* by his subjects, becomes the savior (i.e., analogous with Mohammad or Jesus), and the long-lasting *juche* ideologies of sacrifice become analogous to the Qur'an or the Bible.

Songbun

To egalitarian nations, the North Korean system of assessing a citizen's worthiness (i.e., *songbun*) is perhaps a most offensive ideology. Here, a citizen receives a designation based on a judgment by the ruling class of an individual's loyalty to the nation, government, or the leader. Whereas *yangban* pertained to an achieved designation of a particular social class, *songbun* takes the classification one step further by attributing certain behaviors as more valued than others. How trustworthy is a North Korean citizen to obtain benefits from, or receive protection of, the government? This could include a variety of assistances from the state in the form of jobs, educational opportunities, and even food (Hunter, 1999). In addition, is one worthy enough to join the controlling political party (the Korean Worker's Party, or the KWP)?

Such a system of assessing a citizen's behavior and activities was more prominent before the collapse of the Eastern Bloc of communist nations and particularly of the earlier Soviet Union. Prior to a decline of communism, North Korea received outside funding that allowed generous distribution of goods and services to citizens. One's *songbun* determined who received assistance as well as the kind and amount received. With the rather abrupt reduction of outside assistance, the North Korean citizenry lost government handouts and a famine resulted. Loss of government support led, in part, to the emergence of some capitalism with citizens compelled to rely more on a market economy, even if meager. Nonetheless, such a system that allows the government to measure loyalty and assign various benefits of the ruling party also sets the stage for a system of purging inhabitants almost at will who do not meet government-imposed standards. Categories of citizens include three rather broad groupings of worthiness: core (most worthy), wavering, and hostile. Succeeding the *juche* philosophy of sacrificing one's self to the Korean Worker's Party and to the Great (*suryong*) leader, everyday demonstrations of worthiness must follow. Failure to express worthiness could result in purging (i.e., reduction in *songbun* status or even execution). The government has maintained written records of the loyalty and worthiness of citizens and of the *songbun* status assigned.

MODERN AND ONGOING FEATURES OF SOCIAL ORDER

Ethnic Homogeneity

To the extent that a society exhibits similarity among its inhabitants, it makes common sense to presume that social harmony will more smoothly arise. The opposite is also true; a society that is highly mixed, culturally or otherwise, will be more prone to social conflict. This is clarified in detail in *The Behavior of Law* (Black, 1976), and earlier by Reckless (1961). The restrictive boundaries of North Korea have resulted in a rather ethnically pure Korean society with the exception of a small population of Japanese and Chinese. The population reflects similar physical traits, the same language, and ultimately the citizenry experience and interacts within a similar set of rules and experiences. Thus, the population is both physically and culturally homogeneous, at least as much as would be reflective of a closed society.

Lingering Feudalism

Following a millennium of *juche* and *songbun* traditions, we should not be surprised that feudalistic features persist even with the appearance of some capitalistic practices. A strong ideology of patron allegiance to the property owner (i.e., the government) prevails even though the concept of private property in North Korea lies just beneath the surface. It appears too difficult even for a totalitarian and Marxist oriented government to keep a thumb over millions of citizens spread throughout the nation. It is true that the North Korean ruling establishment technically can claim ultimate ownership of all the land and property. Furthermore, the government has upheld control over the citizenry by providing handouts of resources, mainly food. However, given the diminishing of funding support of mainland China and the prior Soviet Union, along with severe droughts, the handouts of sustenance resources have all but disappeared. Yet, we must conclude that to the extent the ideology and practice of patronage of citizenry to the governing aristocrats over the land and social institutions continues, a condition of extreme social order remains. Stated differently, individual freedoms to exchange goods and services remains relatively stymied, although not totally lacking.

Emergence of Grey Markets

Reports of escapees from the DPRK confirm that a "black" market does persist in North Korea, particularly in regard to such items as foreign movie DVDs, smartphones, notebook computers,. and other electronic gadgets (Tudor & Pearson, 2015). In recent years, the approval of 14 selected spaces within urban areas of the country (i.e., Special Economic Zones, or SEZ's) reveal cracks in the oppressive totalitarian regime, at least in regard to a market economy. Certainly, the country is nowhere near close to a free-market in these zones. However, locals may exchange legally accepted goods for currency. A similar situation emerged with the street or "sidewalk" hawkers found in other Asian nations such as Singapore where the marketing of goods requires a government permit, rather expensive to the poor (Austin, 1987).

Scant research exists on the social organization of the SEZ process or for that matter of the structure and functioning of a single Special Economic Zone. We predict that it must understandably reveal substantial nervousness because buyers and sellers of so many items yet they remain contraband in North Korea. Any clothing, jewelry, or cosmetics associated with the liberal Western nations continue as disallowed products. Wearing of designer blue jeans stays forbidden (Tudor & Pearson, 2015). In what must reveal bartering and under-the-table marketing of desired but illegal goods arguably must unfold with a constant "looking over the shoulder" by scrutinizing government authorities. Such a provisional marketplace provides a fleeting taste of a free or quasi-free market (i.e., grey market) even if only in selected locations. It is reasonable to forecast that extreme rigidity of feudalism and a society based on patronage and the labor of subjects for the benefit of the ruling class cannot endure absent outside funding support of allied socialistic or communistic nations. There are presently few nations willing to support the DPRK.

The failure of crops during the long drought of the 1990s, and with the reduction of outside support from the People's Republic of China and the prior Soviet Union, citizens of North Korea died by the tens of thousands receiving as little as a few hundreds of grams of food handout per person, per day by the government (Hassmann, 2012). Disallowing free exchange of goods and services identifies as a controlling feature of a totalitarian regime.

Communication and Transportation

A denial or even moderate restriction of mobility, whether across land or with an exchange of ideas through communication, ensures social control and order by the ruling government. It remains one of the few truisms in social science that a decrease in mobility accompanies a decrease in norm-breaking and conflict (Black, 1976; cf., Durkheim, 1893). Simply put, to maintain control over a people, a logical move is to restrict physical movement and speech. North Korea epitomizes a nation that denies its citizens such basic freedoms.

The DPRK regulates transportation even for its citizens desirous of moving about within the nation's boundaries. Family members traveling to visit relatives living in diverse regions of North Korea need permission to travel. As previously noted, a desire to depart the nation for visits abroad remains regulated to the extreme. The nation restricts any flow of outside information that may contaminate the mindset of the people. Radios, TV sets, and the Internet remain heavily restricted to the ruling regime's party lines only allowing propaganda emphasizing the government as the prevailing theme. Surfing the Web stays a taboo practice (United Nations, 2014).

One-Party Rule

As a point of emphasis, one should keep in mind that North Korea's "one-party rule" (the Korean Worker's Party) is itself a rather major feature insuring unity and social order. With the supreme leader (Kim Jong-un) assuming the head of the party, both the leader and the party must receive allegiance and submissiveness. Unlike bicameral or multi-systems of governmental control, a single party structure experiences little or no debate. Any dictate of the supreme leader must pass through the party relatively unchallenged. Even during general elections, Kim Jong-un was unopposed in the election. Consequently, to the extent that a nation emerges as authoritarian or as a dictatorship, one would presume low levels of traditional crime. Conversely, extreme democracies with conflicting political parties would expectedly exhibit high levels of internal conflict and high crime rates. Compare, for instance, that for most of its existence, the Singaporean system of "one-party domination" also exhibited low crime rates (see this book's chapter on Singapore).

CRIMES AGAINST HUMANITY

The United Nations concluded a study resulting in a 350-page, single-spaced, document detailing crimes against humanity in the Democratic People's Republic of Korea (United Nations, 2014). Based upon hundreds of interviews with persons fleeing North Korea, the report emphatically criticizes the nation for inhumane conduct. Crimes include extrajudicial killings or "summary executions," prolonged arbitrary detention, and torture (including rape and sexual violence). Targets of such crimes include persons adhering to Christianity or any ideology considered to introduce subversive encouragements. In addition, the U.N. report concludes North Korea guilty of denial of sustenance through discriminatory distribution of food resulting in death of segments of the population. The report claims North Korea continually denies persons repatriation by holding them against their will as a type of enforced disappearances, and determines: "the system is pitiless, pervasive, and with few equivalents in modern international affairs" (United Nations, 2014, p. 352).

LAW ENFORCEMENT

Given the closed nature of North Korea, much information on the precise structure and function of criminal justice remains unclear. We should begin with a comment that the possibility of purely private systems of administering justice found in many other nations appears nonexistent in the DPRK. Even law and order maintained at the village and small town levels still falls under the purview of the national government, and this is pervasive. In addition, the government agencies managing law and order depend on a vast array of informants who provide information on what they see or hear that might be subversive, and they themselves become operatives of the government. We can divide North Korea's formal justice operations into three categories: The Ministry of People's Security (MPS), The State Security Department (SSD), and the Korean People's Army (KPA). Considerable overlap persists between these categories. Although not generally classified as a system of justice, a fourth category of social order remains ever-present—the decrees and wishes of the Supreme Leader. His declarations commonly processed through the single political party in North Korea: The "WPK" or the "Workers' Party of Korea," treat his decrees as inviolate.

The Ministry of People's Security (MPS)

The MPS identifies with what most would associate with basic policing operations, to include traffic control and the investigation of common criminal cases. Moreover, the MPS includes a variety of security operations such as monitoring individual travel, maintenance and protection of government archives, safeguarding public officials, and providing security to government buildings. The MPS also provides management of the prison system for common criminal "non-political" offenders, and observes and keeps records on citizen's political attitudes. Personnel assigned to the MPS number about 144,000 male and female citizens dispersed throughout a dozen provinces, both rural and urban. As a policing system, the personnel wear uniforms and carry out vehicle patrols. The MPS identifies with "internal security" although not a precise classification.

It appears that North Korea's justice system reflects a heavily proactive orientation. Largely, this is dependent upon an informant system that rewards citizen reports of anti-government sentiment and of any illegal activity. Examples of organized efforts to provide informal dispute processing at the neighborhood level appear lacking. In other nations of the region, including Japan, Singapore, the Philippines, and even the bordering People's Republic of China, one finds the emergence of informal justice processing of local disputes. See, for instance, the Singaporean and Philippine networks of informal control discussed in other chapters of this book. However, a social unit termed the *inminban* does exist in North Korea that approaches a neighborhood support group. Comprised of about 30 families within a housing block or neighborhood, this group convenes periodically to discuss local problems that may include street cleaning, public beautification, or collecting food for the military. Importantly, however, this social unit also serves as a channel for transmitting state ideology down to the citizenry. This same unit may also surveil the behavior of locals particularly in regard to politically dissident affairs. The *inminban* operatives may enter a household unannounced and it is said even the number of chopsticks owned by a family may be recorded (Tudor & Pearson, 2015).

The State Security Department (SSD)

Although with some overlap with the MPS and with the North Korean military, the State Security Department (SSD) concerns itself with external affairs. In prior decades, the SSD operations fell under the MPS, but in the early 1970s, the State Security Department emerged to manage counterintelligence matters and any issues associated with political security. The SSD now pertains to what is commonly termed "secret police" (Bermudez, 2001). Functions of the SSD include searching out those charged with anti-state offenses, a category that contains anti-government and nonconforming activities and slander of the political leadership. The SSD manages prison camps for political offenders and concerns itself with counterintelligence operations at home and abroad. In addition, the SSD monitors political attitudes and manages surveillance of persons returning to North Korea.

The Korean People's Army (KPA)

We must classify the North Korean military as rather tangential to what we generally think of as police or law-enforcement elements of the criminal justice system. However, as seen in the case of Singapore, all able-bodied citizens from childhood forward must anticipate serving in some capacity in the armed services, or simply the Korean People's Army. Especially significant with North Korea is the breadth of participation of the citizenry. As an estimation, about six million persons comprise the Korean People's Army. Subdivided into six branches, all operations of the KPA fall under the rule of Kim Jong-un, the Supreme Commander. The branches include Ground Forces, Navy, Air Force, Strategic Rocket Force, Special Operations Forces, and the Worker-Peasant Red Guard. As a type of civil defense division, the Red Guard units form a reliable means of ready assistance to other more traditional policing units at the community level. With the guard units, over three million in number residing at their home areas, they rather automatically encompass a considerable reserve force of government teams who become added eyes and ears of local activities. Consequently, through conscripted service in the military for a minimum of ten years, the nation as a whole permits a substantial portion of the citizenry to perform government obligations. As a type of employment, the youth keep busy and involved in supervised activity, which is considered both a duty and honor. All branches combined, the North Korean military incorporates the largest pool of armed forces in the world (Worden, 2009).

JUDICIAL PROCESSES AND CORRECTIONS

Compared to systems of social order that include police operations, a lesser amount of information exists on the judicial or court systems of North Korea. In such a totalitarian and disciplinary regime, it may be that many of those processed through North Korean courts simply do not live to tell of it. We can say with little reservation that the North Korean judicial processes generally follow from its bordering neighbor to the north—The People's Republic of China. As with the PRC, North Korea maintains a series of courts ranging from so-called people's courts or provincial courts at the small town or more rural regions, to Central Courts in the more urban areas. As with most nations of the world, but unlike the USA, no juries decide guilt or innocence. Rather, judges selected by the Korean Worker's Party that may include several lay assessors, as in the People's Republic of China, decide cases brought by the prosecutor (Worden, 2009).

Judges do not require legal education or experience and appointments appear to be purely political. In addition to processing cases based on law and civil ordinances, a major function of judges concerns the application of political indoctrination and re-education programs. Importantly, North Korea adheres to a strict model of justice that presumes guilt of a party brought to the court by the prosecutor and the police. Although a defendant may voice a defense, whether or not a specific defense council or attorney accompanies a defendant remains unclear. Theoretically, the North Korean judicial system, as with that of the People's Republic of China, follows justice patterns situated somewhere between a Classical and a Positivistic model. Thus, a person accused as a violator of law and presented to the prosecutor by a law enforcement agent of government must accept an assumption of guilt—a very rigid and deterrent-oriented aspect of justice. On the other hand, and at least theoretically, one convicted in North Korean court of a crime must often submit to rather severe political indoctrination schemes that, although are hypothetically rehabilitative, remain ruthlessly punitive. About 20 in number, prison camps remain described as unsanitary and life-threatening, to include torture, starvation, and with public and secret executions (Kang & Rigoulot, 2005; McDonald, 2011; United Nations, 2014).

The prison camps of North Korea contain up to 200,000 prisoners and an estimated 40% die from malnutrition (McDonald, 2011; cf., United Nations, 2014).

SUMMARY

If crime statistics require cautious consideration in Western nations, including the USA, we must conclude that any available statistical information on North Korea must remain discounted. Simply put, the government of North Korea desists from any discussion about illegal activity on the part of its citizens and all reports agree the government sponsors continuous propaganda displaying the nation as faultless. As noted, what we know about North Korea's law and order problems results primarily from persons fleeing the country. We should consider a few speculations even if theoretical. First, at least from a technical point of view, a nation that imprisons so many persons must presumably have a large number of persons in violation of government regulations, even if the rules being broken remain unfounded by many. Thus, from a perspective of the North Korean government, a high rate of illegality must persist. A second sensible perspective holds that North Korea reveals a low crime rate resulting from a deterrent-oriented government apparatus that confines its citizenry to a constricted subservient existence. Restricting mobility and communication must result in keeping citizenry out of sight and out of mind. A third perspective would hold that the poverty-stricken circumstances for so many would logically result in some elevated street-level crime as a matter of survival. The number of street-children and child beggars (i.e., *kotjebi*) have been associated with famines and are predictably associated with some street-level thievery (Tudor & Pearson, 2015; cf., Hassmann, 2012; United Nations, 2014). It makes common sense that adults suffering stress from hunger and oppression may resort to lawbreaking.

The advent of grey and black markets in North Korea also reveal the influx of contraband property from the more liberal South Korea and other Westernized nations (Ruediger, 2017) and reflects an increasingly prospering activity. Additionally, the targeting of young North Korean women for illicit human trafficking, particularly for sex trade markets, frequents the news media and investigative reports (United Nations, 2014). Such illegitimate operations by their very nature increase criminal activity and continue with persistent extortion and bribery operations by North Korean government officials (Perlez, Huang, & Mozur, 2017). Of course, much of the dishonest deviant and unlawful activity falls outside any official North Korean government reports.

DISCUSSION QUESTIONS

1. Why would it be difficult to study and write about the justice system in North Korea?
2. Why would we consider North Korea "off the beaten path"?
3. What historical features of Chinese culture appear to set the stage for strict adherence to regulations and the North Korean leadership?

4. Compared to socialist and communist nations, why would we predict democratic societies would reflect relatively higher crime rates?
5. How and why would we assume North Korea would reveal a homogeneous population?
6. What does feudalism have to do with social control and possibly even rates of crime?
7. How does social mobility apply to North Korean society?
8. What do black or grey economic markets have to do with deviance and lawbreaking?
9. What are crimes against humanity, and what do they have to do with North Korea?

REFERENCES

Abrahamian, A. (2017). Should the United States try to cut tourism to North Korea? *38 North*. Washington, DC: US-Korea Institute at Johns Hopkins (School of Advanced International Studies).

Armstrong, C. (2013). *Tyranny of the weak: North Korea and the world*. Ithaca, NY: Cornell University Press.

Austin, W. T. (1987). Crime and custom in an orderly society: The Singapore prototype. *Criminology*, *25*(2), 279–294.

Bermudez, J. S. (2001). *Shield of the great leader: The Armed Forces of North Korea*. Sydney: Allen & Unwin.

Black, D. (1976). *The behavior of law*. New York: Academic Press.

Central Intelligence Agency. (2017). *The World Factbook*. Washington, DC: U.S. GPO.

Ch'oe, Y-H, Lee, P. H., & de Bary, W. T. (2000). *Sources of Korean Tradition*. Chichester, NY: Columbia University Press.

Deuchler, M. (1995). The Confucian transformation of Korea: A study of society and ideology. (Harvard-Yenching Institute Monograph Series). Harvard University Asia Center.

Durkheim, É. (1893/1964). *The division of labor in society* (G. Simpson, Trans.). New York: Macmillan.

Embassy Pages. (2017). Korea [Democratic Republic] Embassies & Consultants. Retrieved from www.embassypages.com/koreademocratic.php.

Hassmann, R. E. (2012). State Induced Famine and Penal Starvation in North Korea. *Genocide studies and prevention: An international journal*, *7*(2), 146–165.

Hunter, H.-L. (1999). *Kim Il-sung's North Korea*. Westport, CT: Praeger.

Johnson, R. (2013, April 24). A creepy journey to the hidden 5th floor of a Pyongyang hotel. *Business Insider*. New York City.

Kang C.-H., & Rigoulot, P. (2005). *The aquariums of Pyongyang: Ten years in the North Korean Gulag*. New York: Basic Books.

Kim, M. (2010). *Escaping North Korea: Defiance and hope in the world's most repressive country*. Lanham, MD: Rowan & Littlefield.

McDonald, M. (2011, May 4). North Korean prison camps massive and growing. *The New York Times*.

Paris, N., & Morris, H. (2016, May 9). North Korea: How to visit the world's most secretive country. *The Telegraph*. London.

Perlez, J., Huang, Y., & Mozur, P. (2017, May 13). How North Korea managed to defy years of sanctions. *New York Times* (p. A1). New York Times Company.

Reckless, W. (1961). *The crime problem*. New York: Appleton-Century Crofts, Inc.

Ruediger, F. (2017, April 6). "Consumerism in North Korea: The Kwangbok area shopping center. *38 North*. U.S.-Korea Institute, John Hopkins School of Advanced International Studies.

Suh, J.-J. (2012). *Origins of North Korea's* Juche: *Colonialism, war, and development*. Lanham: Lexington Books.

Tudor, D., & Pearson, J. (2015). *North Korea Confidential*. North Clarendon, VT: Tuttle Publishing.

United Nations. (2014). *Report of the detailed findings of the commission of inquiry on human rights in the Democratic People's Republic of Korea*. New York: U.N. Human Rights Council. Department of State. 2016. U.S. Passports and International Travel. (North Korea). Retrieved from https://travel.state.gov/content/passports/en/country/korea-north.html

U.S. Department of State. (2016). *Remarks, press releases, and fact sheets pertaining to North Korea*. Washington, DC: Bureau of Public Affairs.

Wertz, D., Ho, J. J., & Kim, I. (2016). Issue Brief: DPRK Diplomatic Relations. Washington, DC: The National Committee on North Korea.

Williamson, L. (2011). Delving into North Korea's mystical cult of personality. BBC News (Seoul). Retrieved from http://www.bbc.co.uk/news/world-asia-16336991.

Worden, R. L. (2009). *North Korea Country Study*. Washington, DC: Library of Congress.

PART VI

The Hybrid Family of Law

CHAPTER 13

The Philippine Model

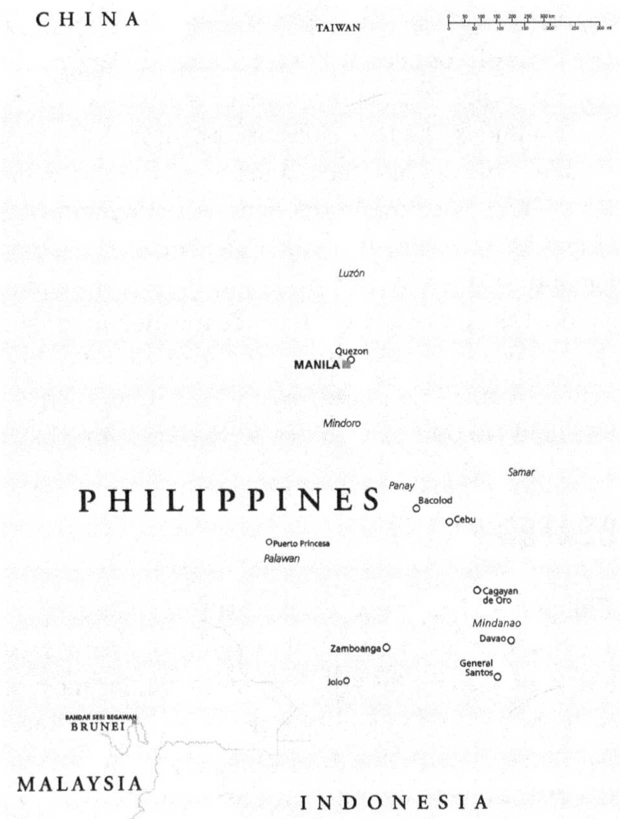

© Peter Hermes Furian/Shutterstock.com

INTRODUCTION

Many nations of the world likely reflect patterns of the "Hybrid" family of laws. However, we feel that The Republic of the Philippines in Southeast Asia, referred to simply as the "Philippines" or the "Philippine Islands" appropriately matches the Hybrid example of law better than most. The Philippine Islands represent a country that has been occupied or colonized by multiple peoples. The most long-lasting occupation began with the conquest of the islands in 1521 A.D. by Ferdinand Magellan under the service of King Philip of Spain, an occupation that lasted for nearly 400 years—thus the origin of the name Philippines. Although Magellan and his mariners claimed the islands after a battle, Magellan was killed by Lapu-Lapu, a Muslim chief. Other occupying nations included the Netherlands, Portugal, Great Britain, Japan, and the United States. Yet, even before Western contact and colonization, influence was felt by Chinese and Islamic cultures, and earlier by settlers drifting in primitive boats from the Malay Peninsula that archaeological evidence suggests occurred as much as 3,000 years ago (Zaide, 1957).

The four centuries of Spanish conquest left its mark most notably by conversion of the population to Catholicism, one of the original purposes of Magellan's early voyage. Today about 83% adhere to Catholic traditions, 9% to various protestant faiths, with about 5% observing Islamic customs that made their way into the islands several centuries before Magellan (CIA World Factbook, 2018). Filipinos celebrate the nation's declaration of independence from Spanish rule dating from 1898. Nonetheless, the independence was not recognized by the latest occupying nation of the United States until July 4, 1946, at the end of World War II. The Republic of the Philippines has existed as an independent nation for only about seven decades and experiences the impact of earlier occupations to the present day. Because the Philippine Islands have been populated and/or occupied by diverse cultures from the East and West hemispheres, the nature of its law and social order is mixed resulting in its hybrid character.

WHY OFF THE BEATEN PATH?

What is it about the Philippine Islands that sets it apart from many other nations as being off the beaten path, or a nation that has been relatively ignored, even if mistakenly by criminal justice scholars? Two reasons account for this. First, as noted, for most of Philippine history, the islands have been subjected to foreign occupation. This rather inevitably relegated the islands to the marginal status of territorial possessions. As such, even though the lands and inhabitants existed as a distinct geo-cultural entity, they were hidden under the wraps of its politically dominant external controllers, particularly the almost four centuries of Spanish occupation and the nearly half-century of United States authority. Even with independence and separation from the USA, the Philippines agreed to an American naval and air base remaining in their country until 1992 (Anderegg, 2005).

Second, we must acknowledge that until rather recently the Philippine Islands remained geographically secluded from mainstream European traditions. This has been likely true of other isolated island cultures that held unique systems of government and also remained sheltered from outside view. Isolation by thousands of miles of ocean understandably relegated the Philippine Island region of Southeast Asia as unfamiliar to more conventional Western audiences that witnessed the birth of criminology.

GEO-DEMOGRAPHIC BACKDROP

Understanding the Philippines must include a discussion of its geography and population features. The nation is comprised of slightly more than 7,100 islands that stretch over 1,000 miles in the South China Sea between Taiwan to the north and Borneo to the south. However, as far as is known, most of the population of over 100 million resides on less than 400 of these islands. If all the islands were squeezed together, the total land mass of the Philippines would approximate that of the state of Arizona. Consequently, we are talking about a highly populated nation; the 12th highest in the world in 2015 (The World Factbook, 2015). With the exception of the metropolitan region of Manila, the capital city, situated on the large northern island of Luzon, and the city of Cebu located in the center island area of the Philippines known as the Visayan region, the nation's bourgeoning population is somewhat disguised by the spread of its people throughout the numerous isles. Mindanao is the large island to the south that is less developed, more rural, and home to Muslim populations that are in periodic conflict with the Catholic majority. Because the hundreds of populated islands are reachable most commonly by boat and by air only between the more populated islands, the nation takes on a rather fragmented arrangement of island cultures sometimes unfamiliar to each other. Such a geography sets the stage for a necessary discussion of the difficulty presented by multiple disconnected island nations especially in regard to the maintenance of social order and national government.

ISLAND COMPLEXITY AND SOCIAL ORDER

It makes common sense that a small, cohesive population would be easier to contain and manage from a legal and governmental standpoint than a nation such as the Philippines with a large population spread throughout hundreds of dispersed islands, many far removed from one another. The dilemma in such a nation is not limited to maintenance of governmental administration. The nation's geography and lack of interisland transportation and even communication for most of its history resulted in the islands developing a multitude of distinct and unique cultures. Estimates differ but some scholars claim about 185 languages are spoken amongst the islands resulting from extended isolation from each other (Lewis, 2015). Even today, a native Filipino traveling to distant islands of the Philippines will commonly experience difficulty or find it impossible to communicate with other Filipinos. Although *Tagalog* was established as a national language in 1987, its use is sporadic or absent in many of the outer islands. The question remaining is how can a cohesive social order be maintained in such a diverse environment? The answer is found in the nature of informal social control present throughout the islands.

THE *BARANGAY* JUSTICE SYSTEM

Any attempt to understand social control in the Philippines must begin with what is now termed barangay justice, *katarungang pambarangay* or community justice in the Tagalog language (Austin, 1999; Silliman, 1991). The term barangay now translates as "community," but is likely derived from the ancient Malay word for boat (*balanghai* or *balangay*). This is significant when we consider that the Philippine Islands were first populated by travelers from the Malay Peninsula. The argument is that sea voyagers, and seafaring people everywhere, form cohesive communities while aboard the ship at sea. Every ship has a captain who must maintain tight control among all passengers and crew while aboard the vessel. However, the argument also presumes that a ship's captain must remain in the good graces of all subordinates. The captain cannot simply place in the brig every deckhand who violates a rule, otherwise maintenance of the ship would eventually suffer. Due to the very nature of being aboard a self-contained ship, a system of peacekeeping logically emphasizes mediation rather than absolute penal servitude. A ship's captain must be respected and even esteemed rather than the often stereotyped image of the punitive tyrant.

Historians suggest that as the boat communities landed in the numerous isles that later became the Philippines, each boat settlement formed a social control network with an elected village captain (Hidalgo, 2002). The captain supervised the island community emphasizing informal justice by maintaining harmony through reconciliation between those in dispute. Throughout the multiple foreign occupations, the one aspect of social organization that appears to have remained rather constant is the informal system of order-maintenance centering on the local village captain, and to this day referred to as the Barangay Captain, presumably a throwback to the days of "balanghai" or boat supervision by the skipper. During the centuries of Spanish occupation, the term "barrio" replaced the original word barangay (i.e., and thus barrio captain). However, in 1978, Philippine president Ferdinand Marcos, through presidential decree, reversed the term barrio to barangay in an effort to reclaim some of the fading native heritage.

If we fast-forward to today, we find slightly more than 42,000 barangays in the Philippines. Each barangay, with an average of several thousand people, reflects a geographic boundary that is considered the lowermost political or governmental district. Multiple adjoining barangays merge to form one of the 1,490 municipalities in the Philippines, and the municipalities coalesce to form the 141 cities of the nation. The cities are subsequently spread throughout

81 provinces of the many Philippine Islands. Every province contains one or more cities and numerous municipalities that are further subdivided into barangays. Technically speaking, even Metro-Manila, a sprawling urban area with a population of about twelve million is itself comprised of 17 cities, many municipalities, and 1,704 barangays (Barangay Justice Handbook, 2013).

Stated differently, if one were to parachute into the Philippines, no matter where they would touch ground, they would technically land in one of the 42,000 barangays whether rural or urban. In the more rural regions, a barangay can be as small as a few hundred households but can reach thousands in major urban areas. Additionally, although it is sometimes overlooked, the average barangay may also be subdivided into smaller units (i.e., *puroks*) best described as neighborhood subdivisions. Even if the barangay is still considered the bottom-most official level of government, at the purok, or more neighborhood level, one may also find an informally elected organizational structure that functions to assist residents with any of numerous necessities, complications, or grievances encountered with daily life.

Such a comprehensive organizational structure has significant benefits. Any assistance desired by a resident or even visitor to the Philippines could start at the barangay or even purok level of organization. Such aid or support might pertain to any of a wide variety of needs, be they in regard to housing, schools, transportation, basic utilities such as water, electricity and sanitation, as well as security issues. Each barangay will typically have an office location where the captain carries out his or her duties (i.e., the Barangay Hall). However, it is likely that a purok organization, especially in the more rural regions, will embody a loosely structured committee operating out of private community residences.

The checkerboard maze of thousands of barangays and puroks should not be viewed as possessing a primary purpose of establishing law and order although that is surely a recognizable function. Rather, the purok committees and barangay halls operate first and foremost as information centers, and places to air citizen concerns at the most local level, whether in the cities or in the distant hinterlands.

JUDICIAL PROCESSES

The laws and various court systems evident today throughout the Philippine Islands result from the many hundreds of years, if not millennia, of settlement by outsiders. All have left their mark. The nearly half century of occupation by the United States is significant, especially in regard to being the most recent outside influence. It left behind English as a second language, and a restructuring of the Philippine Constitution that even today, after a number of Philippine reforms, remains similar in many ways to the American system of justice and law.

Today the Philippine government is structured on a democratic system of popular vote. Yet, the fact remains that the nation still feels the impact from the centuries of feudal colonialism left by the Spanish. Much of the lands of the Philippine Islands were granted by Spanish Kings to lesser aristocrats who came to the islands to supervise political divisions whether locally at the village level or even to occupy provincial governorships. Patterned after the Spanish feudal system, Filipino natives worked the land and haciendas for the overseers, sometimes for wages and in some cases enjoyed the right to work a piece of the land for themselves. Such land tenure by local laborers was, and remains in some places to this day, a complex arrangement of previous inheritors who have been given the right to work the land but with actual ownership of the property murkily linked to a distant but original landlord (Fallows, 1988).

Even after the Philippine Islands were granted to the United States as spoils of the Spanish-American War, democratic elections remained tainted by allegiances to early landlords. The association between voters and the elected officials still reserved some of the feudal traditions of referring to or thinking about the elected officials as patriarchal or matriarchal affiliations rather than as local citizens democratically elected to carry out the people's self-governing aspiration (Pepa, 2013).

During the centuries of Spanish rule in the Philippines, the judicial system was biased by underhanded influence between Spanish landlords and the court system. A revamping of the entire judicial system during the American occupation into more purely democratic institutions still finds substantial perceptions of corruption throughout the government and into the court systems. Ironically, a distrust or fear of excessively strong government by Filipinos may have been enhanced by the American presence until the mid-20th century that still retained as part of its own original heritage a dislike of strong government (See, for instance, Reckless, 1961).

Today, the Philippine Islands observe the three branches of government: legislative, judicial, and executive. The judicial system is comprised of courts that operate throughout the islands. At the top of the hierarchy and situated in the metropolitan Manila area is the Supreme Court with a Chief Justice and 14 Associate Justices who hear cases from the Court of Appeals and issues that pertain to infractions of the constitution. At its discretion, the Supreme Court may sit with three, five, or seven members. The Court of Appeals is headed by a Presiding Justice and 68 Associate Justices as members. Appeals from lower courts may be heard either in the Manila area on the island of Luzon or in the city of Cebu in the Visayan region of the Philippines, or in the city of Cagayan de Oro located on the large southern island of Mindanao. The lower courts are referred to as Regular Courts and are dispersed throughout the islands and classified as either Regional Trial Courts (i.e., that number about 950) in the more urbanized areas, or Municipal Trial Courts (i.e., numbering about 900) generally situated in the smaller towns. There are also Special Courts that receive cases pertaining to tax appeals, or anti-graft and corrupt practices.

Special Courts also include Sharia Courts that operate only in the Muslim populated area on the southern island of Mindanao. With a long and complex history, the Muslim population has remained relatively separate from the Christian majority and have in recent years gained approval to unite five of Mindanao's 25 provinces into a self-governing district referred to as the ARMM (Autonomous Region of Muslim Mindanao), and more recently named the *Bangsamora* (nation and Moro) Autonomous Region (Aquino, 2014). Muslim and Christian populations, particularly on the southern island of Mindanao, have carried on a contentious relationship for centuries. As with other regions of the world the Islamic legal traditions and the Sharia Courts adhere closely to the sacred writings outlined in the Qur'an. The distinctiveness of Islamic law compared to the common law of much of the Western world is one reason the dominant Christian government of the Philippines voted to allow the creation of the Bangsamora Autonomous Region. However, it must be noted that for much of the history of Muslim-Christian relations in the Philippines, the two peoples lived in harmony and even intermarried. Nonetheless, periodic skirmishes resulting in bloodshed leave behind substantial distrust and cynicism between the religious and cultural ideologies in the Southern regions of the islands.

ALTERNATIVE DISPUTE RESOLUTION

Understanding how the Philippine Judicial system works must begin with the fundamental court process embedded in each of the thousands of barangays. At least half of the population of the nation still reside outside the major urban areas and are often far removed even from municipalities. Also, remember that even the cities are subdivided into barangays. Thus, at the most local level, many rely completely on the Barangay Captain to assist with grievances, disputes, and even crimes. It is likely true that most violations of law and the vast number of neighborly disagreements begin with a visit to the Barangay Hall. Because the Barangay Captain is an elected government representative, it makes some sense to presume that the vast majority of judicial processing originates at the barangay level. It is likely that most behavioral infractions that have their start in the local neighborhood puroks and barangays never actually reach the municipal or regional courts. Rather, they are managed in what is now referred to as Alternative Dispute Resolution (ADR), a practice sanctioned by the national government.

As hinted at earlier, it may very well be that reliance on informal resolution of behavioral infractions had its beginning in the earliest boat communities that drifted ashore in the distant past. Regardless, some vestige of informal justice or what might be called out-of-court dispute processing has existed in the thousands of local communities for generations. In earlier decades the process of depending on the barangay captain to manage local conflicts was referred in the Spanish language as *arreglo* (i.e., agreement or understanding) and later as "amicable settlement" or community justice (Austin, 1999; Machado, 1979; Silliman, 1991).

At its most fundamental level in the neighborhoods, the process of Alternative Dispute Resolution can reflect simple mediation by the barangay captain. In such cases, the captain, elected to the position by popular vote and known to all in the community, is frequently able to convince disputing residents to put their differences aside, and if necessary, agree to disagree. The important issue is to maintain harmony in the community. Such a mediation process does not aim to find guilt of either disputing party. The end goal is to convince disputants to reconcile their differences. Successful and popular captains rely on qualities of personal persuasion.

There have been attempts to formalize the barangay captain's unassuming process of mediation between quarreling citizens. For example, the captain is technically given a period of 15 days to resolve disputes through mediation that are brought before the Barangay Hall. If an attempt at reconciliation of disputing parties is unsuccessful, the captain may initiate a process of arbitration with the approval of both sides of the dispute. At this level, a decision would result in a determination of guilt by calling upon selected members of the community to hear both sides of a dispute and to report their findings to the captain. Community members who agree to hear such cases comprise a group (i.e., the *Lupon*) of 10–20 members handpicked by the captain. Each disputing party will have a voice to alternately eliminate members of the Lupon deemed objectionable until a small committee of three persons (i.e., the *Pangkat*) is agreed upon to hear both sides of the case and to arbitrate a final decision. Although this process appears to resemble a small jury, in fact, the term jury is not used.

Over the decades, parties in dispute who choose to have their case go to arbitration at the barangay level do so without legal counsel. The philosophy has been to keep the procedures as relaxed and unceremonious as possible. In the 1980s, the small "barangay halls" where the lupon and pangkat were expected to perform their duties were not often used, and in some cases the buildings were used for other purposes or abandoned. The arbitration process and surely any mediation would more likely take place in a café or under a tree in the more rural communities. Court records are notoriously inadequate at the barangay level (Shoemaker, 1996; cf., Austin, 1999, 2012). Due to the cumbersome process of calling upon a lupon and pangkat for arbitration, it is likely that politically popular barangay captains strive for success at a mediation stage and forego the more complex arbitration procedures. A captain who is influential and successful with mediation will be looked upon favorably at re-election time.

The Alternative Dispute Resolution process is accepted at the national level through congressional legislation as a legitimate practice and an alternative to the higher municipal or city courts (Pangalangan, 2001). Recordkeeping at the "mediation" stage is understandably superficial or even non-existent. It appears clear that any attempt to measure crime rates, particularly at the national level, would fall short when we consider that so many disputes and even issues of lawbreaking are quelled behind the scenes through mediation at the most local neighborhood level. A case that is unresolved at the barangay level can be filed with a municipal trial court. There are no juries in the regular trial courts and all cases represent bench trials decided by a judge after hearing both sides of a case between prosecutorial and defense attorneys. It is also common that some cases thought to be too trivial to a municipal trial judge can be returned to a barangay captain for resolution.

ENFORCING THE LAW

Consider for a moment how difficult it must be to manage law and order in a nation with such a diverse history of colonization and also many hundreds of isolated islands that to this day lack convenient and inexpensive interisland transportation or communication. As recently as 1991 the Philippine Islands united its two national police forces into a single system now referred to as the Philippine National Police or PNP (2015). Today, the PNP boasts about 160,000 officers dispersed throughout the many islands and provinces. However, prior to 1991, and throughout the first half of the 20th century, the Republic of the Philippines provided policing tasks in the municipalities and cities and combined police functions with fire and jail operations under what was known as the Integrated National Police or INP. The INP suffered a lack of smooth operations on so many isolated island locations with their function to maintain law and order in the cities and towns including traffic control. A second national police organization named the Philippine Constabulary (PC) also operated throughout the islands but focused more on major crimes that might involve interisland and distant jurisdictions. Over the past few decades, the earlier INP and the PC activities have been contained in the single Philippine National Police, headquartered in Manila and maintain its operations in all the nation's 81 provinces, and in all cities and major municipalities.

Certainly from hindsight, the organization of various police operations was complicated with the transition from the centuries of Spanish rule, and the transition to American supervision. Also, with the onset of WW II, the Japanese took control of the Philippines between 1941 and 1945 resulting in all policing functions placed under the authority of the Japanese military. To complicate matters, with an effort to provide some kind of systematic law enforcement and military control over Muslim uprisings in Mindanao in the southern islands, and periodic communist rebellion, President Ferdinand Marcos declared martial law that lasted from 1972 until 1981. This basically positioned all policing and military operations under his command, with the legislative and Supreme Court replaced with rule by Presidential Decree.

With the end of Martial Law in 1981, the popularity of President Marcos weakened. After his political rival, Senator Ninoy Aquino was mysteriously assassinated, Marcos called for snap elections and declared himself as winner. Millions took to the streets which led to what was called the "People Power Revolution" of 1986 that elevated Cory Aquino, the wife of assassinated Ninoy Aquino, as President of the Philippines. Soon thereafter the Philippine Constitution was revised and within a few years saw the emergence of the present-day Philippine

National Police. With multiple foreign occupations, a world war, martial law, assassination, and political revolution, it is understandable that providing police functions would be complex and problematic.

Constructing accurate cross-national comparisons of crime rates is problematic at best. Were such possible, we would cautiously predict that the Philippine Islands would still fare reasonably well. Why would this be so? We must again return to a discussion of justice processing at the barangay level.

THE BARANGAY *TANOD*

With the likely exception of the very smallest of the 42,000 barangays, one can expect to find in each of the community organizations a group of persons recruited by the captain to form what is called the "tanod" or guard. Depending on the size and complexity of the community, whether rural or urban, the barangay tanod will vary in size and structure. An average sized barangay of about 2,000 residents may have a barangay force of about six or eight persons, male or female, who assist the captain with such duties as public disorders, emergencies, or anything that may threaten peace or public safety. Throughout the entire nation, there are an estimated 700,000 members of the barangay tanod (Aben, 2004). In the rural areas and more isolated islands, the tanod assemblies represent members of the local community whom the captain can rely upon for assistance. In this sense, they would comprise what to some Westerners are members of a neighborhood watch program. The tanod do not generally wear uniforms although in the more urban areas they can be seen with shirts and caps designating them as tanod, especially when tasked to assist with traffic control. It should be recalled that the barangay captain is also a member of the community elected by popular vote, and who wears no uniform.

Even with a description of the tanod as a loosely structured cadre of neighborhood residents, the fact remains that they exemplify the lowest level of law enforcement in the Philippines. They are not known to carry firearms or to have sworn duties of law enforcement as apply to the Philippine National Police, although they can be deputized by the Philippine National Police as needed. Members of the barangay tanod receive a small stipend from the local government. It is a safe presumption that the more formal municipal and city police would be well aware of what citizens make up the barangay tanod. Indeed, the tanod will surely speak the native dialect of the barangay and would be indispensable to the more regimented police forces sometimes situated in more distant locations.

When at all possible, the successful barangay captain will maintain peace and order within the barangay without having to resort to higher police agencies or the more formal and ritualistic judicial proceedings such as reliance upon the lupon. With the assistance of the tanod, law and order is kept at the neighborhood level. With a reluctance to maintain complete written records of minor infractions and violations of law, crime rates are automatically held to a minimum even if artificially so, particularly in the many rural barangays.

JAILS, PRISONS, AND CORRECTIONS

As of 2013 there were about 10.5 million persons locked up around the world for various crimes. The USA has the highest proportion of its population incarcerated with about 716 per 100,000 persons. Half of the nations of the world have a ratio of less than 150 persons imprisoned per 100,000 persons. The Republic of the Philippines incarcerates about 111 persons per 100,000 for a total of about 108,000 prisoners. This puts the Philippines at the bottom third of nations in regard to incarceration rates (For complete listing and discussion, see Walmsley, 2013; cf., World Prison Brief, 2014). As is true throughout the world, a sizeable proportion of prison populations pertain to persons jailed for pre-trial detention; about 60% in the Philippines. Also, in the Philippines, females account for about 8% of the prison population with juveniles accounting for less than 1% (Institute for Criminal Policy Research, 2014; cf., Austin, 2012).

Prison inmates in the Philippines are kept in seven national prisons and over 1,100 smaller jails and detention facilities spread through the island's provinces, cities, and municipalities. Because of the past centuries of foreign occupation, war, and the isolation of numerous islands, some Philippine prisons do hold notorious reputations. Apparently, the issue of escape from prison was not of much concern in earlier years with prison camps located on remote islands. The western island of Palawan was such a place that held lawbreakers in a prison camp setting where they worked farms and provided for their own well-being. A similar situation applied to the far removed prison camp near Davao City on the southern island of Mindanao. During WW II, the Americans used the camps for holding Japanese prisoners and the same camps held American prisoners of war when the Japanese controlled the islands.

Although the island prisons were presumed to be escape-proof, descriptions of the various detention facilities today suggest a rehabilitative rather than a punitive ideology. Between 1905 and 1989, the various places of incarceration were governed by the National Bureau of Prisons. In 1989, the system was renamed the Bureau of Corrections. All of the larger prisons and prison farms allow inmates to choose among various work specialties, engage in agro-industrial projects to help maintain the prison, and to provide a modest source of income for prisoners (Bureau of Corrections, 2014).

Beginning with the American occupation of the Philippines during the early years of the 20th century, a system of probation and parole was introduced but was not fully established until the 1970s. Today, a highly organized system of community supervision operates in all of the nation's provinces under the Parole and Probation Administration headquartered in Manila. Annually, the administration provides community supervision to about 30,000 probationers and 14,000 parolees (Parole and Probation, 2015).

The viewpoints and goals of community supervision, referred to as a "therapeutic community" by the parole and probation administration, fit well with the barangay justice system of social organization characteristic of the Philippine Islands. A probationer will rather routinely remain in a cohesive community where support from family and neighbors would be more quickly realized than in the more modern urban areas. Even in the densely populated urban areas of the Philippines it should be recalled that tight-knit neighborhoods of the barangay and even purok systems remain intact and can provide some assistance with parolees and also those sentenced to the community on probation rather than prison.

SUMMARY

The Republic of the Philippines reveals a nation whose geography impacts how the justice system developed over the centuries and how law and order is processed into contemporary times. We refer here to the straightforward fact that the Philippines is comprised of over 7,000 atolls and land masses that worked over the years to disperse people such that they formed distinct cultures and even languages. This can be both a positive and a negative in regard to maintaining justice over a combined population surpassing 110 million. On the positive front, we see a nation that has from its very beginning worked to maintain an informal justice system based on the simple fact that residents of often small islands become landlocked, forcing residents to work together as a rather cohesive arrangement of neighborhoods and villages. Justice was, from the very beginning of Spanish occupation of the islands, organized so that neighborhoods elected leaders (captains) to informally oversee disputes and community problems. Generally, such a community-based justice system is considered constructive and encouraging. The negative may be that it then becomes challenging for the geographically distant national government to implement rules and policies deemed best for the large collection of islands. In many cases, isolated islanders may not maintain contact with or care much about national politics.

Consequently, it becomes rather difficult to discuss crime rates in this highly fragmented nation. A case could be made that rates of crime at the village level and in separate islands might be low, compared to high rates of discontent and lawbreaking in the larger urban regions of the capital city of Manila, with over 20 million residents (CIA World Factbook, 2018). Not surprisingly, with overpopulation comes health problems, poverty, and underemployment. After multiple foreign occupations by Spanish, Japanese, and the United States, the Philippines has only in the past eight decades enjoyed political independence. Conflict between Muslims and the dominant Catholic population has experienced intermittent uprisings in recent decades, sometimes prompting national leaders to declare martial law. The current President of the nation, Rodrigo Duterte, from the southern island of Mindanao, is taking a hard-nosed stand to resolve conflict, whether street crime or terrorist activity. His actions have led to polarizing political disagreements among the citizenry (Teehankee, 2016).

DISCUSSION QUESTIONS

1. Why would we place the Republic of the Philippines in the category of the hybrid family of laws?
2. Does it make sense to consider the Philippines as a justice system that is "off the beaten path"?
3. In regard to the overriding issue of maintaining harmony and providing social control for a nation's people, what is it that is relevant at all levels of criminal justice in the Philippines whether we are talking about the police, courts, or a correctional system?
4. Why would we presume that a nation comprised of numerous islands would be problematic in regard to law and order? Is this necessarily true in contemporary times and in highly modernized societies?
5. What is the value of establishing neighborhood systems of dispute processing? How might there be both pros and cons to such a system?
6. What does recordkeeping have to do with crime rates?

REFERENCES

Aben, E. L. (2004, March 12). DILG trains barangay *tanods* as partners of cops in peace drive. *Manila Bulletin.*

Anderegg, C. R. (2005). *The ash warriors.* Air Force History and Museums Programs. Washington, DC: Government Printing Office.

Aquino, N. (2014). Speech of President Aquino at the turnover ceremony of the draft of Bansamoro basic law. Manila: Office of the Presidential Adviser on the Peace Process.

Austin, T. (1999). *Banana justice: Field notes on Philippine crime and custom.* Westport, CT: Praeger.

Austin, T. (2012). Takers keepers, losers weepers: Theft as customary play in the southern Philippines. *Journal of Folklore Research*, *49*(3).

Barangay Justice (*Katarungang Pambarangay*) Handbook. (2013). Department of Interior and Local Government, Quezon City, Philippines.

Bureau of Corrections. (2014). Annual Report. Manila: Department of Justice. Retrieved from www.bucor.gov.ph/

CIA World Factbook. (2018). Langley, VA: Central Intelligence Agency.

Fallows, J. (1988). A damaged culture. *The Atlantic Monthly*, *260*(5), 48–58.

Hidalgo, J. (2002). Cacique democracy and future prospects in the Philippines. In H. M. McFerson (Ed.), *Mixed blessing: The impact of the American colonial experience on politics and society in the Philippines.* Westport, CT: Greenwood Press.

Institute for Criminal Policy Research. (2014). World prison brief. London, England: University of London, School of Law.

Lewis, P. M. (2015). *Ethnologue: Languages of the world* (18th ed.). Dallas, TX: International Linguistics Center.

Machado, K. G. (1979). Politics and dispute processing in the rural Philippines. *Pacific Affairs, 52.*

Pangalangan, P. C. (2001). *Alternative modes of dispute processing.* Institute of Developing Economies. Chibal, Japan: Japan External Trade Organization (IDE-JETRO).

Parole and Probation. (2015). Annual Report. Manila: Department of Justice. Retrieved from www.probation.gov.ph/

Pepa, R. (2013, August 8). Feudalism and colonialism: The case of the Philippines. *News Junkie Post.* Washington, DC: News Junkie Post Publishing.

Philippine National Police (PNP). (2015). Annual report. Quezon City: Philippines. Retrieved from www.pnp.gov.ph

Reckless, W. C. (1961). *The crime problem* (3rd ed.). New York: Appleton-Century-Crofts, Inc.

Shoemaker, D. J. (1996). Juvenile corrections in the Philippines: The barangay system. *Journal of Offender Rehabilitation*, *24*(1), 39–52.

Silliman, G. S. (1991). A political analysis of the Philippines' *katarungang pambarangay* system of informal justice through mediation. *Law & Society Review*, *19*(2), 279–301.

Teehankee, J. C. (2016). Duterte's resurgent nationalism in the Philippines: A discursive institutionalist analysis. *Journal of Currant Southeast Asian Affairs*, *35*(3), 69–89.

Walmsley, R. (2015). *World Prison Population List* (10th ed.). London: International Centre for Prison Studies.

The World Factbook. (2015). Central Intelligence Agency, Washington, DC: Office of Public Affairs.

World Prison Brief (Philippines). (2014). London: Institute for Criminal Policy Research.

Zaide, G. F. (1957). *Philippine Political and Cultural History.* Manila: Philippine Educational Company.

CHAPTER 14

The South Africa Model

© Peter Hermes Furian/Shutterstock.com

INTRODUCTION

The Republic of South Africa lies on the southern tip of Africa. Its western, southern, and eastern borders are the Atlantic and Indian Oceans; and its neighbors to the north and west are Swaziland, Mozambique, Zimbabwe, Botswana, and Namibia. Oddly, the Kingdom of Lesotho is sandwiched around the center of South Africa.

The United Nations estimates the population of South Africa in 2017 to be 55,398,546 million (Worldometers, 2017). The percentages of the racial makeup of the country based on the 2017 World Fact Book is African 80.2%, White 8.4%, Colored 8.8%, Asian 2.5% (The World Factbook). There are 11 official languages in South Africa and several unofficial dialects. As well, there are several religious denominations in the country with protestant being the most dominant—36.6%.

Despite the long period of apartheid from 1948 to the early 1990s (Abel, 1995; Boddy-Evans, 2017), South Africa is highly developed and next to Nigeria, it has the largest economy in the continent of Africa. The country is one of the largest producers of minerals, and it produces close to half of Africa's electricity output. It is the only country in Africa that has been classified as a newly industrialized country (Kuepper, 2017). Newly industrialized countries are countries whose economies are determined by economists to be above those of developing countries, but fall short of being classified as developed.

HISTORY OF SOUTH AFRICAN LAW

One cannot discuss the South African Justice System without discussing its history of colonialism. The Dutch arrived at the Cape of Good Hope in 1652. As part of their settlement process, they introduced Roman-Dutch Law. Roman-Dutch Law was primarily applied in civil cases, even though it dominated South African legal practices for about 150 years despite the fact that judges who enforced the law were neither trained in it, nor in civil law in general.

For the first 150 years of South African colonial history, a variation of civil law was applied in the country. Civil law was used to regulate business transactions but its use morphed into regulating human relationships, particularly those between Europeans and their indigenous servants. A spate in British presence in the country necessitated the opening of a court of criminal appeal in 1808, a circuit court in 1811, and in 1813, judicial proceedings were made open for public observation (Klug, 2002).

With the above transformations, it was only inevitable that English replaced Dutch as the official language, and more English institutions and processes proliferated the country. As an example, in 1827, the Cape Supreme Court was established, and in 1832, a near complete revamp of the judicial system was made. Certain caveats that required the preservation of aspects of Roman-Dutch law were in place; but a series of events including the abolition of slavery, and enlarging the scope of equality among "free coloured persons" made English and English law staples of South Africa (Klug, 2002). Yet, class differences existed and racial segregation was evident, and things only got worse after the parliamentary election of 1948.

The Nationalist Government enacted bills that, in essence, institutionalized apartheid. Citizens were to register their race as this was necessary to keep the races separate. The Unlawful Organizations Act of 1960 banned the African National Congress (ANC) and Pan Africanist Congress (PAC)—organizations that were in place to oppose and combat apartheid. Defiance to apartheid continued with the African National Congress (ANC) spearheading the course. Despite the numerous challenges big and small, riots, and killings, apartheid persisted, but with resilience, shift of attitude toward inclusiveness, and mounting international support for those fighting against apartheid, the end of apartheid was inevitable. In August 1989, The Organization of African Unity adopted the ANC's Harare Declaration, ad hoc guidelines for the country's Bill of Rights. South Africa's 5th Constitution was drawn up in 1994 after apartheid was disbanded, and became effective on February 1997. In efforts to put its sordid history of apartheid in abeyance, the Truth and Reconciliation Commission (TRC) was established in 1996. This commission was tasked with providing restorative justice to victims directly identified as suffering gravely from the scourges of apartheid, and to usher the country into a human rights respecting democratic country.

WHY SOUTH AFRICA IS PART OF THIS STUDY

South Africa's history of colonialism and apartheid, its mix of people, its diversity marked by 11 official languages, and its pluralistic justice system set the country apart. Further, South Africa has produced two of the world's most known human rights activists, both Nobel Peace Prize holders the late President Nelson Mandela and Arch Bishop Desmond Tutu. South Africa has been heralded for its peaceful transition from a coercive and separatist country to a democratic society reveled as Africa's best.

South Africa is the only country in Africa classified as a Newly Industrialized Country (NIC). Its infrastructure and Gross Domestic Product far exceed those of other African countries. The country is among the largest producers of minerals, and at one time was ranked as the 26th "largest trading nation" (Klug, 2002). While its rankings may fluctuate, there is no denying that it remains at the top of Africa's most progressive countries (Klug).

The country is hailed as exemplary in its protection of human rights, although the jury is still out on this. In 1996, South Africa created the Truth and Reconciliation Commission chaired by Arch Bishop Tutu. The commission declared apartheid a crime against humanity.

In 2006, South Africa became the first country in Africa to recognize same sex union, in essence, positioning itself as the most progressive country in the continent. In 2010, South Africa was host to the FIFA World Cup tournament, another first in Africa.

With regard to criminal justice, South Africa is included in this book because of its efforts to modernize its justice system, and again, to be an example in Africa on the most forward-thinking ways to combat crime, even if being exemplary is not its goal. While not yet in its polished state, South Africa's system of justice is superior relatively to those of the majority of African nations. It can at least boast of better intermediate programs; for example, house arrest, probation, and parole. Many of these intermediate programs are non-existent in many African countries.

INTRODUCTION TO SOUTH AFRICA'S SYSTEM OF JUSTICE

The Criminal Justice System of South Africa is relatively progressive especially when examined in the context of other African countries. Given its history, South Africa's criminal justice system is influenced by, and incorporates aspects of, the English, Dutch, and its own indigenous laws. Act number 108 of the 1996 Constitution is the bedrock of South Africa's current criminal justice system. Section 12 of the 1996 Constitution guarantees the people freedom and security; section 14 right to privacy; section 32 right to access of information; section 35 right against self-incrimination, right to counsel, right to speedy trial, right to confront adversaries among others. Besides these constitutional protections, the Criminal Procedure Act of 1977 No. 51 is also instrumental in guiding criminal trials.

As a precursor to the current criminal justice system of South Africa, the 1996 National Crime Prevention Strategy (NCPS) projected crime prevention rather than crime control. Such shift in ideology was necessary to better comprehend the root causes of crime, and to generate better ways of minimizing crime. To this end, the NCPS focused on combating crime through "re-engineering the criminal justice system, reducing crime through environmental design, community values and education," and addressing transnational crime, among other initiatives (Pelser & Rauch, 2001).

The 1998 White Paper on Safety and Security legislation strategic goal was intended to create a springboard for reforms that encompassed improvement on investigative methods by the South Africa Police, utilize the police force in most crucial areas, and address victims' needs, among others. The provisions set forth were to be in effect until 2004. The Department of Justice Vision 2000 document stressed the need for diversity, and the equal treatment of all, with further emphases on upholding the rule of law, and creating more transparency in the administration of justice (South African Government, n.d.). The ministry of justice launched the Justice Vision 2000 in 1997. In 2005 and 2006, the cabinet reviewed some of the initiatives that had been put forth for reform. Among some of the initiatives reviewed were those to reduce violent organized crimes, those to monitor the criminal justice, and much more. These piecemeal reforms and more cumulated to the adoption of the November 7, 2007, "the CJS Seven-Point-Plan."

This criminal justice 7-point plan addressed reforms in all segments of the justice system. The objective of the 7-point plan was to create an "effective, efficient, accessible justice" system (South African Government, n.d.). In his State of the Nation's 2008 address, President Thabo Mbeki affirmed the 2007 7-point CJ reform, and highlighted its vision of progressiveness and efficiency. The reforms embedded in this 7-point plan will be highlighted when each sector of the justice system is discussed below.

THE POLICE

The Department of Police is responsible for all law enforcement services in South Africa. At the top of this establishment is the Ministry of Police. The police force in South Africa had its earliest origins in 1655, by the Dutch Watch paramilitary organization. Following British settlement, they exercised dominion and supervision of the Dutch Watch, and eventually established the Cape Town Police Force in 1840. In the interim prior to 1913, several restructurings of the police force were made with the force being divided into units in the various states. With the country's unification on May 31, 1910, plans were in full fledge to also unify the police force. The South African Police was subsequently established in 1913. Police Act (No. 7) enacted in 1958 by the ruling government at the time extended the sphere of the police to include among other usual police tasks jurisdiction to suppress any riots or subversions or guerrilla warfare. In 1965, further powers were extended to the police by virtue of The Police Amendment Act (No. 70). This act gave the police carte blanche rights to conduct searches and seizures of persons, places, and containers within national borders, and by 1983, officers could conduct such searches and seizures throughout the country. When apartheid ended in the early 1990s, the South African Police (SAP) became known as the South African Police Service (SAPS), and took on restructuring the police force and implementing several reforms.

STRUCTURE OF THE SOUTH AFRICAN POLICE SERVICE

The headquarters of the South African Police Service is in the country's capital of Pretoria. As the main law enforcement entity of the country, the South African Police Service has as its mission to make the country safe for everyone by acting both proactively and reactively to matters of safety. The Minister of Police is the top administrative officer.

The following law enforcement branches (outside of the South African Police Service) report directly to the Ministry of Police: Independent Police Investigative Directorate, Civilian Secretariat for Police, and Private Security Industry Regulatory Authority (South African Government, http:/www.gov.za).

- **Independent Police Directorate (IPID):** Vested with the responsibility of investigating complaints against the South African Police Service as well as the metropolitan police services (Google search, n.d.).
- **Civilian Secretariat for Police**: As a technical advisor to the Minister of Police, this agency advises the ministry on community issues and crime prevention, auditing, policy implications from evidence-based research, and a host of other issues (About Us/Civilian Secretariat for Police, n.d.).

- **Private Security Industry Regulatory Authority:** This sector reports on business matters, regulatory issues, contractual agreements between the Security Board and any business, fees violations, and other issues (Untitled, n.d.).

The South African Police Service has among its objectives to combat organized crimes, crimes that affect women and children, espionage and terrorism, to secure the country's border, to participate in community policing, and to provide any services that protect the people, government, and country.

- Community Police Forums: The South African policy and legislation created these forums to improve police relations with the community. These forums are liaisons that promote the understanding of the purposes of community policing. However, success of the forums has been highly debated (Pelser & Rauch, 2001).

The South African Police Service is divided into six divisions which include:

1. **The Crime Combating and Investigation Division:** This division's responsibilities are vast and varied. They are responsible for supervising crime records, commercial crime unit sector, minerals and contraband, stock and combustible units, automobile theft unit, missing persons unit, and murder and robbery units.
2. **The Visible Policing Division:** This division is responsible for protecting high government officials, and their offices and residences. As well, the division has the task of protecting railways and the country's borders. Strategically, this unit is also equipped with special task forces to combat any types of insurgencies.
3. **The Internal Stability Division:** This unit, as its name suggests, is responsible for preventing and addressing domestic disturbances, and to participate in nationwide attempts at fighting crime.
4. **The Community Relations Division:** This unit primarily tackles human rights violations of all types, and works in concert with other divisions to curb acts intended to attack the dignity of other humans.
5. **The Supporting Service Division:** This unit is the recordkeeping sector in charge of administrative, legal, and fiscal issues.
6. **The Human Resource Management Division:** This unit is in charge of personnel, recruiting, and training.

It is worthy of note that the SAPS also has metropolitan police that serve each city in the country.

Qualifications to Be a South African Police Officer

In order to become a police officer in South Africa, a candidate must be a citizen of the country, and is generally required to have at least a high school diploma and pass physical and psychological tests. One, who successfully applies and is accepted, has to undergo an intense theoretical and field training program in one of the six special police colleges in the country. Upon the expiration of the 6 months, the trainee acquires the lowest entry rank of student constable. The pupil constable is presumed to still be in training as he/she gets more experience with the public by working in a community service center. This position requires that the pupil wear an officer's uniform and play the role of an officer for 3 months, and then is transferred to another jurisdiction to serve for another 3 months. This full year of training is followed by another year of field training as part of the South African Police Service. Upon faring well with the job challenges during this time, the pupil will then be accepted as a full member of the South African Police Service. Promotions to higher echelons are based on merit and statutory time limits.

South African Police Service Ranks of Officers as of April 1, 2010

Senior Management Commissioned Offices:
General
Lieutenant-General
Major-General
Brigadier

Commissioned Officers:
Colonel
Lieutenant-Colonel
Major
Captain
Lieutenant

Non-Commissioned Positions:
Warrant Officer
Sergeant
Constable

Requirements for Promotion

In order to be promoted from **Constable to Sergeant**, the officer has to have served a minimum of 7 years in that capacity, and this time does not include years of pupilage.

To be promoted from **Sergeant to warrant officer**, the officer must meet one of two qualifications:

1. The officer must attain a National Qualifications Framework 6 Qualification, and service record of at least 2 years as a sergeant. This system of National Qualifications Framework (NQF) was established following Act 67 of 2008. The Minister of Higher Education and Training approved the NQF as a method of classifying candidates or applicants so as to avoid discrimination and promote equal, essential education and training to candidates. OR
2. The officer must have a minimum of 5 years as a sergeant.

Qualifications for promotion from **warrant officer to ranks above it up to that of colonel** include a minimum of 2 continuous years of service in that rank. OR at least 5 years of continuous service in addition to NQF 4 qualification.

Promotions above the rank of **colonel up to that of lieutenant general** are supervised by the National Instruction of 4/2010. Detailed qualifications and expectations of the position are listed at the time of announcement for applications.

Worthy of note as well is the fact that availability of funds also at times determines if candidates would be promoted to the next level (DoP:SAPS, 2010).

THE SOUTH AFRICAN JUDICIARY

Legal Concepts

South Africa today represents a country whose legal system is shaped by its multi-colonial heritage, foreign settlements, and indigenous practices. In this hybrid system, civil law inherited from the Dutch, common law from the British, and customary laws from indigenous Africans apply in the country. Customary laws in most African countries, and that is the case in South Africa, vary giving the multiplicity of tribes and customs within a country. Application of customary law in South Africa is recognized under Section 211 of the country's Constitution (See, *Bhe v. Magistrate, Khayelitsha & Others* 2004, where the court upheld the legality of customary law). As Du Bois (2007), explains, common-law practices and customary practices in South Africa at times converge in procedural applications, while Roman-Dutch civil law is evident in substantive practices. The type of cases to which common law is mostly used are criminal law, evidence, criminal procedure, constitutional law, and company law. Roman-Dutch law is mostly used in tort law, property law, family law, and contract law.

Customary law differs from both common and civil laws in that reliance is placed entirely on the practice of the people. It in essence is passed down from generation to generation through memorized practices, and since it is not codified, it is not static. A chief or village head, or some respectable person in the community usually would be responsible for presiding over the customary court. Prior to colonization and the introduction of European laws, family issues, land disputes, contractual obligations, and more were settled based on existing norms. For instance, inheritance issues invariably were, and are still settled under many customary laws based on primogeniture rules. While custom identifies a people, and some of its practices promote good values, it at times is without fault. Some like Time (2017) and Wall (2015) have written against customary practices and laws that subjugate and disenfranchise women and children in Africa, and recommend that coercive customary practices should be eradicated.

When in doubt as to customary law, the Constitutional Court in South Africa has stepped in to untangle the contradictions. In *Alexkor Ltd and Another v. the Richtersveld Community and Others* (2003), the Constitutional Court stipulated that as an independent source of law, Customary law had to be interpreted by its own merit and not "through the common law lens," as well, it was only enforceable as long as it complied with the Constitution and any relevant legislations (*Alexkor Ltd and Another v. the Richtersveld Community and Others*, 2003).

South African courts are independent entities from governmental influence, and are only required to submit to the dictates of the Constitution and law. The Constitution of 1996 remains the Supreme law of the country. Bloemfontein is the judicial capital of South Africa. Even though the main languages spoken in court are English and Afrikaans, the move has been to open indigenous language courts throughout the country. This move has the benefits of speeding up justice by not relying on interpreters, as well as, improving the quality of justice by having adjudicators hear directly from litigants and not from interpreters (African languages in SA Courts/Brand South Africa, 12 Mar 2009).

When South Africa decided to put its history of apartheid in abeyance, it established a Truth and Reconciliation Commission (TRC) which had to investigate atrocities that were perpetrated on Blacks, and to issue amnesty to the guilty ones. This was a unique and singular fact-finding judicial body split into hearings that (a) investigated human rights infringements; (b) had perpetrators accept their roles in the violations; and (c) advised government on reparations to be paid to victims.

Cases tried based on common-law practices are adversarial while civil law cases are inquisitorial (see Chapters 1–2). Even though use of jury in trials is associated with common-law practice, South Africa abolished jury trials in 1969. Among some of the reasons given for abolishing jury trials are public hesitance to serve, the Minister of Justice's prerogative to order bench trials, and apprehension of racial prejudice, among others (Adwar, 2014).

A Law Commission ordered by government comprising legal experts, administrators, and researchers is responsible for conducting research and coming up with relevant legislation (Pelser & Rauch, 2001). Some of what the commission has accomplished includes work on juvenile justice and questions relating to prosecutorial appeals, among others (Pelser & Rauch).

Following the requirements of the 1996 Constitution, the country has the following courts:

> Constitutional Court, Supreme Court of Appeal, High Courts, Magistrate Courts, and any other courts that Parliament deems fit to open. In addition, there are several civil courts such as tax courts, labor courts, land claims courts, and small claims courts, among others.

STRUCTURE OF COURTS IN SOUTH AFRICA

Constitutional Court

This is the highest court of the land. The court reviews all matters of constitutional relevance forwarded to it from the Supreme Court of Appeal. The Court is also responsible for reviewing and endorsing any decisions of the High Court relating to a national statute or to presidential action before the action becomes applicable (Klug, 2002).

Supreme Court of Appeal

This is a court of last resort for all matters except constitutional issues; that is, the court has jurisdiction to review appeals of cases that do not involve constitutional questions.

High Courts:

The High Court reviews appeals from the Magistrate Courts, and has original jurisdiction for high felonies and of civil cases over stipulated amounts than what the Magistrate Court has jurisdiction over.

Magistrate Courts:

These are district courts of first instance that handle petty offences, gross misdemeanors, and lower level felonies. As well, these courts have jurisdiction over civil cases for which damages do not exceed R300,000 (approximately $22,699, on July 14, 2017) (South African Court Hierarchy, n.d.). The country is divided into 350 magisterial districts with each its own court; in addition to regional magistrate courts (South African Court Hierarchy).

Local Tribunals:

These local courts consist of Small Claims Courts, Chiefs' Courts, and Headmaster's Courts (South African Court Hierarchy, n.d.).

Other Specialist Courts:

There are several courts that handle specific issues involving property, social, contractual, and military issues. For example, there are Land Claims Courts, Labor Courts, Tax Courts, Electoral Courts, and Military Courts (South African Court Hierarchy, n.d.).

LEGAL ACTORS

In order to become a lawyer in South Africa, a law degree is required (LL.B., which is the equivalent of a J.D. in the United States). Thereafter, individuals planning on practicing law (becoming an advocate) become a pupil in a law office for at least a year, and pass the bar examination. Aspiring legal practitioners must either serve as a pupil, or reduce this requirement by doing community legal service, or attend legal training course. A professional examination set by provincial law society is thereafter taken. There are speculations of revising these conditions (Practicing Law in SA, n.d.).

Worthy of note is the fact that following the British system, attorneys in South Africa are classified as barristers and solicitors. Barristers comply with all the requirements listed above, and can thereafter argue cases in high courts and above, while those not admitted to the bar are solicitors and cannot argue cases in high courts. Klug (2002) opines that the distinction between barristers and solicitors will subsequently become a thing of the past in that both categories of lawyers will have equal opportunity to be advocates in any and every court.

Judicial appointments in South Africa are based on Constitutional requirements. The President of the country makes appointments of judges in Constitutional Courts after vetting a list of candidates submitted by the Judicial Service Commission (JSC), and with involvement in the process of political leaders of the National Assembly.

Judges of the Supreme Court of Appeal and those of the High Courts are appointed by the president following counsel of the Judicial Service Commission. The Minister of Justice appoints magistrates with advice from a Magistrates Commission (Klug, 2002).

CORRECTIONS

The Department of Justice and Correctional Services supervises corrections in South Africa. The minister heads the department and has two deputies who help run the Correctional Services that has a staff of approximately 34,000, about 240 prisons housing approximately 189,748 prisoners (Department of Justice and Correctional Services-Wikipedia, n.d.). Makou, Skosana, and Hopkins (2017) place the number of prisons in the country at 243, of which 236 are operational, and of this number 6 are women's prisons and 14 youth facilities. Prior to the sentencing of an offender, the probation officer or a correctional official must draft a pre-sentence report, and this report guides the judge on what sentence to administer to the offender.

Prison categories mirror those of most nations; that is, maximum, medium, and minimum security depending on the caliber of the inmate and his/her crime.

PRISON CLASSIFICATIONS

It is not uncommon to have all three levels of prison in one large facility.

- **Maximum Security Prisons:** These house the worst types of criminals—murderers, incorrigible criminals, violent gang dealers, and opponents of apartheid like late President Mandela, among others. These prisons like eBongweni C-Max in Kwazulu Natal, have modern surveillance features like CCTV, steel doors, and other electronic monitoring devices (TYI, 2017).
- **Medium Security Prisons:** These prisons like Drakenstein, Paarl, house lesser violent offenders than those in maximum security, but experience overcrowding, drug and gang related issues, and violence (TYI, 2017).
- **Minimum Security Prisons:** These prisons house low level criminals and defendants awaiting trial. Overcrowding and other deplorable conditions are of profound concern (Dissel, 1996).

The Department of Correctional Services is also responsible for rehabilitative programs, inmate release/probation, parole and re-integration of convicts into society (Pelser & Rauch, 2001). Inmates in South Africa are accorded several rights just as those accorded inmates in the United States. Some of them have the right to healthcare, right to education, right to humane treatment, and right to religious freedoms, among others (Correctional Services/South African Government, n.d.). As well, the department of corrections there suffers some of the challenges that many departments of corrections in many countries suffer: prison crowding, insufficient rehabilitative programs, AIDS and HIV infections, and so forth (Pelser &

Rauch). With regard to juvenile offenders, the Department of Welfare is responsible for ensuring their safe custody (Pelser & Rauch).

The death penalty was abolished in South Africa in 1995, in favor of life sentences or maximum sentences. As opposed to lengthy sentences which offer little therapeutic effects, the South African Correctional Services tries to place inmates in correctional programs with emphases of rehabilitation. For instance, in 2015–2016, the department sentenced about 75,595 offenders through such programs (Correctional Services/South African Government, n.d.).

In its quest for progressiveness, South Africa promotes rehabilitation of inmates as its foremost purpose of incarceration (Correctional Services/South African Government, n.d.). The White Paper on Corrections in South Africa, 2004 (derivative reforms from the 1996 Constitution), and the Correctional Services Act (Act No 11 of 1998) is a revised document that advocates more humane treatment for prisoners that will enable their transition to life in society after incarceration. The Correctional Services' goals are listed as ensuring the protection of society, reintegrating offenders to society, and managing the process effectively (Correctional Services/South African Government).

ALTERNATIVES TO INCARCERATION

On August 15, 1991, South Africa lunched its community corrections program in hopes of creating a smooth integration of inmates to society under supervision of correctional officers. To effectuate community corrections, the Community Corrections Office must organize quarterly meetings with the community to address concerns citizens may have about probationers and parolees and how they would be supervised and monitored. There must be assurances from family and friends to provide requisite financial, residential, moral, and other kinds of support to the probationer or parolee prior to release. For probationers or parolees who may not get the requisite financial backing, the government provides some money and other necessities as a head start for the probationer or parolee. Community-based corrections are not a right; hence, violations may lead to revocation, which means confinement in prison. Among the community based programs are:

- **HOUSE ARREST:** Risk of recidivism is taken into consideration before a convict is put on house arrest. Flexibility is given to accommodate the probationer's work schedule and other activities like church attendance and shopping with the probation officer/correctional supervisor.
- **RESTRICTION TO MAGISTERIAL DISTRICT:** This condition is restricted to probationers who must reside in areas where they can be monitored.

- **VICTIM COMPENSATION:** This is a court-ordered sanction for the offender/probationer to pay a specified amount of money to the victim. The head of the Community Corrections Office coordinates payments from probationer to victim. Failure to make payment is immediately reported to the court which has discretion to impose other sanctions.
- **COMMUNITY SERVICE:** The probationer is ordered to do something symbolic to society by way of work in schools, nursing/senior living homes, parks, or any establishment that the court deems fit. The court specifies the duration of the community service.
- **CORRECTIONAL PROGRAMMES AND LECTURES:** The offender/probationer is ordered by the court to attend and listen to lectures by specialists on topics pertinent to the probationer's criminality; for instance, alcohol and drug abuse, relationship issues, and work ethic, among others. Such lectures are given by experts at the Community Corrections Office, or by invited specialists.
- **OTHER CONDITIONS:** There are mandatory conditions for probationers, as for instance, get and retain a job, do not be transient unless with permission from the head of Community Corrections, maintain constant and frequent contact with the head of Community Corrections, and refrain from any type of criminal behavior, among others.
- **PAROLE:** The Commissioner of Correctional Services puts forth the conditions of parole, which among others include no commission of new crimes, constant reporting to the Community Corrections Office, must engage in worthwhile approved activities, and must have a job, among others (these conditions relate to probationers as well). The parolee must not default on any of the conditions. During the time of parole, the parolee is closely monitored by the Commissioner of Correctional Services or any parole officers that the Commissioner delegates (Correctional Services, n.d.). Similarly to what occurs in the United States, probationers and parolees are monitored via phone calls, unannounced visits to workplace or home, mandatory reports to the office of Community Corrections, and any other means deemed fit by authorities. As well, the level and intensity of monitoring the probationer or parolee depends on risk assessment factors. South Africa divides such levels of supervision into "maximum intensive monitoring, medium intensive monitoring, and minimum monitoring" (Correctional Services).

REVOCATION OF PROBATION AND PAROLE

Single or minor violations of probation or parole do not automatically lead to revocation of that conditional release. Warnings and probable cause hearings are first held. Further violations and the commission of a new crime may lead to revocation which means reinstating a prison sentence, or to the imposition of other sanctions.

QUALIFICATIONS TO WORK WITH THE CORRECTIONAL SERVICES

In order to work as a correctional officer, there are several requirements to overcome. On the basic level, the applicant must fill out an application form, be a citizen, must have a minimum of high school or secondary school education "Standard 10/Grade 12 Certificate," or Training Certificate NQF or National Certificate in Vocational Studies (Level 4), and must not be a felon (SA Learnerships, 2013). Accepted applicants must spend 1 year in training doing both theoretical and field training. Theoretical training comprises studies in use of weapons, self-defense, and other basic steps needed to work with inmates. Trainees will be placed in accredited training colleges with room, board, and uniforms paid by government. Seventy percent of trainees' time, however, is devoted to field work at Correctional and Social Reintegration Centers (SA Learnerships, 2013). At this point, trainees are schooled on inmate rehabilitative and security programs. Since trainees would at this time be given monthly stipends, government would no longer be amenable for room and board and other personal expenses that government absorbed.

SUMMARY

South Africa lies in the Southern tip of Africa. It is a democratic country which today is Africa's most progressive country, despite its checkered past with apartheid. Even though the Dutch introduced civil law in the country it was overshadowed by common law introduced by the British colonizers.

The police force of South Africa has six units with the National Headquarters in Pretoria. The police force has several units and several branches including the Independent Police Investigative Directorate, Civilian Secretariat for Police, and Private Security Industry.

The country's judicial system is hybrid, blending common law, civil law, and indigenous customary practices. Act number 108 of the 1996 Constitution is the foundation of South Africa's criminal justice system with other Acts providing other legal protections. In 2008, President Mbeki approved a drastic reform to a 2007 seven-part reform plan in all three agencies of the criminal justice system. Following the English heritage, attorneys in South Africa are either solicitors or barristers who argue cases in court.

A minister and two deputies under the domain of the Department of Justice and Correctional Services head corrections in South Africa. The Community Corrections Programs in the country were launched on August 15, 1991. The Department of Corrections is responsible for rehabilitative programs, probation and parole.

DISCUSSION QUESTIONS

1. The South African Criminal Justice 7-Point Plan is to create an "effective, efficient, accessible criminal justice system."
   a. What do you think makes a criminal justice system "effective and efficient"?
   b. Do you think the criminal justice system of South Africa is effective and efficient?
2. What makes the criminal justice system of South Africa a mixed or hybrid system?
3. Discuss the various units that comprise the South African Police Service.
4. Explain the judicial system of South Africa.
5. What are the requirements to work with the Correctional Services of South Africa?

REFERENCES

Abel, R. (1995). *Politics by other means: Law in the struggle against apartheid 1980–1994.* New York: Routledge.

About Us/Civilian Secretariat for Police. (n.d.). Retrieved from http://www.policesecretariat.gov.za/about/about.php

Adwar, C. (2014, April 3). Here's why nobody in South Africa gets a jury trial including Oscar Pistotius. *Business Insider.* Retrieved from http://www.businessinsider.com/heres-why-oscar-pistorious-won't-get-a-jury-trial-2014-4

African Languages in SA Courts/Brand South Africa. (2009, March 12). Retrieved from https://www.brandsouthafrica.com/people/indigenous-languages-in-sa-courts

Boddy-Evans, A. (2017). Understanding South Africa's apartheid era. Thoughtco.com. Apartheid FAQ: Common Questions about South Africa's Apartheid Era. Retrieved from https://www.thoughtco.com/common-questions-about-apartheid-era-4070234

Correctional Services. (n.d.). Retrieved from http://www.dcs.gov.za/Services/Community-Corrections.aspx

Correctional Services/South African Government. (n.d.). Retrieved from http://www.gov.za/about-government-system/justice-system/correctional-services

Department of Justice and Correctional Services-Wikipedia. (n.d.). Retrieved from https://en.m.wikipedia.org/wiki/Department_of_justice_and_Correctional_Services

Dissel, A. (1996). South Africa's prison conditions: The inmates talk. *Imbizo*, (2), 4–10.

DoP:SAPS. (2010). Parliamentary Question: DoP:SAPS ranks/defenceWeb. Retrieved from http://www.defenceweb.co.za/index.php?option=com_content&task=view&id=11136&Itemid=187

Du Bois, W. E. B. (2007). *The world and Africa.* H. L. Gates, Jr. (Ed.). United Kingdom: Oxford University Press.

George, W. (1970). *Wille's Principles of South African Law.* 9th ed. Du Bois Francois (ed.) (2007). Cape Town: JutaPublishing.

Google Search. (n.d.). What is the independent police investigative directorate? Google Search. Retrieved from https://www.google.com/search?q=what+is+independent+police+investigative+directorate&ie=UTF-8&oe=UTF-8&hl=en&client=safari

Klug, H. (2002). South Africa. In H. Kritzer (Ed.), *Legal Systems of the World: A Political, Social, and Cultural Encyclopedia* (pp. 1483–1491). Santa Barbara, California: ABC-CLIO Publishing.

Kuepper, J. (2017). What are newly industrialized countries (NICs)? Retrieved from https://www.the balance.com/what-are-newly-industralized-countries-nics-1978978

Makou, G., Skosana, I., & Hopkins, R. (2017, July 18). Fact Sheet: The state of South Africa's prisons. *Daily Maverick.* Retrieved from http://www.dailymaverick.co.za/article/2017-07-18-fact-sheet-the-state-of-south-africas-prisons/#.WXGNKBj3arU

Pelser, E., & Rauch, J. (2001). South Africa's criminal justice system: Policy and priorities. Paper presented at the South African Sociological Association (SASA) Annual Congress, Globalization, Inequality and Identity, July 1–4.

Practicing Law in SA/Faculty of Law. (n.d.). Retrieved from http://www.law.uct.ac.za/law/about/lawinSA

SA Learnerships. (2013, July 15). Correctional Services Learnership 2017–2018. South Africa Learnership Programmes. Retrieved from http://salearnership.co.za/correctional-services-learnership-2014/

South African Court Hierarchy. (n.d.). Retrieved from http://www.hierarchystructure.com/south-african-courts-hierarchy

South African Government. (n.d.). Justice Vision 2000: Executive Summary/South African Government. Retrieved from http://www.gov.za/af/documents/justice-vision-2000-executive-summary

South African Government. (n.d.). Police, defence and intelligence. Retrieved from http://www.gov.za/about-sa/safety-security-defence

Time, V. (2017). *Women's social and legal issues in African current affairs: Lifting the barriers.* Lanham: Lexington Books.

TYI. (2017). 9 of the worst prisons in SA/The young independents. Retrieved from https://www.tyi.co.za/education-and-work/news-education/9-of-the-worst-prisons-in-sa

Untitled. (n.d.). Private Security Industry Regulatory Authority Act (56/2001) [25 November 2011]. Retrieved from http://us-cdn.creamermedia.con.za/assets/articles/attachments/36626_n833.pdf

Wall, D. (2015, June 15). Customary law in South Africa: Historical development as a legal system and its relation to women's rights. *South African History Online.*

The World Fact Book—Central Intelligence Agency (CIA). (2017). South Africa. Retrieved from https://www.cia.gov/library/publications/the-world-factbook/geos/sf.html

Worldometers. (2017). South Africa Population (2017). Retrieved from http://www.worldometers.info/world-population/south-africa-population

CASES

Alexkor Ltd and Another v. Richtersveld Community and Others. (2003). Constitutional Court of South Africa.

Bhe v. Magistrate, Khavelitsha & Others. (2004). Constitutional Court Case CCT 49/03.

PART VII

Canon Law/Roman Catholic

CHAPTER 15

Vatican City and The Vatican Model

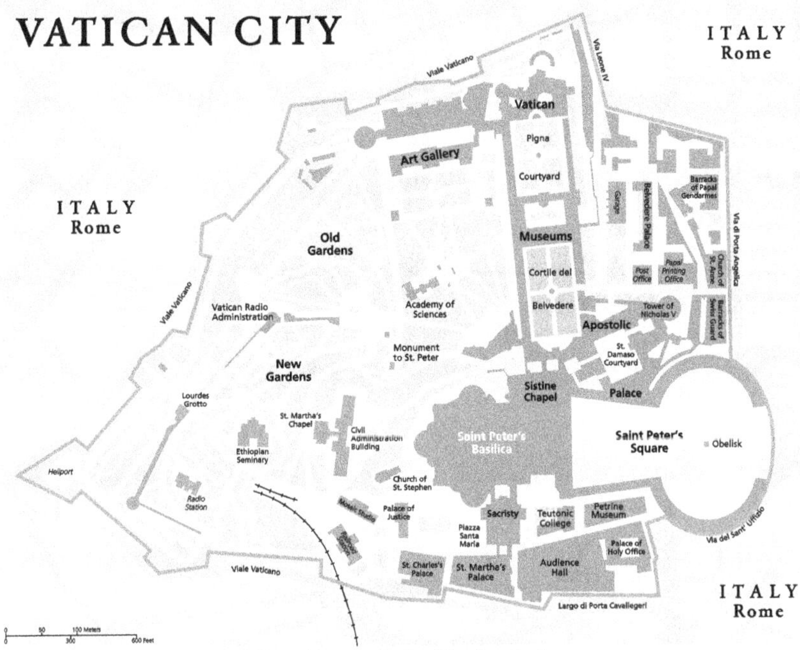

© Peter Hermes Furian/Shutterstock.com

INTRODUCTION

The Vatican City is not only the smallest sovereign state worldwide, it is also the headquarters of the Roman Catholic Church, and abode of the Pope, and the Office of the Secretariat. What is known as the Holy See refers to the government of the Catholic Church, which operates from the Vatican City. The Vatican City covers an area of 108.7 acres (Shelledy, 2002), and has a population of about 1,000 people following a 2017 estimate (CIA

World Fact Book, 2017). It is a landlocked enclave in Rome, Italy. The Vatican's authority spans 23 sites within Rome, five outside of Rome comprising the Pope's summer home—the Pontifical Palace in Castel Gandolfo (CIA World Fact Book).

A multitude of languages including Italian, Latin, French, and Spanish, among others are spoken by the Pope and other residents of the Vatican. The Vatican City has its own post office, banking and phone systems, pharmacy, radio and television stations, and a newspaper service.

The history of the Vatican City is traced to 1929 after discord between a succession of Popes and the Italian government over territory and control of internal affairs was finally resolved. The issue between the Popes and the Italian government, which lasted from 1870–1929, was known as the "Roman Question." The Lateran Treaty signed on February 11, 1929, between the Holy See and the Italian government, gave prominence to Roman Catholicism in Italy and established the Vatican City's independence by ceding to it 108.7 acres (Shelledy, 2002). The treaty and other provisions (some consider these three treaties) include:

1. Recognizing the independence and sovereignty of the Holy See and creating the State of the Vatican City (Treaty of Conciliation, see Shea, 2012).
2. A concordant defining the relations between the government and the church within Italy. In 1984 an Amendment was made to the Lateran Treaty, but this change did not affect the terms of the concordant.
3. A financial convention providing the Holy See with compensation for its losses in 1870 (U.S. State Department, 2001).

The Vatican City, pursuant to the Treaty, recognized the Italian government.

Following the 1929 Lateran treaty, the Vatican drew up a Constitution that was revised in 1963, and tweaked in 2001. The Constitution, signed in 1929, comprised six fundamental laws: Fundamental Law of the City of the Vatican; Law of the Source of Laws; Law on the Rights of Citizenship and Sojourn; Law on Administrative Organization; Law on Economic, Commercial, and Professional Organization; and Law of Public Security (Shea, 2012).

In 2013, the current Pope—Francis—put in place a council of nine cardinals to begin the process of reforms of the administrative domain of the Vatican, and with a broader task of writing an entirely new Constitution. In order for Amendments to be made to the laws of the Vatican, the wordings of Article 4 of the Fundamental Law of the Vatican have to be revisited. According to Article 4, the Pontifical Commission for the Vatican City must approve any Amendments to the Constitution, and the draft legislation must be reviewed by the secretariat of state before the Pope can consider its passing.

While the Holy See is revered and garners much respect, the establishment has been marred by scandals over the years. Pope Benedict XVI's voluntary resignation in 2013 was something that had not happened in 600 years. Embroiled by scandals emanating from the impropriety and crimes of priests, the Holy See needed a change. Pope Francis, current Pope since March 13, 2013—seems to be a breadth of fresh air—one to restore the good name of the papacy.

The Pope is chief of state. The Pope is elected by cardinals who are usually not older than 80 years, and must comprise 120. A two-thirds majority must elect the Pope. If this majority cannot agree within 3 days, then after the third day, a simple majority vote would suffice. The Secretary of State is the Head of Government. The cabinet comprises the Pontifical Commission for the State of the Vatican City. The Pope appoints this commission, which comprises Cardinals with term limits of 5 years. The President of this commission is vested with executive powers. However, such powers do not go unchecked, because in important issues a unilateral decision cannot be made until after the secretariat of the state has been consulted. The secretary assigns day-to-day issues of little magnitude to a special delegate (Shelledy, 2002).

WHY THE VATICAN CITY IS PART OF THIS STUDY

Unlike the other countries discussed in this book that fall under one of the six families of law, the Vatican City is unique. Its uniqueness stems from the fact that it is a city-state headed by the spiritual leader of the Roman Catholic Church. Its leader, the Pope, is not a political leader, nor does the Vatican City have any political parties. As an independent entity, and with a system different from that of Italy, and indeed, of the entire world, the Vatican City's inclusion in any book dealing with systems of law must be deliberate and not fortuitous. Its system of law is religion-based (canon law) and while it occasionally defers to Italian Civil law, such deferment only occurs when there is no conflict with laws of the Vatican.

Of significant importance is the fact that this small state hosts millions of Roman Catholics and tourists annually, and uses its non-political platform to participate in important international organizations that promote the peace and well-being of mankind. In this vein, the Holy See is a member of the World Health Organization (WHO), United Nations Education and Scientific Organization (UNESCO), International Labor Organization (ILO), World Trade Organization (WTO), International Atomic Energy Agency (IAEA), Interpol, and a host of others, and is also observer to several more organizations, among which are the United Nations, Union Latina, Organization of American States, and European Community, among several others. The message of peace that is sent out from the Vatican City by the Pope provides hope, comfort, and détente, not only to the billions of Catholics worldwide, but its message is far-reaching even to politicians and heads of states. The Pope's approach to international affairs is marked by its neutrality and conciliatory stance, which at times seems coddling, yet its message for the most part seems effective.

The Vatican City is to Christians a most sacred place, a pilgrimage destination, and for non-Christians, a place to soak in the splendor of the ensemble of architecture, gardens, and history. With at least 1.2 billion visitors annually (see Vatican City, n.d.), it attracts a lot more people than most nations—that speaks to its relevance and makes it a compelling addition to the book. Further, it is worthwhile highlighting the system of law and workings of the justice system of the Vatican, because ignorance of the law would not be an excuse even at the most sacred place in the world. The Vatican is an economic giant, providing Rome in particular, and Italy in general a gigantic financial portfolio based on revenues accrued from tourists.

As the seat of Catholicism, messages transmitted from the Vatican City provide moral and spiritual lessons to Christians and to others who look for messages of hope and an avenue that anchors their hopelessness and fears. In this regard, the Holy See is not sectarian; consequently, the Pope's message strives to promote inclusiveness, peace, and brotherhood to all mankind. Political leaders may harbor similar thoughts and utter similar messages, but they seldom are effective since they seldom remain neutral in the face of adversity.

LEGAL CONCEPTS

As a religious and nonpolitical entity, the Holy See is based on Christian philosophies. Canon Law governs the life of those who live and work in the Vatican City. The Pope is entrusted with absolute executive, legislative, and judicial powers. As Shelledy (2002) explains, three major factors delineate the legal system of the Vatican:

1. The Pope is a religious leader of the Roman Catholic Church. As the head of the Church, the Pope is responsible for setting the tone of how things work in the Vatican City. Many of the precepts of Roman Catholicism are borrowed from Canon Law, but the Holy See remains the religious pillar.

2. The Pope is an elected "absolute monarch." Based upon the Constitution, the Pope is vested with leadership over all three conventional branches of government: legislative, executive, and judiciary. Even though persons assigned by the Pope run the judiciary, the Pope still retains powers to override or rescind any actions taken.

3. Despite its status as an independent entity, the Vatican City draws a lot from the legal system of Italy. Not only does the court structure of the Vatican mirror that of Italy, the Vatican reverts to Italian law in matters not espoused in laws of the Vatican City. Based on the Law of the Source of Laws adopted after the signing of the Lateran Treaty, Canon Law Code, laws put in place by the Pope or anyone he delegates are applicable in the Vatican City. Article 3 of the Law of the Source of Laws allows the Vatican City to apply Italian Law, Roman law, and municipal laws as long as they do not clash

with canon law, or divine law (Shea, 2012). The Vatican City reserves the right to defer criminal cases (crimes committed within the confines of the Vatican City) to Italian Courts. As well, just as Italy provides security, that is, police presence in St. Peter's Square, it also grants legal protection to the Pope.

LAW ENFORCEMENT

It is easy to distinguish two main types of police in the Vatican City: Police Force *Corpo di Vigilanze* and Swiss Guard. There is also a fire Brigade at the Vatican City.

The Police force of the Vatican City (*Corpo di Vigilanze*) is responsible for criminal investigation, order maintenance, and border and traffic control. Based on Article 3 of the 1929 Lateran Treaty, Italian police may patrol parts of the Vatican City, but such patrolling is not to exceed the steps to the basilica (see Crime in Vatican City, n.d.).

Pope Pius VII established the Gendarmerie force in 1816 at the Vatican City, which was to complement the Swiss Guard. While accounts hold that Pope Paul VI dissolved the gendarmerie corps instituted in 1816 (see Gendarmerie Corps, n.d.) that is not entirely correct. The gendarmes are simply the police force that is responsible for law enforcement and criminal investigation. On July 16, 2002, Pope John Paul II established a Directorate for Security Services and Civil Defense, headed by the Chief of the Corps of Gendarmes and Fire Brigade. This directorate oversees the police force (Gendarmerie Corps).

The Swiss Guard: This body, comprising a little over 100 members (130 members) (Squires, 2011), in the force has full responsibility of protecting the Pope (Shelledy, 2002), and is responsible for the security of the Apostolic Palace. They also serve as a ceremonial unit. Their striped blue, red, and gold uniforms make it easy to spot this unit.

Qualifications to Be a Police/Gendarme

In order to become a gendarmerie at the Vatican City, one has to be an Italian (Squires, 2011). In addition, one has to be Catholic between the ages of 21 and 25. The recruit must have at least a high school certificate, and must be at least 5 feet 8 inches tall (Taylor, 2015).

Qualifications to Become a Swiss Guard

Use of the Swiss Guards can be traced to 1506 when Pope Julius II utilized the services of Swiss mercenaries who were looking for work in foreign countries. Today, the Vatican City still employs Swiss trained citizens to provide security to the Pope and to the Papal residence.

Members of this unit must be between the ages of 19 and 30; must be at least 5 feet 8 inches tall; must be unmarried, must be morally upstanding, and must complete training in a Swiss military academy (Squires, 2011).

THE JUDICIAL SYSTEM

The Pope has the ultimate authority in issues that arise within the Vatican City. On June 7, 1929, Pope Pius XI set up a system of law, which has been thrice revised in 1932, 1946, and 1987. The prerogative of such revisions is the Pope's, and he publishes such revision(s) in the Vatican newsletter. The November 21, 1987, revision by Pope John Paul II that was titled *Quo Civium iura* was, at the time, the last revision of Vatican laws (Shelledy, 2002). On November 26, 2000, Pope John Paul II promulgated the Fundamental Law of the Vatican City (Wikipedia.org, n.d.). The Fundamental Law/Constitutional Law consists of 20 articles. On October 1, 2008, Pope Benedict signed a new statute, Law No. LXXI *Legge sulle fonti del diritto*, which enabled just a carefully selected Italian legislation to be adopted and applied in Vatican courts.

The Courts

The court system of the Vatican City has four tiers based on a hierarchy: The Court of Limited Jurisdiction—Sole Judge (*Giudice Unico*), Court of General Jurisdiction—Tribunal (*Tribunale*), Court of Appeal (*Corte d'Appello*), and Supreme Court (*Corte di Cassazione*).

1. Court of Limited Jurisdiction (Sole Judge—*Giudice Unico*)

   The Court of Limited Jurisdiction is presided over by one judge who must be a citizen of the Vatican City (Shelledy, 2002). The jurisdiction of this judge and court is over petty offenses, traffic violations, small claims issues, matrimonial issues, and minor issues that require judicial attention. The judge in this court may also serve in the next court level, which is the Tribunal.

2. Tribunal (Court of General Jurisdiction—*Tribunale*)

   At the head of the Tribunal is the president who presides with two other judges present (Shelledy, 2002). These judges are not legally trained; they are appointees of the Pope. In this court as well, the Pope appoints a promoter of justice/*promotore di giustizia* (guardian of the law), whose responsibilities are akin to those of a prosecutor, in that the promoter brings a case against the law violator. This court handles both criminal and civil cases. A General Jurisdiction Court handles gross misdemeanors and felonies. The promoter may elect to try the cases at the Vatican City, or may waive the cases to Italian courts.

3. Court of Appeals (*Corte d'Appello*)

   The composition of this court includes a president and three judges. These judges are nominated by the Pope to serve a 5-year term. As well as serving on the Court of Appeals, these judges also serve on the Roma Rota, responsible to govern the ecclesiastical domain. Very few cases make their way to this level. Included in its other duties are the duties to provide discipline among the Vatican's lawyers, and attending to employment controversies stemming from the Office of Work of the Apostolic See.

4. Supreme Court of Appeals (*Corte di Cassazione*)

   Three judges review cases in this court, which is the highest court in the Vatican See. The president of the Supreme Court is a cardinal, who is also head of the Apostolic *Signatura* (the highest canon law court in the Catholic Church) (see Shelledy, 2002). He, along with two other cardinals, are responsible for decision-making in the Supreme Court. These cardinals are also members of the Apostolic *Signatura*. Besides hearing appellate cases from the Court of Appeal, the Court has original jurisdiction in criminal issues against cardinals and Bishops not handled by the Pope.

The Legal Profession

There are no law schools in the Vatican City; consequently, those that handle legal cases in the Vatican Courts are trained somewhere else or must be canon lawyers. The Sole judge, and those of the Tribunal, are required to fulfill the following eligibility requirements: (1) their names must be on the official list kept by the tribunal; (2) they must belong to the Order of Rotal Lawyers; (3) they must have a civil law degree (Shea, 2012; Shelledy, 2002).

Lawyers who practice in the Court of Appeals may be enrolled to practice at that court; however, the president of the Court of Appeal has discretion to enlist a lawyer who has a desired specialty. As well, on a case-by-case basis, or as needed, the president of the appellate court may appoint lawyers who are not on the official list (Shelledy, 2002). Eligibility to practice before the Supreme Court requires that the lawyer has experience teaching civil or ecclesiastical law at a university, or must be a consistory lawyer (Shelledy).

CORRECTIONS

Except for detention cells in police posts in the Vatican City, there are no prisons. Convicts in Vatican City courts are incarcerated in Italian prisons with the Vatican footing the bills (Crime in Vatican City, n.d.). This arrangement is embodied in Article 22 of the Lateran Treaty of 1929. The Vatican had abolished the death penalty in 1969, so only jail or prison sentences can be administered to persons who perpetuate crimes in the Vatican City.

SUMMARY

This chapter explains the legal system of the Vatican City. How the Vatican City became an independent entity from Italy after the Roman Question was settled in 1929 was discussed.

The Vatican City is the smallest sovereign state. The Pope is not only leader of the Holy See, and of the Roman Catholic Church, he is also the head of the Vatican City. Following the Lateran Treaty of 1929, a constitution outlining the fundamental law of the Vatican City was drawn. Executive, legislative, and judicial powers rest with the Pope.

Security of The Vatican city rests on Vatican Police, while the Swiss Guard is responsible for the security of the Pope and of the papal palace.

Courts in The Vatican City, like those in most countries, are based on a hierarchy, with cases moving from the Sole Judge Court to the Tribunal, and then to the Court of Appeals, and finally to the Supreme Court of Appeals. Lawyers who practice law in the Vatican Courts have to be versed in Canon law, be experienced in teaching civil or ecclesiastic law, or be on the Rota list. Law violators can either be tried in Vatican Courts or waived to Italian Courts.

Persons found guilty of minor offenses may be locked up in police cells at the Vatican City, while gross misdemeanants and felons are sent to prisons in Italy.

DISCUSSION QUESTIONS

1. Do you agree that it is relevant to include a discussion of the Vatican City as a separate chapter in this book? What makes the inclusion of the Vatican City in this book relevant?

2. Explain the legal system of the Vatican City. Do you think that because the Vatican City occasionally applies Italian law, it should be considered a hybrid legal system?

3. What are the requirements to be an appellate judge at the Vatican City?

4. Is the Vatican City and the Holy See the same? Explain your response.
5. Explain what the "Roman Question" is. How was this question answered?

REFERENCES

CIA World Fact Book. (2017). Vatican City. Retrieved from http://theodora.com/wfbcurrent/holy_see_geography.html

Crime in Vatican City. (n.d.). Retrieved from http://en.wikipedia.org/wiki/Crime_in_Vatican_City

Gerndarme Corps. (n.d.). Retrieved from https://www.vaticanstate.va/content/vaticanstate/en/stato-e-governo/structura-del-governatorato/corpo-della-gendarmerie.html

Shea, A. (2012). Update: Researching the law of the Vatican City State. Retrieved from www.nyulawglobal.org

Shelledy, R. (2002). Vatican. In H. M. Kritzer (Ed.), *Legal systems of the world: A political, social, and cultural encyclopedia* (Vol. IV: S–Z, pp. 1734–1738). Santa Barbara: ABC-CLIO.

Squires, N. (2011). A history of the Vatican's Swiss Guard. Telegraph.co.uk. Retrieved from https://www.telegraph.co.uk/news/worldnews/europe/vaticancityandholysee/8873853/A-history-of-the-Vaticans-Swiss-Guard.html

Taylor, A. (2015). Yes, the Pope has a police force. Here's how the Vatican lays down the law. Retrieved from http://www.washingtonpost.com/news/worldviews/wp/2015/11/03/yes-the-police-force-heres-how-the-vatican-lays-down-the-law/?utm_erm=.863c0f5ff7f2

U.S. State Department. (2001). Holy See History. Retrieved from http://workmall.com/wfb2001/holy_see_/holy_see_history.html

Vatican City. (n.d.). History.com. Vatican City Facts and Summary. Retrieved from http://www.history.com/topics/vatican-city

Wikipedia.org. (n.d.). Law of the Vatican City. Retrieved from https://en.wikipedia.org/wiki/law_of_Vatican_City

CHAPTER 16

Closing Thoughts

Completing this book proved more challenging than anticipated with each of the chapters requiring independent research. For instance, writing about the justice system in Cuba may be much different than Singapore, Brazil, or Iran. In other words, each chapter stands on its own requiring original thought and effort. As authors, considerable time was spent carrying out the tedious background investigation for each chapter. In some cases, we could draw upon on-site fieldwork or previous visits to the cultural area explored, such as Singapore or the Philippines. Other chapters were assisted by discussion with persons who had emigrated from the area examined which was the case for Iran and Cuba. Yet, most chapters required old-fashioned archival research sifting through sometimes obscure sources.

Other factors caught us by surprise. Because the book took several years to complete, the findings of one earlier finished subject area occasionally experienced changes as the months unfolded that required a return to the chapter for slight alterations. What was true for Cuba, the Philippines, or North Korea witnessed, and continue to witness, fluctuations over the course of a year. Constantly shifting cultures makes any writing on comparative justice challenging. Problematic, and always on our minds as authors, was that our choice of nations to represent families of law may not satisfy all readers. Of the approximately 200 countries of the world, one might choose from a variety of nations to represent any of the six traditional families of law, whether Common, Civil (Napoleonic), Civil (Germanic), Islamic, Socialist, or Hybrid categories. Although not so much a surprise, our suspicion was confirmed that any attempt to fit a nation into a single grouping of pure features results in some perplexity. In fact, in recent years most nations arguably fit the hybrid family of law, one way or another. We also decided to add a discussion of the Vatican City. Not only is the Vatican City the smallest sovereign state worldwide, more importantly, it is the headquarters of the Roman Catholic Church. With over a billion Catholics globally, and with millions of tourists flocking to the Vatican City annually, we thought an addition of a discussion of Canon law of the Catholic Church was necessary and justified.

Although our selection of nations reveals models of the families of law, even if roughly so, we hasten to add that understanding any nation's justice system requires delving deeper into the society than the legal system. That is, the underlying context of a justice system in any nation necessitates scrutiny of the society's entire backdrop of its social institutions. We must look at a nation's family and demographic profile, its public health, occupational, and educational system, and sometimes its religious character and even its military, perhaps among others. As a result, this volume becomes sociological and anthropological as much as it is legalistic or criminal justice in scope. We see this as a positive, not a negative.

In all our chapters, we find justice systems clearly incorporate a mixing of formal with informal systems of justice processing. For example, in the Philippines, we find a most clear example of informal or neighborhood based systems of law enforcement. In other societies, such as the Republic of Yemen, we find most of the people reside in small villages where the processing of disputes is managed through tribal laws without a need for formal, government judicial systems. Also, in some societies, such as North Korea and Yemen, we find the use of government incarceration and torture of offenders most common, compared to other nations more intent on providing rehabilitation. If anything, our selection of chapters reveals the great diversity of justice systems around the globe while incorporating multiple families of law.

During the writing of this volume, it became clear to us that no nation in our selection can remain for long in isolation from the rest of the world. Rather, various factors (e.g., economic, political, religious, social, etc.), work to keep countries connected and on a particular pathway. How a nation may remain off a beaten path is a matter of degree and may change over time. Surely, the United States has had profound effect on the viability of many other nations as populations migrate between and among the continents. Or, religion may become the glue holding nations together such as with Sharia law as illustrated here by Iran and Yemen. Socialism has worked over the years to connect North Korea and Cuba with Russia or with China, and so forth, and on a certain path with other nations.

As authors, we have no doubt that some readers will express surprise or disagreement with our sample of nations. We all will have our favorite cultural areas to discuss when thinking comparatively, and our selection of a dozen nations is not the only listing of nations to reflect the families of law. Additionally, does our sample clearly reflect places that have been out of the mainstream of comparative justice? Some areas in our listing leave no doubt, such as North Korea. Others may raise an eyebrow, such as Brazil, Italy, or Singapore. We do not stress over this and encourage others to arrive at their own selection. Unquestionably, justification exists for additional volumes to augment this one. However, we do argue with no sense of reticence that our discussion of nations provides a starting point, if not a stimulating supplement, to thinking about comparative justice.

INDEX

D

E

F

G

Q

R

www.ingramcontent.com/pod-product-compliance
Lightning Source LLC
Jackson TN
JSHW060344180725
87711JS00002B/3
* 9 7 8 1 5 2 4 9 6 9 0 7 3 *